TRANSITIONS BETWEEN CONSCIOUSNESS AND UNCONSCIOUSNESS

The empirical study of consciousness is in constant progress. New ideas and approaches arise, methods are being debated and refined, and experimental research over the last two decades has produced a rich body of data, acquired in the aim to better understand consciousness and its neural underpinnings. This volume synthesizes these data, focusing on how to understand the relations and transitions between consciousness and unconsciousness alongside exploring and distinguishing conscious experience of sensory stimuli and unconscious states.

Bringing together leading academics and promising young scientists from across the fields of psychology and neuroscience, *Transitions between Consciousness and Unconsciousness* discusses controversial topics and ideas, providing an overview of current research trends and opinions, as well as perspectives on theoretical and methodological questions.

This is an essential volume for consciousness researchers and students from across psychology, neuroscience, and philosophy, as well as those researching modes of visual processing.

Guido Hesselmann is a Professor of General and Biological Psychology at the Psychologische Hochschule Berlin (PHB), Germany.

Current Issues in Consciousness Research
Series Editor: Morten Overgaard

Current Issues in Consciousness Research is a series of edited books that will reflect the state of the art in areas of current and emerging interest in the psychological and philosophical study of consciousness.

Each volume will be tightly focused on a particular topic and will consist of six to ten chapters contributed by international experts. The editors of individual volumes will be leading figures in their areas and will provide an introductory overview.

Example topics include consciousness and metacognition, consciousness and free will, neural correlates of consciousness, disorders of consciousness, and conscious sensation of movement.

Sensation of Movement
Edited by Thor Grünbaum and Mark Schram Christensen

TRANSITIONS BETWEEN CONSCIOUSNESS AND UNCONSCIOUSNESS

Edited by Guido Hesselmann

LONDON AND NEW YORK

First published 2019
by Routledge
2 Park Square, Milton Park, Abingdon, Oxon OX14 4RN

and by Routledge
52 Vanderbilt Avenue, New York, NY 10017

Routledge is an imprint of the Taylor & Francis Group, an informa business

© 2019 selection and editorial matter, Guido Hesselmann; individual chapters, the contributors

The right of Guido Hesselmann to be identified as the author of the editorial material, and of the authors for their individual chapters, has been asserted in accordance with sections 77 and 78 of the Copyright, Designs and Patents Act 1988.

All rights reserved. No part of this book may be reprinted or reproduced or utilised in any form or by any electronic, mechanical, or other means, now known or hereafter invented, including photocopying and recording, or in any information storage or retrieval system, without permission in writing from the publishers.

Trademark notice: Product or corporate names may be trademarks or registered trademarks, and are used only for identification and explanation without intent to infringe.

British Library Cataloguing-in-Publication Data
A catalogue record for this book is available from the British Library

Library of Congress Cataloging-in-Publication Data
Names: Hesselmann, Guido, editor.
Title: Transitions between consciousness and unconsciousness / edited by Guido Hesselmann.
Description: 1 Edition. | New York : Routledge, 2019.
Identifiers: LCCN 2019005866 |
Subjects: LCSH: Consciousness. | Subconsciousness.
Classification: LCC BF311 .T7173 2019 | DDC 155.4/13—dc23
LC record available at https://lccn.loc.gov/2019005866

ISBN: 978-1-138-60222-9 (hbk)
ISBN: 978-1-138-60226-7 (pbk)
ISBN: 978-0-429-46968-8 (ebk)

Typeset in Bembo
by Swales & Willis Ltd, Exeter, Devon, UK

 Printed in the United Kingdom by Henry Ling Limited

CONTENTS

	Foreword *Guido Hesselmann*	*vi*
1	The breaking continuous flash suppression paradigm: review, evaluation, and outlook *Timo Stein*	1
2	What's up with high-level processing during continuous flash suppression? *Pieter Moors*	39
3	Unconscious visual processing: how a neuro-functional hierarchy can guide future research *Bruno Breitmeyer and Guido Hesselmann*	71
4	The unconscious processing of social information *Apoorva Rajiv Madipakkam and Marcus Rothkirch*	92
5	Studying the benefits and costs of conscious perception with the liminal-prime paradigm *Dominique Lamy, Eyal A. Ophir, and Maayan Avneon*	118
6	From aliens to invisible limbs: the transitions that never make it into conscious experience *Jaan Aru*	148
	Index	*163*

FOREWORD

Guido Hesselmann

DEPARTMENT OF GENERAL AND BIOLOGICAL PSYCHOLOGY, PSYCHOLOGISCHE
HOCHSCHULE BERLIN

As all scientific disciplines and endeavors, the empirical study of consciousness is in constant progress. New ideas and approaches arise, methods are being permanently debated and refined, more and more experimental data are gathered at ever increasing speed, and widely accepted conceptions are frequently questioned and sometimes revised. Over recent years, diverse empirical work has been devoted to distinguishing conscious experience of sensory stimuli and unconscious states. Shared by many consciousness researchers is the notion that a deep understanding of that which specifically characterizes conscious sensory states, including neural correlates and cognitive functions, may crucially inform the ambition of understanding the relation between subjective experience and the physical world. Different methodological traditions and choices have led to quite different answers about how conscious and unconscious states relate. Current viewpoints are diverse and include such different positions as the idea that unconscious states are associated with the very same functional characteristics as conscious states, and the idea that no informational state that is available for action can be completely unconscious. This book, titled *Transitions between Consciousness and Unconsciousness*, is therefore devoted to this particular question, how to understand the relations and transitions between consciousness and unconsciousness. Its main objective is to provide a "snapshot" of the current state of affairs in this fast-moving research area. It intends to provide an overview of current research trends and opinions, as well as perspectives on theoretical and methodological questions. In their respective chapters, the authors synthesize the state-of-the-art knowledge about the transitions between consciousness and unconsciousness, and their main empirical focus will be on results from psychophysical experiments with healthy human participants.

One of the most appealing questions in the field of consciousness research is whether stimuli that cannot be consciously perceived by the observer can nevertheless influence the observer's behavior. About ten years ago, interest in this long-standing research question was invigorated by the introduction of a new and powerful psychophysical "blinding" technique, i.e. a psychophysical method that can be applied in the laboratory to render normally visible stimuli invisible to the observer. Since then, continuous flash suppression (CFS), and in particular, its variant called breaking CFS, have become widely used and highly influential methods in the fields of visual perception, cognitive psychology, and cognitive neuroscience. The key idea behind breaking CFS is surprisingly simple: unconscious processing is inferred from the time different stimuli need to overcome suppression and break into awareness (i.e. the time it takes stimuli to transit from unconscious to conscious processing). A large and steadily growing body of experiments using breaking CFS now seems to suggest that the extent of unconscious processing is much greater than previously thought. In the first chapter, Timo Stein presents a comprehensive and critical overview of what can really be learned from that immensely popular CFS "transition" paradigm. His review shows that most findings from breaking CFS studies may have been confounded by perceptual and post-perceptual influences unrelated to unconscious processing. As a constructive outlook, Timo Stein proposes two novel approaches that can help to avoid these confounds in future studies.

Early empirical studies relying on the CFS paradigm have frequently reported evidence for so-called integrated, semantic, or high-level processing of invisible stimuli. These findings have led some researchers to believe that unconscious processing is possible for virtually any high-level stimulus property (e.g. the context of a complex visual scene, or the meaning of a written sentence). In the second chapter, Pieter Moors presents an in-depth summary of the large and diverse CFS literature suggesting various high-level unconscious processes, including results from more classical priming studies that have used CFS to efficiently mask visual prime stimuli. It becomes clear that following a "first wave" of CFS studies reporting mostly positive and often thought-provoking results, a series of CFS studies compellingly challenged many of these initial findings either through failing to replicate them, or by showing that the previously observed effects can be explained more parsimoniously by low-level stimulus confounds. As Pieter Moors nicely shows, this "second wave" of CFS studies also reflects the ongoing change in research practices in psychology, which are in favor of more transparency, openness, and cooperation. He then explains how the results of rather limited unconscious processing fit within a broader theoretical framework of interocular suppression, of which CFS is a potent variant. The chapter ends on a personal note – the author reflects about how principles of open and transparent science have influenced his work as a PhD student, and he provides some recommendations for young and early-career researchers on how studies investigating unconscious visual processing should be designed and performed to be maximally informative.

CFS is by far not the only suppression method available and, as briefly mentioned above, it is even among the youngest "blinding" techniques, having been introduced in 2005. Many further psychophysical methods exist to render visual stimuli invisible, i.e. inaccessible to conscious report. In the third chapter,

viii Foreword

Breitmeyer and Hesselmann further elaborate the notion – originally proposed by Breitmeyer – that that the various suppression methods (e.g. binocular rivalry, backward masking) suppress conscious visual processing at different depths or levels of visual processing. In principle, comparing what sorts of visual information could or could not be suppressed by the various blinding methods should allow one to infer a psychophysically determined functional hierarchy of unconscious visual processing. This functional hierarchy is defined by the relative order of "blinding" methods with respect to the level of unconscious stimulus processing. The levels vary from very early ones, presumably occurring as early as striate cortex, or even earlier, to stages higher up in the visual cognition hierarchy, such as those associated with feature integration, object recognition, and selective attention. For example, backward masking is ranked higher than binocular rivalry, because unconscious semantic processing has been established for the former, but not the latter. Breitmeyer and Hesselmann elaborate on the notion of a neurofunctional hierarchical scheme: although psychophysical studies can determine relative functional levels of unconscious processing, neuroimaging studies are needed to clarify and pinpoint the actual anatomical levels of cortical processing associated with psychophysically determined functional levels. Such a neurofunctional hierarchy will allow the formulation of predictions on the level of unconscious processing that can be expected in a specific experimental setup, and thus it can guide future empirical research. Without such prior assumptions on the depth of visual suppression, every new single study reporting unconscious processing would be equally weighted, independently of the accumulated and meta-analytic knowledge about the applied suppression method, and the boundaries of unconscious processing would then – inevitably and prematurely – be pushed further and further.

Another long-standing and controversial question in the realm of consciousness research is to what extent social information can still be processed in the absence of awareness, given that the rapid processing of social information is critical for human interaction. For example, facial characteristics like an emotional expression or the direction of eye gaze convey information so that the observer can immediately judge whether the counterpart is hostile or sympathetic. In the fourth chapter, Apoorva Madipakkam and Marcus Rothkirch provide a comprehensive review of the evidence for unconscious processing of social information, including research on the processing of emotional face expressions, the learned relevance of faces, and eye gaze. They focus on studies investigating whether socially relevant information is processed even when it is entirely suppressed from visual awareness, and on studies addressing the question whether social information has privileged access to visual awareness, i.e. whether it transits faster from unconscious to conscious processing in breaking CFS paradigms. Based on their review, they formulate a simple scheme in which the effects of the unconscious processing of social information typically decrease with an increasing level of complexity, ranging from single features, like eye gaze, to complex features (e.g. a person's identity as revealed by holistic face processing). This review is complemented with a nuanced discussion of the highly influential notion of a so-called "low road" of visual processing, supposedly underlying the unconscious processing of social information. In the second part of their chapter, the authors address the important question of how the investigation of abnormal unconscious processing in patients with psychiatric disorders can lead to a better understanding of these disorders. For example, they report on their own research showing that adults with autism spectrum disorder exhibit no preference towards unconsciously presented faces with direct gaze, while typically developed adults preferentially process direct in comparison to averted gaze outside of awareness. These and other findings raise hopes for new therapy options for psychiatric disorders, inspired and informed by research on the transitions between conscious and unconscious processing.

From its beginnings, heated controversies over what counts as conscious and unconscious perception have accompanied the study of unconscious processing, and they have not abated to this day. At its core, this controversy is about methodology, and the distinction between objective and subjective measures of awareness (including their combined use in various different experimental paradigms). According to the objective awareness criterion, forced-choice detection or discrimination performance at chance level indicates the absence of awareness. Subjective measures of awareness, by contrast, are based on participants' introspective reports of their perceptual states (e.g. whether they saw a visual stimulus clearly or only vaguely). In the fifth chapter, Dominique Lamy, Eyal Ophir, and Maayan Avneon propose that unconscious processing can optimally be studied using a subjective measure of awareness in the so-called liminal-prime paradigm. In this paradigm, subjective perception of the prime is measured on every trial, while the impact of the prime on responses to the target (i.e. the priming effect) is concomitantly assessed. Based on post-hoc trial sorting, the priming effect can be assessed for each level of reported prime visibility. The authors first describe the paradigm and discuss its advantages and drawbacks, and then illustrate how it can be employed to determine the extent to which different processes depend on conscious processing. They also suggest that the liminal-prime paradigm can be used to investigate the cost of consciously perceiving an event on the processing of a trailing event (i.e. the "costs of awareness"). The chapter concludes with a set of guidelines for using the liminal-prime paradigm in future studies.

Imagine that you had to explain the current state of affairs in consciousness research to a visiting group of alien scientists, and that you had to pick a selection of scientific papers. This unusual scenario is the starting point of the sixth and final chapter. Jaan Aru brings up this imagined situation to ask some of the most fundamental questions: Where do we stand in understanding consciousness? What progress has been made? The author then lays out his rather pessimistic view on the progress of the science of consciousness, attacking the so-called contrastive analysis that underlies many previous and ongoing experiments. In this widely used approach, trials with and without conscious perception are contrasted to unravel the neural processes that differ between the two conditions. As the author points out, however, this method cannot reveal the true mechanisms underlying consciousness, simply because it will always bring along neural processes that reflect unconscious prerequisites and consequences, in a manner and extent that is specific to the experimental paradigm used. Jaan Aru proposes that a new promising approach will be to explore the mechanisms that maintain the continuity of consciousness by preventing certain transitions in the environment (e.g. eye blinks) from entering conscious experience. Continuity of consciousness is not in the focus of current theories of consciousness. The chapter reviews ongoing studies conducted in virtual reality environments suggesting that one mechanism supporting the continuity of consciousness is the withdrawal of attention from the specific predictable sensory activity. It is then discussed how the suppression of self-generated transients can be explained by active inference theory, a possible candidate for explaining some phenomena of conscious experience better than current theories of consciousness. The chapter concludes with the author's appeal for radically new experimental approaches, and for the leaving behind of the paradigms that were applied when the scientific study of consciousness was started.

In addition to providing a "snapshot" of current research on consciousness, the six chapters of this book are meant to illustrate that research on the transitions between consciousness and unconsciousness is characterized by a large diversity of approaches, methods, and measures. I hope that the reader will find this book both informative and thought-provoking, and that it will stimulate and contribute to the scientific debate.

1

THE BREAKING CONTINUOUS FLASH SUPPRESSION PARADIGM

Review, evaluation, and outlook

Timo Stein

BRAIN AND COGNITION, DEPARTMENT OF PSYCHOLOGY,
UNIVERSITY OF AMSTERDAM

Understanding the function and neural basis of conscious awareness is one of the major challenges of cognitive psychology and neuroscience. One promising approach to is to map out those perceptual and cognitive functions that can take place outside of conscious awareness, i.e. unconsciously (Kouider & Faivre, 2017). Ultimately, this research program could yield a set of functions that cannot occur unconsciously and are tightly linked to conscious awareness, which would provide important insights into the functional role of conscious awareness (Baars, 1988). Alternatively, it may turn out that virtually all perceptual and cognitive processes can transpire unconsciously, rendering conscious awareness an epiphenomenon.

However, a consensus on the scope and potential limits of unconscious processing seems currently out of reach. The reason for this is not simply a lack of studies testing whether certain perceptual or cognitive functions depend on conscious awareness. Rather, based on the same published data some researchers conclude that unconscious processing can carry out basically any high-level function (Hassin, 2013), whereas others are more skeptical, proposing that unconscious processing is quite limited (Hesselmann & Moors, 2015). This disagreement stems partly from different definitions of the term "unconscious" in social psychology (where it is often used interchangeably with "implicit", i.e. without conscious knowledge of an experimental manipulation) and cognitive psychology (where it is mostly used to refer to a "non-reportable" stimulus feature during its presentation).

But even within experimental psychology and cognitive neuroscience some authors conclude that there is no evidence even for very basic unconscious visual perception (Peters & Lau, 2015), while others propose that even complex semantic integration can occur unconsciously (Sklar, Deouell, & Hassin, 2018). Much of this controversy is due to the use of a range of widely differing experimental approaches to unconscious processing. Different researchers adopt different experimental paradigms, different psychophysical techniques for presenting stimuli outside of conscious awareness, and different measures to demonstrate the absence of conscious perception. Some of these approaches, such as the classical dissociation paradigm, are grounded in a long history of experimentation, have high face validity, and a large literature discussing their theoretical underpinnings (e.g. Erdelyi, 1986; Greenwald & Draine, 1998; Merikle, Smilek, & Eastwood, 2001; Schmidt & Vorberg, 2006; Snodgrass, Bernat, & Shevrin, 2004). Other, more recently developed approaches, such as the "breaking CFS" paradigm discussed in this chapter, are currently widely applied although their underlying rationale has not yet been fully developed. Not all researchers consider findings obtained with these novel approaches convincing evidence for unconscious processing.

1 Continuous flash suppression (CFS)

In the domain of vision, the development of a novel psychophysical technique, named continuous flash suppression (CFS; Tsuchiya & Koch, 2005) has sparked a tidal wave of interest in unconscious processing (see Figure 1.1). CFS is a strong

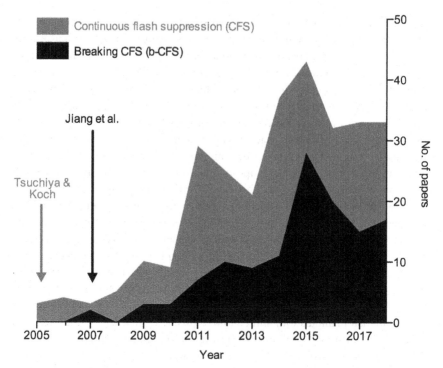

FIGURE 1.1 Number of CFS publications per year, from the publication by Tsuchiya and Koch (2005) who developed the technique of CFS to August 2018. Also plotted is the subset of papers that adopted some variant of the "breaking CFS" paradigm first introduced by Jiang, Costello, and He (2007). Publications are based on data from the website of Pieter Moors (www.gestaltrevision.be/s/cfs, retrieved August 10, 2018).

interocular suppression technique, in which the presentation of flashing, high-contrast dynamic masks to one eye can render an image (the target) presented to the other eye invisible for up to several seconds. Because CFS is straightforward to implement and allows for long periods of subjective invisibility of complex visual stimuli, this technique has been widely adopted to study unconscious processing. While many studies have combined CFS with traditional dissociation paradigms for studying unconscious processing, the technique also inspired the development of a novel paradigm, the so-called "breaking CFS" (b-CFS; Jiang, Costello, & He, 2007; Stein, Hebart, & Sterzer, 2011a) paradigm.

Although nearly half of all studies using the psychophysical technique of CFS adopted some variant of the b-CFS paradigm (see Figure 1.1), it is currently debated whether this paradigm is indeed measuring unconscious processing (Gayet, Van der Stigchel, & Paffen, 2014; Stein et al., 2011a; Stein & Sterzer, 2014; Yang, Brascamp, Kang, & Blake, 2014). In this chapter, I will first compare the rationale of the b-CFS paradigm to classic dissociation paradigms (sections 2 and 3). I will then review how the paradigm has been applied to study unconscious processing, including an overview of the most common b-CFS tasks and measures. This review will include a critical evaluation of what can be concluded from findings obtained with b-CFS, and how control conditions and additional paradigms might or might not be helpful in interpreting b-CFS results (section 4). In the final part, I will propose possible future avenues for embedding the b-CFS paradigm in the classical dissociation framework (section 5).

2 The classic dissociation paradigm

To better illustrate why the b-CFS paradigm represents a novel, uncommon way of measuring unconscious visual processing, it is necessary to briefly describe the most common approach to unconscious visual processing, the classic dissociation paradigm (Erdelyi, 1986). This approach is very intuitive: a stimulus is rendered invisible and two measures are collected, one measure of stimulus awareness and one measure of stimulus processing. According to the simple dissociation logic (Schmidt & Vorberg, 2006), unconscious processing is demonstrated when the awareness measure shows null sensitivity while the processing measure shows some sensitivity. For the present purpose, it is helpful to distinguish between two variants of the classic dissociation paradigm, which I term the "direct-indirect" dissociation paradigm, often used in "priming-like" studies and the "direct-direct" dissociation paradigm, often used in "blindsight-like" studies.

2.1 The direct-indirect dissociation paradigm in "priming-like" studies

This approach contrasts a direct task assessing stimulus awareness (with the instructions explicitly referring to the invisible stimulus) with an indirect task assessing incidental stimulus processing (Figure 1.2a). There are many different measures of

4 Timo Stein

stimulus processing, the most popular being priming, where the invisible stimulus exerts an influence on the response to a subsequent visible stimulus. Other common measures of stimulus processing include attentional cueing, adaptation aftereffects, and recordings of neural activity. There are also many different ways of assessing stimulus awareness, each with their own advantages and disadvantages. Some researchers use subjective awareness measures in which participants simply indicate whether they did or did not see a stimulus, rate stimulus visibility, or their confidence. Other researchers prefer objective awareness measures to show that participants are unable to either detect the invisible stimulus or to discriminate certain stimulus features. The pros and cons of subjective and objective measures have been discussed elsewhere (e.g. Cheesman & Merikle, 1986; Kunimoto, Miller, & Pashler, 2001; Schmidt, 2015; Snodgrass et al., 2004). Suffice it to say that subjective measures may be too liberal, as they tend to underestimate stimulus awareness and thus may overestimate the extent of unconscious processing, while objective measures may be too conservative and thus may underestimate the extent of unconscious processing.

2.2 The direct-direct dissociation paradigm in "blindsight-like" studies

In this less commonly used variant of the dissociation paradigm, two direct tasks are contrasted, one assessing stimulus awareness and the other stimulus processing (Figure 1.2b). Here, both tasks explicitly refer to the invisible stimulus. Although this approach has a long tradition and was adopted long before the discovery of "blindsight" (e.g. Sidis, 1898) it seems intuitive to label it "blindsight-like" because the basic idea is reminiscent of the behavior of certain patients with visual cortex lesions. These blindsight patients report no awareness of a visual stimulus that they can nevertheless detect and discriminate with high accuracy (Weiskrantz, 1986). Similarly, with healthy subjects a subjective measure of stimulus awareness, such as a seen/unseen judgment or a visibility rating, can be contrasted with an objective measure of stimulus processing, such as discrimination of a stimulus feature (e.g. Soto, Mäntylä, & Silvanto, 2011). One important concern with this approach is that subjective measures require subjects to set an arbitrary criterion for reporting stimulus awareness. This criterion may be too conservative, such that weakly conscious stimuli are categorized as unconscious. Performance without subjective awareness could thus reflect weakly conscious rather than truly unconscious processing (e.g. Eriksen, 1960; Peters & Lau, 2005; Stein, Kaiser, & Hesselmann, 2016).

Aside from these methodological concerns, it is interesting to note that even within the classic dissociation paradigm the same task can be used to index either conscious or unconscious processing. In the direct-indirect variant of the dissociation paradigm a direct, objective task, such as stimulus detection, often serves to measure awareness, whereas in the direct-direct variant of the dissociation paradigm the same direct, objective task could serve to measure stimulus processing. This inconsistent usage of tasks and measures contributes to the difficulty of aggregating data from different paradigms into a general theory of unconscious processing.

2.3 CFS studies adopting the classic dissociation paradigm

Before the development of CFS, most studies adopting the direct-indirect variant of the dissociation paradigm used some form of backward masking, where the visibility of very brief, binocularly presented stimuli is degraded by the presentation of a succeeding visual pattern (Breitmeyer & Öğmen, 2006). This approach has yielded evidence for high-level semantic unconscious processing under backward masking (Kouider & Dehaene, 2007; Van den Bussche, Van den Noortgate, & Reynvoet, 2009). Initial priming and adaptation aftereffect studies using CFS, by contrast, showed that unconscious processing is comparably limited (e.g. Almeida, Mahon, Nakayama, & Caramazza, 2008; Moradi, Koch, & Shimojo, 2005). By now, the CFS literature using the classic direct-indirect dissociation paradigm has become increasingly complex. Although a review is beyond the scope of this chapter, it is useful to highlight the discrepancy between findings obtained with the direct-indirect dissociation paradigm and the b-CFS paradigm with one select example: A number of behavioral studies adopting the direct-indirect dissociation paradigm have found little evidence for unconscious processing of facial attributes (other than emotional expression) under CFS (Amihai, Deouell, & Bentin, 2011; Shin, Stolte, & Chong, 2009; Stein, Peelen, & Sterzer, 2012a; Stein & Sterzer, 2011; Xu, Zhang, & Geng, 2018; but see Hung, Nieh, & Hsieh, 2016; Xu, Zhang, & Geng, 2011). In contrast, as reviewed below, b-CFS studies have provided evidence for unconscious processing of various facial attributes (section 4.1.2). This can be seen as evidence that the b-CFS paradigm is more sensitive to unconscious processing than the direct-indirect dissociation paradigm.

Comparably far less CFS studies have adopted the direct-direct dissociation paradigm. Only a handful of behavioral studies compared a subjective awareness measure to an objective performance measure (for an fMRI study, see Hesselmann, Hebart, & Malach, 2011). These studies found, even for subjectively unconscious stimuli, above-chance localization (Oliver, Mao, & Mitchell, 2015; Vieira, Wen, Oliver, & Mitchell, 2017; Bergström & Eriksson, 2015, 2018) and discrimination (Bergström & Eriksson, 2015, 2018; Song & Hao, 2016). However, all of these studies suffer from the criterion problem mentioned above: participants may have categorized weakly conscious stimuli as unconscious. Recent work using criterion-free measures of subjective awareness and backward masking found no evidence for unconscious processing when this criterion issue was ruled out (Peters & Lau, 2015). Thus, the direct-direct dissociation paradigm seems comparably insensitive to unconscious processing, even with backward masking. Nevertheless, I believe that there are elegant ways for including modified versions of the direct-direct dissociation logic in improved future versions of the b-CFS paradigm, and will propose a way of incorporating this method in b-CFS at the end of this chapter (section 5.2).

6 Timo Stein

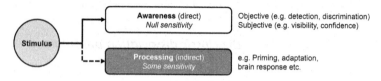

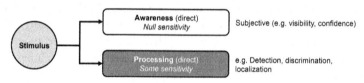

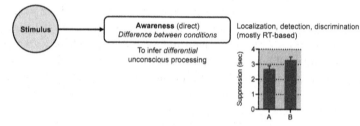

FIGURE 1.2 The three most popular paradigms for measuring unconscious visual processing. (a) In the direct-indirect dissociation paradigm a direct measure of awareness is contrasted with an indirect measure of stimulus processing and unconscious processing is inferred when the former shows null sensitivity while the latter shows some sensitivity. (b) In the direct-direct dissociation paradigm a direct measure of subjective awareness is contrasted with a direct measure of stimulus processing (which can be the same as the direct measure of awareness in the direct-indirect dissociation paradigm) and unconscious processing is inferred when the former shows null sensitivity while the latter shows some sensitivity. (c) In the b-CFS paradigm, only one direct measure of awareness is collected. Differences between stimulus conditions in this measure are thought to reflect differential unconscious processing.

3 The breaking CFS (b-CFS) paradigm

The b-CFS paradigm differs fundamentally from the variants of the dissociation paradigm. In its basic form, the b-CFS paradigm consists of only one direct task rather than two tasks or measures, and no attempt is being made to contrast and dissociate different measures. This single direct task capitalizes on the fact that CFS can render a stimulus (the "target") invisible for up to several seconds, but eventually the stimulus will perceptually "break" through the CFS masks and enter awareness. The b-CFS paradigm aims to track the time different target stimuli need to overcome CFS and break into awareness, most commonly through speeded localization or detection responses (see section 4.2). Localization or detection latencies are taken as estimates of the duration of perceptual suppression. Differences in suppression time between different target conditions are thought to reflect differences in unconscious processing the stimuli receive while still being suppressed (Figure 1.2c). Shorter suppression times are believed to indicate enhanced, faster, or more fluent unconscious processing.

The b-CFS paradigm is used to infer *differential unconscious processing* of one condition relative to another condition. This is different from the classic dissociation paradigm which could, in principle, be used to study unconscious processing with one suppressed stimulus only, e.g. by testing priming from one particular stimulus exemplar (e.g. one face identity). The b-CFS paradigm requires the comparison of at least two different, initially suppressed targets. In the first published b-CFS study, Jiang and colleagues (2007) compared suppression times of upright to inverted faces (i.e. rotated by 180 degrees) and found that upright faces break into awareness more quickly. According to the b-CFS logic this shows that upright and inverted faces receive differential unconscious processing while still being fully suppressed. This indicates that information about face orientation can be represented unconsciously. Clearly, for this reasoning to be valid the two target conditions should not differ along any other dimension. For example, higher luminance contrast in one condition would trivially account for shorter suppression times. Indeed, as discussed below (section 4.1.1), differences in such low-level stimulus properties represent a major difficulty in interpreting b-CFS findings, especially for studies comparing target stimuli that have inherent, uncontrollable physical differences, such as faces with different emotional expressions (see section 4.1.2).

The more general conceptual issue with the b-CFS paradigm is that its basic logic seems at odds with previous and more common ways of measuring unconscious processing, such as the classic dissociation paradigm. The one measure collected in b-CFS studies is a direct measure of stimulus awareness. In most studies, this measure is a speeded response, i.e. a subjective measure (participants need to decide when they have enough sensory evidence to press a button; see section 4.2). In both the direct-indirect and the direct-direct version of the classic dissociation paradigm this direct task would represent a measure of stimulus awareness, not a measure of unconscious stimulus processing. Why, then, are differences in this direct measure in b-CFS paradigms used to measure differential unconscious processing? Two different underlying rationales are adopted in the b-CFS literature. As these are rarely made fully explicit (but see Stein & Sterzer, 2014), it is useful to flesh them out in some detail.

3.1 Differences in detectability reflect differential unconscious processing

One rationale is that differences in the time target stimuli need to break into awareness simply reflect differences in preceding unconscious processing. This view is based on the idea of a temporal sequence from unconscious processing to conscious awareness. It also assumes that there is a more or less discrete transition from unconscious processing to conscious awareness that can be tracked with high precision, for example, by using simple (speeded) localization or detection responses. Because of the assumed sequential stream from unconscious processing to conscious awareness, differences between stimuli in transition times must imply differences in unconscious processing.

It is interesting that this logic is commonly adopted in b-CFS studies but only very rarely when other psychophysical techniques are used. In fact, the same logic could in principle be applied to any experiment measuring differences in stimulus detectability, irrespective of whether CFS or backward masking, or any other psychophysical technique (e.g. crowding, visual search, rapid serial visual presentation, simultaneous noise masking, etc.) is used (Dijksterhuis & Aarts, 2003; Gaillard, Del Cul, Naccache, Vinckier, Cohen, & Dehaene, 2006). With CFS, this logic may be more readily adopted because stimuli remain invisible for up to several seconds before they enter awareness, and this may be suggestive of an extended period of unconscious processing. With other techniques, such as backward masking, this time can be in the order of several milliseconds only. This comparably short period, however, does not exclude differential responses to different stimuli, for example, in a rapid feedforward sweep of visual processing (Van Rullen, 2007). Although stimulus detection most likely involves different neural processes for different psychophysical techniques, this is not directly relevant for the basic logic assuming (a) an unconscious-conscious sequence and (b) a precise measure of the transition point. As such, this logic could be similarly applied to other techniques.

Independent of the psychophysical technique, researchers adopting this logic need to address several challenges. One of the most obvious problems is that it is debated whether a discrete transition point from unconscious processing to conscious awareness exists, with a whole literature investigating the question whether consciousness is gradual or dichotomous (e.g. Asplund, Fougnie, Zughni, Martin, & Marois, 2014; Nieuwenhuis & de Kleijn, 2011; Overgaard, Rote, Mouridsen, & Ramsøy, 2006; Sergent & Dehaene, 2004). Furthermore, even if such a transition point existed, it is questionable whether any particular behavioral response could be used to track this point with sufficient precision. A particularly pressing issue with the tasks commonly used in b-CFS studies is that responses may be influenced by perceptual processes that occur after the transition into awareness (e.g. categorization, exemplar-level identification, etc.) or even by later non-perceptual processes (e.g. naming, decision, response selection, etc.). Below I will review which tasks and responses are currently used in b-CFS studies (section 4.2), how researchers attempt to control post-perceptual processes by non-CFS control conditions (section 4.3), and give some recommendations for future research (section 5).

3.2 CFS-specific unconscious processing differences

An alternative rationale in the b-CFS literature is to base any conclusion about unconscious processing on a comparison with a non-CFS control condition. As we described previously (Stein & Sterzer, 2014), on this account unconscious processing is inferred from b-CFS only *because* CFS is used to render a stimulus invisible. That is, differences in target detectability are attributed to differential processing that took place specifically under CFS, i.e. to *CFS-specific* differences. For this reasoning to be valid, *non CFS-specific* differences in stimulus detectability need to be excluded as a cause for differences in suppression times.

To isolate CFS-specific processing, suppression times are compared to a binocular or monocular control condition, in which the same task as in b-CFS is implemented, but stimuli are presented in a way that does not induce interocular suppression. The target is most commonly gradually blended in on top of the flashing CFS masks. Targets and masks are presented either to both eyes or to one eye only, with the other eye receiving no visual stimulation. The control condition is intended to perceptually resemble b-CFS and to capture all non-CFS specific differences in stimulus detectability that might have contributed to differences in suppression times. Following this logic, CFS-specific unconscious processing differences are inferred when the difference in suppression times is larger than the effect obtained in the control condition.

We have argued that this conclusion is unwarranted (Stein et al., 2011a; Stein & Sterzer, 2014) because it seems impossible to develop a control condition that captures all aspects of non CFS-specific processing that might contribute to differences in suppression times. For example, in b-CFS perceptual uncertainty about target appearance tends to be much greater than in control conditions (see section 4.3), and participants can easily tell b-CFS and control conditions apart, demonstrating that they are not perceptually matched (Stein et al., 2011a). Thus, at least in its present form, the logic of comparing b-CFS to control conditions cannot provide unequivocal evidence for CFS-specific unconscious processing.

There may be one exception, namely when significant differences between stimulus conditions are obtained both in b-CFS and in the control condition, but with the effect going in opposite directions in the two conditions (see Stein & Sterzer, 2014). Such opposite effects would render CFS-specific unconscious processing differences as a cause for differences in suppression times more likely. To date there has only been one such finding in the literature: Prioli and Kahan (2015) found that in b-CFS neutral words were identified faster than negative words, whereas in the control condition negative words were identified faster than neutral words. However, this study used an RT-based identification task that can strongly be affected by post-perceptual biases (see section 4.2.1), and their influence may differ between b-CFS and the control condition. Also, this study adopted a between-subject design with different participants in b-CFS and in the control condition, and the critical interaction effect just crossed the threshold for statistical significance, thus calling for independent replication.

4 Review of b-CFS studies

From the above summary of the two different rationales that are commonly used to infer unconscious processing from b-CFS it is clear that the exact implementation of the paradigm is of critical importance. In the following, I will review the most common experimental manipulations used in published b-CFS studies, summarize the key findings (section 4.1), critically evaluate the tasks and measures that have been employed (section 4.2), and review whether and how control conditions have been implemented, and to what extent b-CFS results have been compared to other psychophysical techniques (section 4.3).

For Figure 1.1, I identified 125 publications that used some version of the b-CFS paradigm in a broad sense. This also included studies that did not explicitly compare suppression times for different stimulus conditions but used b-CFS paradigms to measure eye dominance (Ding, Naber, Gayet, Van der Stigchel, & Paffen, 2018; Yang, Blake, & McDonald, 2010) or to probe into the influence of visual properties of the CFS mask, such as its orientation, spatial frequency, color, flash frequency, pattern, and similarity with visual properties of the target (Drewes, Zhu, & Melcher, 2018; Han & Alais, 2018; Han, Blake, & Alais, 2018; Han, Lunghi, & Alais, 2016; Hong & Blake, 2009; Kaunitz, Fracasso, Skujevskis, & Melcher, 2014; Moors, Wagemans, & de-Wit, 2014; Zhan, Engelen, & de Gelder, 2018). While these studies are of foundational importance for our understanding of the CFS technique itself, in the following review I only included those 115 b-CFS publications that compared suppression times for different target stimuli.

4.1 Topics and experimental manipulations

4.1.1 Visual features

Although the debate on the extent of unconscious processing revolves around the processing of "higher-level" (i.e. semantic or conceptual) stimulus dimensions, b-CFS has also widely been used to measure visual processing of "lower-level" visual stimulus properties. These studies found that suppression times are shorter for targets that have higher contrast (e.g. Akechi, Stein, Senju, Kikuchi, Tojo, Osanai, & Hasegawa, 2014; Akechi, Stein, Yikuchi, Tojo, Osanai, & Hasegawa, 2015; Kaunitz et al., 2014; Song & Yao, 2016), larger retinal size (Heyman & Moors, 2014), higher spatial frequency (Yang & Blake, 2012), radial rather than tangential orientation or motion (Hong, 2015), higher moving speed (Ananyev, Penney, & Hsieh, 2017), higher motion and form coherence (Chung & Khuu, 2014; Kaunitz, Fracasso, Lingnau, & Melcher, 2013), collinear rather than orthogonal contours (Li & Li, 2015), and for targets that contain a hole (Meng, Cui, Zhou, Chen, & Ma, 2012; Zhu, Drewes, & Melcher, 2016). Taken together, these findings indicate that most manipulations that increase a target's visual salience are associated with shorter suppression times.

Another important factor is target-mask similarity: the more similar the visual features of the target and the CFS mask the longer the suppression time (Han & Alais, 2018; Yang & Blake 2012; but not for moving speed, see Ananyev et al., 2017). Interestingly, this influence of target-mask similarity is not limited to visual features alone. When CFS masks consist of images from object categories that have similar representations in higher-level visual cortex as the target object (e.g. buildings and cars) suppression times are longer than when representations are comparably dissimilar (e.g. building and bodies; Cohen, Nakayama, Konkle, Stantić, & Alvarez, 2015). While these effects related to target-mask similarity and to lower-level physical visual features are not directly relevant for answering whether higher-level stimulus properties affect suppression times, it is important to consider these influences when comparing physically different stimuli.

To illustrate, one b-CFS study found that "pacmen" stimuli oriented in a way that created a Kanisza surface broke suppression faster than rotated control stimuli (Wang, Weng, & He, 2012). Originally, this was interpreted as showing that certain aspects of perceptual grouping could occur unconsciously, thereby representing one example of a b-CFS finding that was at odds with results from CFS experiments adopting the classic dissociation paradigm, which showed no evidence for unconscious perceptual grouping (Harris, Schwarzkopf, Song, Bahrami, & Rees, 2011). However, subsequent experiments revealed that the advantage of Kanisza targets was unrelated to the perception of a Kanisza surface but instead reflected lower-level confounding factors such as collinear edges and the presence of certain orientations (Moors, Wagemans, van Ee, & de-Wit, 2016c). This demonstrates the importance of matching b-CFS target conditions on all potentially relevant lower-level properties before inferring high-level unconscious processing differences.

Although this particular study suggests that there is little influence of inferred visual properties (the Kanisza surface) on b-CFS, other work has recently shown that stimuli which are consciously perceived as causal events (a moving disc launching the movement of another disc) are associated with shorter suppression times than nearly identical stimuli that elicit less of a causal percept (Moors, Wagemans, & de-Wit, 2017). To conclusively determine whether such inferred stimulus properties can influence suppression time, more b-CFS studies using ambiguous stimuli or visual "illusions" are required.

4.1.2 Faces, objects, and emotional stimuli

Since the first b-CFS publication that reported a strong effect of face inversion (Jiang et al., 2007) many studies replicated this finding (e.g. Akechi et al., 2015; Gayet & Stein, 2017; Kobylka, Persike, & Meinhardt, 2017; Moors, Wagemans, & de-Wit, 2016b; Stein et al., 2011a). Subsequent studies used the inversion manipulation both to study unconscious object processing as well as to control for low-level physical differences among stimuli. Image inversion is an elegant manipulation as it keeps physical properties (pixel values) intact, while it disrupts the stimuli's meaningfulness, configuration, or structure. Inversion effects in b-CFS have been found to be larger for faces and human bodies than for houses (Zhou, Zhang, Liu, Yang, & Qu, 2010a) or for other animate and inanimate objects (Stein, Sterzer, & Peelen, 2012b). This indicates some face- and body-specific unconscious processing, and most likely reflects an effect of visual experience or expertise, as inversion effects are also larger for faces seen under natural lighting conditions (Stein, Peelen, & Sterzer, 2011b), for faces from one's own race and age group (Stein, End, & Sterzer, 2014), and for objects of expertise (Stein, Reeder, & Peelen, 2016).

One topic that has attracted a lot of research interest is whether emotional or socially relevant stimuli receive privileged unconscious processing, perhaps mediated by a specialized subcortical pathway to the amygdala (e.g. Pessoa & Adolphs, 2010; Tamietto & de Gelder, 2010; also see Madipakkam & Rothkirch, Chapter 4 in this volume). Already the second published b-CFS study showed an advantage of fearful over neutral and happy faces, but this fear advantage was similarly present for inverted faces (Yang, Zald, & Blake, 2007). If this effect was related to differences in emotional meaning one would expect a smaller effect for inverted faces, as it is more difficult to extract emotional meaning from inverted faces. A full-strength effect for inverted faces indicates that low-level physical differences between faces – which are fully preserved in inverted faces – caused the effect. Many subsequent b-CFS studies manipulated facial expressions, consistently finding an advantage of fearful expressions (e.g. Capitão, Underdown, Vile, Yang, Harmer, & Murphy, 2014; Oliver, Mao, & Mitchell, 2015; Zhan, Hortensius, & de Gelder, 2015). Other studies showed that this effect does not rely on a specialized subcortical pathway to the amygdala (Stein, Seymour, Hebart, & Sterzer, 2014; Tsuchiya, Moradi, Felsen, Yamazaki, & Adolphs, 2009) but reflects specific physical differences between stimuli that are unrelated to emotion per se (Gray, Adams, Hedger, Newton, & Garner, 2013; Hedger, Adams, & Garner, 2015; also see Stein & Sterzer, 2012).

Many other properties of faces have been studied using b-CFS (also see Axelrod, Bar, & Rees, 2015). These studies found shorter suppression times for faces making eye contact (Chen & Yeh, 2012; Madipakkam, Rothkirch, Guggenmos, Heinz, & Sterzer, 2015; Stein, Senju, Peelen, & Sterzer, 2011c; Yokoyama, Noguchi, & Kita, 2013), for faces turned towards the viewer (Gobbini, Gors, Halchenko, Hughes, Cipolli, 2013a), for trustworthy and non-dominant faces (Abir, Sklar, Dotsch, Todorov, & Hassin, 2018; Getov, Kanai, Bahrami, & Rees, 2015; Stein, Awad, Gayet, & Peelen, 2018; Stewart, Ajina, Getov, Bahrami, Todorov, & Rees, 2012), for attractive faces (Hung et al., 2016; Nakamura & Kawabata, 2018), male adult and female baby faces compared to male baby and female adult faces (Zheng, Luo, Hu, & Peng, 2018), for faces of friends compared to strangers (Gobbini, Gors, Halchenko, Rogers, Guntupalli, Hughes, & Cipolli, 2013b), and for one's own face compared to famous faces (Geng, Zhang, Li, Tao, & Xu, 2012). However, these studies either did not use an inversion control (Geng et al., 2012; Getov et al., 2015; Gobbini et al., 2013a, 2013b; Hung et al., 2016; Madipakkam et al., 2015; Stewart et al., 2012; Yokoyama et al., 2013; Zheng et al., 2018) or found similar effects for inverted faces (Abir et al., 2018; Chen & Yeh, 2012; Nakamura & Kawabata, 2018; Stein et al., 2011c, 2018), such that differences in suppression times could have reflected physical differences rather than differential processing of the facial property per se. Similarly, differences in suppression times between different emotional body

The b-CFS paradigm **13**

postures (Zhan et al., 2015) or between snakes and birds (Gomes, Silva, Silva, & Soares, 2017; Gomes, Soares, Silva, & Silva, 2018) could reflect confounding physical differences between stimuli (for recent evidence supporting this view, see Stein et al., 2018, and Gayet, Stein, & Peelen, 2019).

Thus, even when accepting the b-CFS rationale that suppression time differences reflect unconscious processing differences, it is not yet clear whether these facial attributes or affective stimulus properties are indeed registered under suppression. Alternatively, some uncontrolled physical difference among stimuli could have caused these effects. Some studies addressed this issue by showing that b-CFS effects correlated with questionnaire-based personality traits (Capitão et al., 2014; Oliver et al., 2015; Schmack, Burk, Haynes, & Sterzer, 2016; Stewart et al., 2012). Here, the idea is that the individual significance of a stimulus determines the extent of unconscious processing. For example, the advantage of spiders over flowers in b-CFS was correlated with self-reported spider phobia symptoms (Schmack et al., 2016), and the b-CFS disadvantage of dominant faces with less self-reported propensity to trust (Stewart et al., 2012). Although these correlations are typically weak and sometimes not replicable (Stein et al., 2018, failed to replicate Stewart et al., 2012), this may represent a promising approach to unconscious processing of behaviorally relevant stimuli.

In summary, b-CFS experiments with faces and objects show that suppression times are influenced by familiarity, meaningfulness, or visual expertise, with more familiar stimuli having privileged access to awareness. Future studies implementing more stringent low-level controls are required to answer whether other properties related to a face's or object's emotional or social significance can indeed influence suppression times.

4.1.3 Words and phrases

Similar to faces, also suppression times for words are influenced by familiarity. A participant's familiarity with a writing system (Chinese, English, Hebrew) results in shorter suppression times (Jiang et al., 2007; Rabagliati, Robertson, & Carmel, 2018), and a b-CFS inversion effect exists for words as well (Kerr, Hesselmann, Räling, Wartenburger, & Sterzer, 2017; Yang, Tien, Yang, & Yeh, 2017; Yang & Yeh, 2011, 2014; but see Heyman & Moors, 2014). Surprisingly, no consistent effect of word frequency on suppression times has been found (Heyman & Moors, 2014; Prioli & Kahan, 2015), and one study even failed to find differences between real words and pseudo-words (Heyman & Moors, 2014). This may indicate that the influence of familiarity (as evidenced by the inversion effect) is limited to the processing of single upright vs. inverted letters, while integration into whole words might be disrupted by CFS.

Above and beyond familiarity, the use of words or phrases as stimuli offers unique possibilities to test for influences of self-relevance, emotional content, and semantics on suppression times while minimizing differences in low-level physical factors. Unfortunately, the b-CFS literature is far from consistent regarding the existence of such higher-level effects. While there are no differences between words denoting attributed that were judged to be self-related or not (Noel, Blanke, Serino, & Salomon, 2017), two studies found an effect of a word's emotional meaning, with negative Chinese and English single words taking longer than neutral words to break suppression (Prioli & Kahan, 2015; Yang & Yeh, 2011), an effect akin to "perceptual defense" (Postman, Bronson, & Gropper, 1953). Yang and Yeh (2011) also included an inversion control, such that physical differences between negative and neutral words were an unlikely cause for the effect.

While these studies investigated the processing of single words, another study received much attention for being the first to provide evidence that suppression times could be influenced by the semantic relationship among multiple words, i.e. phrases (Sklar, Levy, Goldstein, Mandel, Maril, & Hassin, 2012). This study found *shorter* suppression times for negative phrases (e.g. electric chair) than for neutral phrases (e.g. dining table), a finding that is difficult to reconcile with evidence for perceptual defense for single negative words. Furthermore, this study also found *shorter* suppression times for semantically incoherent phrases (e.g. I ironed the coffee) than for coherent phrases (e.g. I drank coffee), a result that is at odds with the more commonly reported b-CFS advantage of familiar stimuli. While these results were considered the first evidence for multi-word integration under CFS ("reading"), a recent large-scale replication failed to replicate these findings (Rabagliati et al., 2018; for another conceptual replication failure see Yang et al., 2017).

Thus, also for words there is good evidence that visual familiarity influences suppression times, although this effect may be related to single-letter processing. Semantic effects, by contrast, seem limited, although the study by Yang and Yeh (2011) provides some initial evidence for an effect of valence that is specific to upright words. In the light of recent failures to replicate high-profile b-CFS findings (Rabagliati et al., 2018; Moors, Boelens, van Overwalle, & Wagemans, 2016a; also see below), these interesting findings require independent replication.

4.1.4 Perceptual and affective learning

One elegant way of ruling out confounding low-level physical stimulus differences is to record suppression times for stimuli that differ only with regard to their learning history. However, there is not much evidence for an effect of perceptual learning on b-CFS. In one study, several blocks of detecting gratings with a particular orientation did not result in shorter suppression times for this specific orientation (Mastropasqua, Tse, & Turatto, 2015). Similarly, perceptual learning of a particular motion direction was not associated with faster breakthrough (Paffen, Gayet, Heilbron, & Van der Stigchel, 2018). Rather, observer's overall suppression times got shorter over time, and this effect was specific to the eye of target presentation (Mastropasqua et al., 2015), but not specific to the trained feature.

In order to elicit feature-specific effects through learning, these features need to be associated with threat. One study measured suppression times for gratings that had been paired with electric shocks in a classical fear conditioning procedure (Gayet, Paffen, Belopolsky, Theeuwes, & Van der Stigchel, 2016). Fear-conditioned orientations broke suppression faster, indicating enhanced unconscious processing for stimuli that signal threat. Similar results have been obtained with fear-conditioned faces (Vieira, Wen, Oliver, & Mitchell, 2017).

This effect of affective learning seems limited to classical conditioning involving threatening unconditioned stimuli. Two studies that used an affective learning procedure in which participants learned to associate faces with negative, neutral, or positive autobiographical stories failed to obtain effects on b-CFS (Rabovsky, Stein, & Rahman, 2016; Stein, Grubb, Bertrand, Suh, & Verosky, 2017). Similarly, associating stimuli with self-relevant information (which is known to affect performance in more complex discrimination tasks) did not influence b-CFS with a standard simple localization task (Stein, Siebold, & van Zoest, 2016). Another b-CFS study found an effect of self-relevancy with an identification task (Macrae, Visokomogilski, Golubickis, Cunningham, & Sahraie, 2017), which taps into later perceptual processes and is more prone to the influence of post-perceptual factors, such that this effect may not reflect a genuine difference in transition times (see section 4.2).

4.1.5 Priming, working memory, and attention

Suppression times for identical stimuli do not only differ as a function of affective learning history, but also depending on the context in which they are presented (for an in-depth review of contextual influences, see Gayet et al., 2014). Several studies investigated how priming affects suppression times. Note that this priming procedure is different from the classical dissociation paradigm. These priming b-CFS studies measured the effect of a conscious prime on the suppression time of a subsequent target stimulus. Suppression times are shorter when prime words or images predict a target's object identity, object category, or color (Forder, Taylor, Mankin, Scott, & Franklin, 2016; Lupyan & Ward, 2013; Ostarek & Huettig, 2017; Pinto, van Gaal, de Lange, Lamme, & Seth, 2015; Stein & Peelen, 2015; Stein, Thoma, & Sterzer, 2015; Sun, Cai, & Lu, 2015). Priming can occur even on a purely semantic level. For example, a word prime (e.g. "sock") leads to shorter suppression times for semantically related targets (e.g. "shoe") than for unrelated targets (e.g. "tape"; Costello, Jiang, Baartman, McGlennen, & He, 2009; also see Kerr et al., 2017). Similar priming effects have been obtained for target words that syntactically matched a preceding prime word sequence, independent of semantics (Hung & Hsieh, 2015). Such findings indicate that unconscious processing can be influenced by conscious visual, semantic, and abstract information.

Some of these priming effects may be rather short-lived and seem to disappear when the temporal interval between prime and target is increased to more than one second (Ostarek & Huettig, 2017; but see Stein et al., 2015). Longer-lasting effects from conscious information on suppression times have been obtained in studies manipulating working memory content. Keeping a specific color, shape, face identity, or emotional facial expression in mind over the course of a b-CFS trial is associated with shorter suppression times for targets matching the content of working memory (Gayet, Paffen, & Van der Stigchel, 2013; Gayet, van Maanen, Heilbron, Paffen, & van der Stigchel, 2016; Liu, Wang, Wang, & Jiang, 2016; Pan, Lin, Zhao, & Soto, 2014). Similarly, inducing or adopting a particular attentional set or adding attentional load can influence suppression times (De Loof, Poppe, Cleeremans, Gevers, & Van Opstal 2015; Sun, Cant, & Ferber, 2016), and these attentional influences can even be eye-specific (Zhang, Jiang, & He, 2012). Thus, top-down influences seem to be capable of reaching the earliest, monocular levels of visual processing during b-CFS.

4.1.6 Multimodal integration

Another way of testing contextual influences on b-CFS is to present matching or mismatching information through other modalities. For example, smelling an odorant (the smell of the rose) during a b-CFS trial shortens suppression times for a matching target (an image of a rose) relative to a mismatching target (an image of a pen marker; Zhou, Jiang, He, & Chen, 2010b). Such findings could be taken to suggest that nonvisual sensory information can be integrated with unconscious visual information.

Several studies adopting a similar approach for the auditory modality arrived at partly inconsistent conclusions. One study found no effect from concurrent auditory stimulation (Moors, Huygelier, Wagemans, de-Wit, & van Ee, 2015), another found that a sound shortened suppression times, but that congruence between the pitch of a tone and the target's visual field location did not lead to additional benefits (Mustonen, Nuutinen, Vainio, & Häkkinen, 2018). Other studies found shorter suppression times when sounds were spatially congruent with b-CFS targets (Aller, Giani, Conrad, Watanabe, & Noppeney, 2015; Yang & Yeh, 2014), and modulations of suppression times when a sound was in or out of synch with the contrast modulation of a target grating (Hong & Shim, 2016). Evidence for such audiovisual integration has been obtained with more complex stimuli as well: Suppression times are shorter for congruent shape-sound pairings (Hung, Styles, & Hsieh, 2017), for talking faces with matched auditory sentences (Alsius & Munhall, 2013), and for images and video clips of scenes with matching scenery soundtracks (Cox & Hong, 2015; Tan & Yeh, 2015). Importantly, some of these findings are unlikely to be explained by semantic priming alone, because effects disappeared when the auditory stimulus was presented before rather than concurrently with the b-CFS target (Cox & Hong, 2015; Tan & Yeh, 2015).

Similar evidence for multimodal integration in b-CFS has been obtained for other modalities beyond audition and olfaction. One study found shorter suppression times for dots moving out of synch with a touch to participant's back (Salomon, Galli, Lukowska, Faivre, Ruiz, & Blanke, 2016a) Another study found that touching a haptic grating shortens suppression times for gratings with congruent orientations (Lunghi, Lo Verde, & Alais, 2017). Such benefits have also been found when matching vestibular signals (participant's rotation direction on a rotating chair) with the direction of optic flow targets (Salomon, Kaliuzhna, Herbelin, & Blanke, 2015). For proprioception, there is currently evidence for and against integration with visual information in b-CFS. One study found that b-CFS targets presented against an irrelevant hand background broke suppression faster when the observer's hand was in a congruent position (Salomon, Lim, Herbelin, Hesselmann, & Blanke, 2013). Another study did not find an effect of matching observer's voluntary or spontaneous facial expressions with face targets displaying emotional expression (Korb, Osimo, Suran, Goldstein, & Rumiati, 2017).

While some of these findings could reflect semantic priming or participants figuring out the purpose of the study (demand characteristics), this is unlikely to be the case for a final, particularly intriguing finding, showing that even interoceptive signals can be integrated with visual information in b-CFS: flashing targets presented in synch with participant's heartbeat were found to be associated with longer suppression times than targets presented out of synch (Salomon et al., 2016b, 2018). Importantly, this happened despite participants being unable to tell whether flashing targets (presented without CFS) were in or out of synch with their heartbeat.

4.1.7 Clinical studies

The b-CFS paradigm has also been used to study altered unconscious processing in clinical populations. All of these studies used faces or emotional stimuli as b-CFS targets, thus testing whether certain mental disorders were associated with biases in unconscious processing of socially relevant stimuli (also see Madipakkam & Rothkirch, Chapter 4 of this volume). Indeed, one study found evidence for so-called mood-congruent biases, with suppression times for sad faces being reduced in patients with major depressive disorder (Sterzer, Hilgenfeldt, Freudenberg, Bermpohl, & Adli, 2011), but a later study did not replicate this finding (Münkler, Rothkirch, Dalati, Schmack, & Sterzer, 2015). Two studies found evidence that psychopathic traits were related to longer suppression times for fearful faces (Jusyte, Mayer, Künzel, Hautzinger, & Schönenberg, 2015; Sylvers, Brennan, & Lilienfeld, 2011), which is in line with the "fearlessness" hypothesis of psychopathy (Lykken, 1957), locating its origin in impaired unconscious visual processing. Three studies tested individuals with autism spectrum disorder. While face inversion effects were found to be normal (Akechi et al., 2015), in contrast to healthy participants there was no evidence for shorter suppression times for faces making eye contact (Akechi et al., 2014) or for rewarding social scenes (Gray, Haffey, Mihaylova, & Chakrabarti, 2018). Individuals with schizophrenia, however, showed a normal b-CFS advantage for faces making eye contact (Seymour, Rhodes, Stein, & Langdon, 2016).

4.1.8 Visual integration and replication issues

The recent failure to replicate two high-profile b-CFS studies caused a debate on the possibility of unconscious visual integration under CFS (Moors, Hesselmann,

Wagemans, & van Ee, 2017; Sklar et al., 2018; Moors et al., 2019). As reviewed above, one study found suppression time modulations from multi-word phrases (Sklar et al., 2012), indicating unconscious integration of spatially separate words ("reading"). The other study showed that scenes with incongruent objects (e.g. a chessboard in the oven) broke CFS more quickly than scenes with congruent objects (Mudrik, Breska, Lamy, & Deouell, 2011). Both original findings (advantage of incoherent phrases and of incongruent scenes) were inconsistent with the general b-CFS advantage of more familiar, typical, or meaningful stimuli and both findings failed to replicate in recent large-scale replication attempts (Moors et al., 2016a; Rabagliati et al., 2018). One other study provided evidence that pairs of objects placed in normal (congruent) spatial configurations (e.g. lamp above a table) break suppression *faster* than objects placed in uncommon configurations (e.g. lamp below a table; Stein, Kaiser, & Peelen, 2015). This effect, however, may not require explicit integration, because such typical configurations of object pairs may be processed as one perceptual unit by the visual system (Kaiser, Stein, & Peelen, 2014). Future work is required to answer whether suppression times can be influenced by target conditions where two or more distinct visual stimuli need to be integrated into a whole.

The more general issue raised by these failures to replicate highly influential b-CFS findings is to clarify whether and why b-CFS studies are prone to produce false positives. Two recent papers have highlighted how "researcher degrees of freedom" (Simmons, Nelson, & Simonsohn, 2011) may be of particular concern with the b-CFS paradigm (Kerr et al., 2017; Rabagliati et al., 2018). In brief, most b-CFS studies use RT measures (see below) and b-CFS RT distributions have positive skew and kurtosis, with an extremely long tail. Deriving an appropriate measure of central tendency is therefore not trivial, and different researchers use a wide range of different transformation and data exclusion methods (Kerr et al., 2017; also see Gayet & Stein, 2017). Future b-CFS work would greatly benefit from pre-registered, openly available, or even standardized analysis pipelines (Rothkirch & Hesselmann, 2017).

4.2 Tasks and measures

Before discussing different tasks and measures used in b-CFS studies it is important to recall that suppression times should ideally provide an accurate estimate of the transition from unconscious processing to conscious awareness. Perceptual or post-perceptual processes that occur after this transition into awareness should not influence an ideal measure of suppression times.

4.2.1 Speeded RT-based measures

As can be seen in Figure 1.3, the vast majority of b-CFS studies followed the seminal study by Jiang and colleagues (2007) and adopted RT-based localization tasks, in which participants indicate as quickly and accurately as possible in which of two or four possible spatial locations a target appears. The second most common way of quantifying suppression times in b-CFS studies are RT-based detection tasks, where participants indicate as quickly and accurately as possible the appearance of a target. This detection task is sometimes followed by an additional localization task. Intuitively, stimulus detection or localization captures the transition into awareness well, while being relatively immune to later (post-)perceptual influences. As soon as one is aware of a stimulus, one should be able to report its presence or location. At the same time, neither detection nor localization requires later recognition or identification.

However, the RT-based, speeded nature of these tasks requires subjects to set some arbitrary criterion for providing their localization or detection response through a button press. The required sensory evidence will inevitably vary within and between participants (e.g. depending on motivation, exact instruction, speed-accuracy tradeoff etc.) and, more importantly, between experimental conditions. For example, it is conceivable that less sensory evidence is required to make a localization/detection response for familiar stimuli (e.g. upright faces) than for less familiar stimuli (e.g. inverted faces). In this scenario, actual transition times could be similar but recorded suppression times would differ as a function of different decision criteria. More broadly speaking, RT-based measures are susceptible to post-perceptual influences that are beyond the control of the experimenter, and can therefore not be taken as valid measures of the transition into awareness. In addition to post-perceptual decisional influences, it is also possible that later perceptual processes influence recorded suppression times. There is simply no way to tell if subjects fail to comply with instructions and, for example, decide to withhold their detection or localization response until they can partly or fully recognize and identify an initially suppressed stimulus. It is not even known whether human observers are capable of providing a speeded response to precisely indicate target localization or detection before having identified a stimulus or stimulus parts. Again, such later perceptual processes may vary between conditions (e.g. upright faces are easier to identify than inverted faces) and could influence recorded suppression times. Thus, due to the very nature of speeded RT-based tasks, differences in suppression times obtained with RT-based localization or detection tasks cannot be taken as evidence for differential unconscious processing. Any measured difference in suppression times could stem from later perceptual and even post-perceptual processes.

Some of these issues are exacerbated when RT-based discrimination or identification tasks are used (see Figure 1.3), especially when the required discrimination is not fully orthogonal to the experimental manipulation. When the required discrimination is very basic (e.g. judging the orientation of a grating) and the experimental manipulation is fully orthogonal (e.g. influence of the color of the annulus surrounding the grating on b-CFS, see Gayet et al., 2016), discrimination-based RTs are similar to localization-/detection-based RTs. However, when the required discrimination (e.g. judging the orientation of a grating) is directly related to the experimental manipulation (e.g. touching a haptic grating with congruent or incongruent orientation, see Lunghi et al., 2017), any recorded effect could be entirely related to later perceptual processes of stimulus identification (which may be speeded e.g. in the congruent cases) rather than breakthrough into awareness. Furthermore, with non-orthogonal discrimination tasks the confounding influence of post-perceptual decisional and strategic factors could be larger as well. Thus, none of these RT-based measures can be considered a valid index of a target's transition into awareness.

4.2.2 Non-speeded accuracy-based measures

A solution to some of these issues lies in adopting non-speeded accuracy-based localization or detection tasks. Such tasks can be used to derive criterion-free measures of perceptual sensitivity, for example using signal detection theory. Dependent measures in these studies include performance scores (e.g. proportion correct or d') and estimates of detection or localization thresholds from adaptive staircase procedures. Only a handful of b-CFS studies used such accuracy-based detection or localization tasks instead or in addition to RT-based tasks (see Figure 1.3). The key difference in comparison with RT-based b-CFS tasks lies in fixing the duration of a trial. In RT-based tasks a trial is terminated when the subject responds, whereas in accuracy-based tasks stimuli are presented for a fixed duration and subjects respond without speed pressure. Different response criteria for different conditions should thus not affect response accuracy, such that post-perceptual influences are ruled out.

Given this advantage, why are accuracy-based tasks not more widely adopted in b-CFS studies? First, while RT-based tasks are straightforward to implement, it can be challenging and time-consuming to set up and run accuracy-based b-CFS tasks. As suppression times are highly variable within and between individuals (e.g. Stein et al., 2011a; Gayet & Stein, 2017), it can be difficult to avoid floor or ceiling effects with fixed presentation times. Staircase procedures offer a part solution by adaptively adjusting presentation times or stimulus energy based on performance (see Hung et al., 2016; Moors et al., 2015; Stein et al., 2011a). Second, RT-based measures may have more intuitive appeal. After subtracting a few hundred milliseconds for motor preparation, RTs seem to provide a direct estimate of the time it took different stimuli to enter awareness. In comparison, it may be more difficult to make sense of some estimated threshold value from a staircase procedure that converges to, say, 75 percent correct. Clearly, this should not preclude the use of accuracy-based tasks in b-CFS experiments given that such threshold estimates and estimates of associated psychometric functions are the most common dependent measures in visual psychophysics.

Finally, some researchers seem concerned that forced-choice localization performance or criterion-free measures of detection sensitivity may not capture transition into awareness, but may instead tap into blindsight-like unconscious perception (Gayet et al., 2014). Here, the issue is not that the measure may be influenced by (post-)perceptual processes that occur after the transition point but that the measure could reflect unconscious processes that occur beforehand, while

The b-CFS paradigm **21**

not being related to stimulus awareness or reportability. Indeed, if this were the case one assumption of this approach to unconscious processing, namely a precise measure of the transition point, would not be met. However, in my view, this possibility represents an advantage rather than a problem for accuracy-based tasks. If a difference between experimental conditions in such accuracy-based tasks indeed reflected differences in preceding unconscious processing, this version of the b-CFS paradigm would actually measure what it had been developed to measure in the first place, namely differential unconscious processing. One could then also relax the assumption that a precise measure of the transition point is required to infer unconscious processing. If a measure is only tapping into processes that occur *before* rather than after the hypothetical transition point, any influence on this measure must, by definition, be unconscious.

Thus, accuracy-based tasks represent a solution to many of the issues related to RT-based measures of suppression times discussed above. Nevertheless, the actual implementation is important. Some studies fixed presentation times but combined an accuracy-based with an RT-based task, taking RTs, hit rates, and detection sensitivity (d') as dependent measures (e.g. Forder et al., 2016; Lupyan & Ward, 2013; Ostarek & Huettig, 2017; Sun et al., 2015). Here, additional speeded response requirements could have interfered with perceptual sensitivity, such that differences in response criteria between conditions could inadvertently have had an effect on detection sensitivity. It would be preferable to entirely remove any speeded response requirements and take detection sensitivity or localization accuracy as the only dependent measure.

Furthermore, even when post-perceptual influences are ruled out by using non-speeded tasks, later perceptual processes may play an undesired role. Although largely unexplored, it seems possible in principle that accuracy-based, criterion-free localization or detection measures could ("recursively") be influenced by later conscious stimulus recognition or identification (e.g. Hochstein & Ahissar, 2002). This could represent a problem for the b-CFS notion of a sequential (hierarchical) stream from unconscious processing to conscious perception. In particular, when localization or detection sensitivity is relatively high (i.e. d' well above 0), it is very likely that in many trials stimuli were not only successfully localized or detected but also consciously identified. If successful identification could recursively influence localization or detection performance (e.g. by increasing confidence), and if identification performance differed between conditions (e.g. upright vs. inverted faces, or validly vs. invalidly primed objects), this would have a confounding influence on suppression time estimates from accuracy-based detection or localization tasks. At the end of this chapter (sections 5.1 and 5.2) I will propose two ways of avoiding this potential issue in future, improved accuracy-based b-CFS studies.

In summary, RT-based measures of suppression times are straightforward to implement but cannot provide a valid estimate of the transition into awareness. Future b-CFS studies should instead implement non-speeded detection or localization tasks to derive criterion-free measures of detection sensitivity or localization accuracy.

Tasks and measures in b-CFS studies

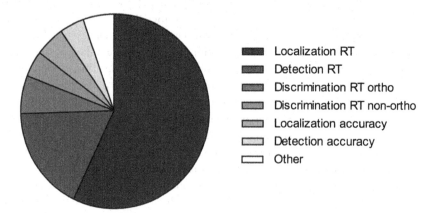

FIGURE 1.3 Tasks and measures used in b-CFS studies. The 115 b-CFS publications included in the present review were categorized according to the tasks and measures they adopted. When several tasks or measures were used in a single paper, we included the one task or measure on which the most important conclusions of the study were based. "Localization" refers to tasks requiring participants to indicate a target's location. "Detection" refers to tasks requiring participants to indicate target appearance (and sometimes, to indicate target absence). "Discrimination" refers to tasks requiring participants to categorize the target e.g. based on its features. "Ortho" means that discrimination tasks were orthogonal to the experimental manipulation (e.g. Gayet et al., 2016; response to grating orientation but study measured the influence of the color of a surrounding annulus). "Non-ortho" means that the discrimination tasks were not fully orthogonal to the experimental manipulation (e.g. Lunghi et al., 2017; response to grating orientation and study measured the influence of congruence between haptic and visual orientation). "RT" means that the primary outcome measure was response time. "Accuracy" means that some non-RT-based measure was at least one of the primary outcome measures, such as detection d' (e.g. Kaunitz et al., 2013), proportion correct in localization (e.g. Oliver et al., 2015), staircase thresholds for localizability (e.g. Moors et al., 2015), or staircase threshold for detectability (e.g. Hung et al., 2016). "Other" refers to measures that do not naturally fall into any of these categories, e.g. accuracy-based discrimination tasks, or subjective confidence ratings.

4.3 Control conditions and other psychophysical techniques

Forty-six out of the 115 b-CFS studies reviewed here included a non-CFS binocular or monocular control condition. With one exception (Sun et al., 2015), all of these b-CFS studies used purely RT-based tasks in both the b-CFS and in the control condition. As can be seen in Figure 1.4, nearly all of these studies obtained a significant effect in the b-CFS condition. In the control condition, by contrast,

The b-CFS paradigm **23**

effects were either absent or strongly reduced. This may indicate that most studies were successful in controlling for the factor the control condition was intended to control for. However, I believe that this demonstrates that control conditions simply have rather poor sensitivity for measuring differences between conditions, and that this represents a serious concern for b-CFS studies that base their conclusions on a comparison with the results from such control conditions.

Control conditions have been employed in two ways. Many RT-based b-CFS studies attempted to control for the effect of post-perceptual factors on suppression times. Other b-CFS studies used control conditions to isolate CFS-specific unconscious processing differences as a cause for differences in suppression times. However, because control conditions differ from b-CFS conditions in many ways, including subjective perceptual experience, target appearance, perceptual uncertainty, and target predictability, both approaches lack validity.

4.3.1 Control for post-perceptual factors

As described above (section 4.2.1), post-perceptual factors such as differences in response criteria or motor preparation can influence RT-based measures of suppression times. Although it might be possible in principle to design a control condition that captures all post-perceptual factors that might have played a role in b-CFS, it is unlikely that control conditions that have been employed in the literature were successful in doing so. In fact, control conditions fail to mimic the rather unique perceptual experience under CFS (see Stein et al., 2011a). Subjectively, the impression of an abrupt, all-or-none transition of the target stimulus into awareness is rare in b-CFS, and partial suppression and piecemeal breakthrough are common. Because of the stochastic fluctuations of interocular suppression (Blake & Logothetis, 2002) target appearance in b-CFS is unpredictable and associated with a high degree of perceptual uncertainty. In control conditions, by contrast, targets are usually slowly blended into the CFS masks, such that subjective target appearance differs from b-CFS and is highly predictable. Indeed, b-CFS RT distributions have much more spread and much longer tails than control RT distributions.

Therefore, b-CFS may be associated with a higher degree of perceptual uncertainty than control conditions. With high perceptual uncertainty the influence of different response criteria for different conditions on recorded RT differences may be particularly strong, and may thus contribute to the sometimes surprisingly large effects obtained with b-CFS. For example, large effects have been obtained when comparing familiar (or cued, primed, predicted) stimuli, which may be associated with a lower response criterion, to unfamiliar (or non-cued, non-primed, non-predicted) stimuli (e.g. RT differences between upright and inverted faces in a simple localization task of >800 ms, see Stein et al., 2011a). In the control condition, where target appearance is highly predictable, participants may adopt a different response strategy, such that RTs may be less influenced by differential response criteria, and this may contribute to reduced or absent effects. Independent of these speculations, the mere fact that b-CFS and control conditions differ along many dimensions other than just the presence or absence of interocular suppression renders their comparison invalid. To conclusively rule out the influence of post-perceptual factors in b-CFS researchers should replace RT measures of suppression times with non-speeded, accuracy-based detection or localization tasks.

4.3.2 Isolating CFS-specific processing

The other approach of using control conditions goes beyond controlling just for post-perceptual factors. Here, an attempt is being made to show that any difference in target detectability resulted from CFS-specific differences in unconscious processing, rather than from general differences in stimulus detectability (see section 3.2). Thus, the control condition needs to measure all non-CFS specific differences in stimulus detectability that might have contributed to the b-CFS effect. As discussed above, this reasoning is unwarranted because it is unlikely that the control condition captures all of the relevant factors. In fact, standard b-CFS control conditions seem to represent a rather poor way of measuring non-CFS specific differences in stimulus detectability. For example, the detection advantage for upright over inverted faces has been obtained with several psychophysical techniques other than b-CFS (e.g. Garrido, Duchaine, & Nakayama, 2008; Purcell & Stewart, 1988), but b-CFS control conditions have repeatedly failed to yield a significant inversion effect. Again, the mere fact that control conditions are

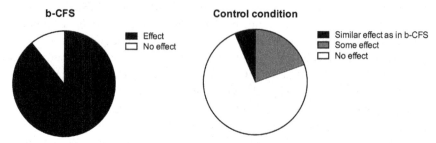

FIGURE 1.4 Effects and null effects in b-CFS studies with control conditions. Left panel: The 46 b-CFS studies that included a control condition were categorized according to whether a significant effect was obtained in the b-CFS condition or not. Studies that failed to obtain a significant effect in their main analysis but found some other effect were categorized as "no effect" (e.g. Korb et al., 2017, focused on integration with interoception but found effect from facial expressions). Right panel: Results from control conditions were categorized as "no effect" when there was no significant difference, as "some effect" when the effect was significantly smaller than in the b-CFS condition or when only some effect that was not of primary interest to the study was significant, or as "similar effect as in the b-CFS condition".

The b-CFS paradigm **25**

not fully comparable to b-CFS renders their comparison invalid, and conclusions about CFS-specific unconscious processing differences based on their comparison are unwarranted.

4.3.3 Comparisons with other psychophysical techniques

Only twelve b-CFS studies took the opposite approach and sought to generalize their b-CFS findings to other psychophysical techniques. These studies tested whether similar differences in stimulus detectability or early stimulus processing could be obtained with standard binocular rivalry (Stein et al., 2017; Zhou et al., 2010b), backward or sandwich masking (Hedger et al., 2015; Hung et al., 2017; Stein et al., 2014, 2015) visual search (Tsuchiya et al., 2009), inattentional blindness (Li et al., 2015), rapid serial visual presentation (Cohen et al., 2015; Gobbini et al., 2013), crowding (Salomon et al., 2016b), or attentional capture (Zheng et al., 2018). Interestingly, all eleven out of these twelve studies that obtained an effect in the b-CFS experiment also obtained some (often quite similar) effect with these other psychophysical techniques.

This illustrates two points. First, it seems that at least some of the effects obtained with b-CFS are not related to CFS-specific unconscious processing. Second, the fact that standard b-CFS control conditions usually produce null results while these other non-CFS detection measures yield significant effects suggests that control conditions indeed have rather poor sensitivity for measuring differences between conditions. Together, this adds to the concerns regarding any conclusions about CFS-specific unconscious processing (section 3.2). A more promising avenue for future studies consists in comparing effects obtained with – preferably accuracy-based, non-speeded – b-CFS detection or localization tasks to other psychophysical techniques measuring stimulus detection or localization. If differences in stimulus detectability are taken to reflect differences in preceding unconscious processing (section 3.1) the same logic should be applied to findings obtained with other psychophysical techniques.

5 Recommendations and future avenues

The b-CFS paradigm represents a novel approach to unconscious processing, fundamentally different from previous, established approaches adopting the dissociation paradigm. It remains to be seen if its underlying logic will find broad acceptance in the field. This chapter represents an attempt to flesh out and clarify the paradigm's underlying logic. Perhaps most importantly, any user of the b-CFS paradigm necessarily adopts certain assumptions, some of which might or might not be valid. Inferring CFS-specific unconscious processing from a comparison with a control condition rests on the assumption that the control condition is comparable to b-CFS. This assumption is invalid (see sections 3.2 and 4.3.2; Stein et al., 2011a; Stein & Sterzer, 2014). Inferences about CFS-specific unconscious processing are therefore unwarranted.

But even inferring unconscious processing differences from detection differences – with no claim about CFS-specificity – rests on a set of assumptions that are rarely spelled out in the literature. To reiterate (section 3.1), these are (a) a temporal sequence from unconscious processing to conscious perception and (b) a precise measure of the transition point from unconscious processing to conscious perception, or a measure that is influenced only by processes preceding the hypothetical transition point. As reviewed in the previous sections, for this reasoning to be valid suppression times need not be influenced by later perceptual processes or by post-perceptual factors.

Ruling out influences from post-perceptual factors can be achieved through non-speeded, accuracy-based detection or localization tasks (see sections 4.2 and 4.3.1). Ruling out influences from perceptual processes that only take place after the transition into awareness but may nevertheless influence suppression times is more challenging. In the final sections, I will propose two ways that may be useful for ruling out such undesirable later perceptual influences in future studies. These recommendations are not specific to b-CFS but similarly apply when other psychophysical techniques are used to measure differences in stimulus detectability.

5.1 Proposal I: Detection at threshold

One concern, even with non-speeded, accuracy-based detection or localization measures is that later perceptual processes that take place only after the transition into awareness (e.g. conscious stimulus discrimination or identification) could affect performance. As touched upon previously (section 4.2.2), it is possible in principle that a difference between conditions related to these later processes contributes to differences in detectability. Especially when overall detection or localization performance is relatively high (i.e. d' well above 0) it is likely that conscious stimulus identification occurs at least in a subset of trials. Conversely, when overall detection or localization performance is around chance level (i.e. $d' \approx 0$) conscious stimulus identification is very unlikely or impossible, assuming that discrimination and identification can occur only after initial detection.

Accordingly, one way to avoid the potentially confounding influence of later perceptual processes is to present stimuli at the (absolute) threshold for detection, such that performance is around chance level for condition A (e.g. inverted faces). This allows testing whether some manipulation hypothesized to influence the initial detection stage is associated with a lower (absolute) threshold, i.e. whether performance for condition B (e.g. upright faces) is just above chance level. A convincing demonstration of detection differences uncontaminated by later perceptual processing would establish (a) chance level performance (i.e. $d' \approx 0$) for condition A, (b) above-chance level performance (i.e. $d' > 0$) for condition B, and (c) significantly better performance for condition B than for condition A (see Figure 1.5a). Here, any difference between conditions must reflect an initial detection advantage.

This would represent a scenario where an experimental manipulation "boosts" one target stimulus into awareness (condition B, $d' > 0$), while the other remains unconscious (condition A, $d' \approx 0$). This idea of "boosting" a stimulus into awareness was coined previously in the title of the seminal paper by Lupyan and Ward (2013) who concluded that primes boosted congruent targets into awareness. However, in this study overall detection performance was very high ($d' > 1.5$), meaning that incongruent targets were consciously perceived in most trials as well. The priming effect could thus have been related to later perceptual processes. The same is true for most other b-CFS studies using accuracy-based tasks. It is thus quite possible that some of the effects reported in the literature disappear when stimuli are presented at threshold. For example, the b-CFS detection advantage for coherent radial motion relative to random walk motion, which was obtained at high levels of overall performance ($d' \approx 2$), disappeared at lower levels of overall performance ($d' \approx 0.5$; Kaunitz et al., 2013).

As the strength of CFS strongly varies between and within participants, it may be difficult in practice to present target stimuli at the threshold for detection. Although chance performance may be achieved by presenting targets for rather short presentation times and with low energy, this also risks floor effects, such that differences between conditions would be missed. Adjusting presentation parameters for each observer individually may be one solution, but trial-to-trial fluctuations in suppression strength and overall weakening of suppression strength over time (e.g. Ludwig, Sterzer, Kathmann, Franz, & Hesselmann, 2013; Mastropasqua et al., 2015; Paffen et al., 2018) represent procedural challenges. It may therefore be sensible to replace CFS with other psychophysical techniques, such as backward masking. As I have argued above, the logic of inferring unconscious processing differences from differences in detectability is not tied to the technique of CFS but can similarly be applied to other psychophysical techniques. With backward masking, for example, stimulation parameters can be more easily calibrated to present targets with maximum strength around the detection threshold.

5.2 Proposal II: Detection-discrimination dissociation

Another way to rule out any confounding influence from later perceptual processes is to demonstrate that participants cannot discriminate the relevant stimulus dimension. If the critical experimental manipulation could not be accessed but nevertheless affected detectability, this would provide convincing evidence for an initial detection difference uncontaminated by later perceptual processing. In addition, it would show that the relevant stimulus dimension was indeed truly unconscious, while still affecting detectability; thereby providing direct evidence that unconscious processing differences yielded the effect. To illustrate, if upright faces were detected better than inverted faces while participants could not discriminate between upright and inverted faces ($d' \approx 0$) this would demonstrate truly unconscious processing of the critical manipulated stimulus dimension, i.e. of face orientation. This logic could be applied to any b-CFS experiment, including studies on contextual influences, for example, by demonstrating that congruently primed targets were detected better than incongruently primed targets but participants could not discriminate between congruent and incongruent trials ($d' \approx 0$).

This approach would effectively turn the b-CFS paradigm into a direct-direct dissociation paradigm (see Figure 1.5b). One direct measure of stimulus awareness (accuracy-based, non-speeded detection or localization) would be contrasted with a direct measure of "manipulation awareness" (accuracy-based, non-speeded discrimination of the critical experimental manipulation). Thus, on every trial, two measures would be collected, one measure of detection or localization and one measure of stimulus discriminability. There is already some b-CFS evidence that localization performance can be better than discrimination performance. Kobylka and colleagues (2017) found localization performance for faces and houses to be superior to face-house discrimination performance, and their study also revealed

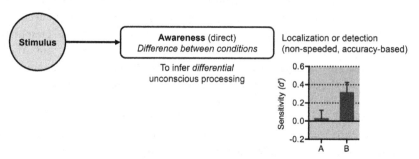

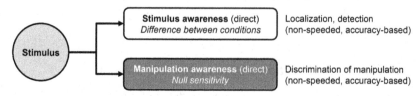

FIGURE 1.5 Two proposals for improved future detection paradigms that could provide evidence for unconscious processing differences. These proposals are not tied to the psychophysical technique of CFS but could be similarly used with other psychophysical techniques, such as backward masking. (a) In the detection-at-threshold paradigm one experimental condition (A) cannot be detected above chance ($d' \approx 0$), while the other condition (B) is detected above chance ($d' > 0$). This would virtually rule out the potentially confounding influence of later perceptual processes on detection measures. (b) In the detection-discrimination dissociation paradigm, experimental conditions differ in detectability but participants cannot discriminate between conditions. This would show that the experimental manipulation was truly unconscious but nevertheless caused a difference in target detectability.

a face inversion effect even when discrimination ability was rather low ($d' \approx 0.5$). Note that this study did not fit the criteria of the detection-discrimination paradigm proposed here, because the discrimination task did not measure the critical stimulus manipulation (upright vs. inverted faces) and discrimination performance was significantly greater than chance.

As with the detection-at-threshold proposal, the procedural challenge lies in finding appropriate stimulus presentation parameters, in particular when using CFS. The target needs to be displayed at a level that (a) yields null sensitivity in the discrimination task but (b) some sensitivity in the detection or localization task and (c) a difference between conditions in the detection or localization task. Backward masking might be preferable over CFS to test whether such a novel dissociation can be achieved in practice.

5.3 Conclusion

Although the b-CFS paradigm has been widely adopted to study unconscious processing, its underlying assumptions have rarely been spelled out. Because b-CFS is fundamentally different from conventional dissociation approaches to unconscious processing, it is important to consider the validity of its logic. Here, I have shown that b-CFS cannot be used to infer CFS-specific unconscious processing. But even when using b-CFS to infer unconscious processing differences – independent of their CFS-specificity – confounding influences from later perceptual or post-perceptual processes need to be ruled out. Results from published b-CFS studies could have been contaminated by such factors. I have proposed two novel approaches that future studies could adopt to avoid these problems. Both the detection-at-threshold paradigm and the detection-discrimination dissociation paradigm can be used to demonstrate that a difference in stimulus detectability was caused by unconscious processing differences. Perhaps ironically, psychophysical techniques other than CFS, such as backward masking, could similarly be used to implement these novel paradigms in future studies on unconscious visual processing.

References

Abir, Y., Sklar, A. Y., Dotsch, R., Todorov, A., & Hassin, R. R. (2018). The determinants of consciousness of human faces. *Nature Human Behavior, 2*, 194–9.

Akechi, H., Stein, T., Kikuchi, Y., Tojo, Y., Osanai, H., & Hasegawa, T. (2015). Preferential awareness of protofacial stimuli in autism. *Cognition, 143*, 129–34.

Akechi, H., Stein, T., Senju, A., Kikuchi, Y., Tojo, Y., Osanai, H., & Hasegawa, T. (2014). Absence of preferential unconscious processing of eye contact in adolescents with autism spectrum disorder. *Autism Research, 7*, 590–7.

Aller, M., Giani, A., Conrad, V., Watanabe, M., & Noppeney, U. (2015). A spatially collocated sound thrusts a flash into awareness. *Frontiers in Integrative Neuroscience, 9*, 16.

Almeida, J., Mahon, B. Z., Nakayama, K., & Caramazza, A. (2008). Unconscious processing dissociates along categorical lines. *Proceedings of the National Academy of Sciences USA, 105*, 15214–18.

Alsius, A., & Munhall, K. G. (2013). Detection of audiovisual speech correspondences without visual awareness. *Psychological Science, 24*, 423–31.

Amihai, I., Deouell, L., & Bentin, S. (2011). Conscious awareness is necessary for processing race and gender information from faces. *Consciousness and Cognition, 20*, 269–79.

Ananyev, E., Penney, T. B., & Hsieh, P. J. (2017). Separate requirements for detection and perceptual stability of motion in interocular suppression. *Scientific Reports, 7*, 7230.

Asplund, C. L., Fougnie, D., Zughni, S., Martin, J. W., & Marois, R. (2014). The attentional blink reveals the probabilistic nature of discrete conscious perception. *Psychological Science, 25*, 824–31.

Axelrod, V., Bar, M., & Rees, G. (2015). Exploring the unconscious using faces. *Trends in Cognitive Sciences, 19*, 35–45.

Baars, B. J. (1988). *A Cognitive Theory of Consciousness.* Cambridge, MA: Cambridge University Press.

Bergström, F., & Eriksson, J. (2015). The conjunction of non-consciously perceived object identity and spatial position can be retained during a visual short-term memory task. *Frontiers in Psychology, 6*, 1470.

Bergström, F., & Eriksson, J. (2018). Neural evidence for non-conscious working memory. *Cerebral Cortex, 28*, 3217–28.

Blake, R., & Logothetis, N. K. (2002). Visual competition. *Nature Reviews Neuroscience, 3*, 13–21.

Breitmeyer, B. G., & Öğmen, H. (2006). *Visual Masking: Time Slices through Conscious and Unconscious Vision.* Oxford: Oxford University Press.

Capitão, L. P., Underdown, S. J. V., Vile, S., Yang, E., Harmer, C. J., & Murphy, S. E. (2014). Anxiety increases breakthrough of threat stimuli in continuous flash suppression. *Emotion, 14*, 1027–36.

Cheesman, J., & Merikle, P. M. (1986). Distinguishing conscious from unconscious perceptual processes. *Canadian Journal of Psychology, 40*, 343–67.

Chen, Y. C., & Yeh, S. L. (2012). Look into my eyes and I will see you: Unconscious processing of human gaze. *Consciousness and Cognition, 21*, 1703–10.

Chung, C. Y. L., & Khuu, S. K. (2014). The processing of coherent global form and motion patterns without visual awareness. *Frontiers in Psychology, 5*, 195.

Cohen, M. A., Nakayama, K., Konkle, T., Stantić, M., & Alvarez, G. A. (2015). Visual awareness is limited by the representational architecture of the visual system. *Journal of Cognitive Neuroscience, 27*, 2240–52.

Costello, P., Jiang, Y., Baartman, B., McGlennen, K., & He, S. (2009). Semantic and subword priming during binocular suppression. *Consciousness and Cognition, 18*, 375–82.

Cox, D., & Hong, S. W. (2015). Semantic-based crossmodal processing during visual suppression. *Frontiers in Psychology, 6*, 722.

De Loof, E., Poppe, L., Cleeremans, A., Gevers, W., & Van Opstal, F. (2015). Different effects of executive and visuospatial working memory on visual consciousness. *Attention, Perception, and Psychophysics, 77*, 2523–8.

del Río, M., Greenlee, M. W., & Volberg, G. (2018). Neural dynamics of breaking continuous flash suppression. *Neuroimage, 176*, 277–389.

Dijksterhuis, A., & Aarts, H. (2003). On wildebeests and humans: The preferential detection of negative stimuli. *Psychological Science, 14*, 14–18.

Ding, Y., Naber, M., Gayet, S., Van der Stigchel, S., & Paffen, C. L. E. (2018). Assessing the generalizability of eye dominance across binocular rivalry, onset rivalry, and continuous flash suppression. *Journal of Vision, 18*(6)6, 1–13.

Drewes, J., Zhu, W., & Melcher, D. (2018). The edge of awareness: Mask spatial density, but not color, determines optimal temporal frequency for continuous flash suppression. *Journal of Vision, 18*(1)12, 1–15.

Erdelyi, M. H. (1986). Experimental indeterminacies in the dissociation paradigm of subliminal perception. *Behavioral and Brain Sciences, 9*, 30–1.

Eriksen, C. W. (1960). Discrimination and learning without awareness: A methodological survey and evaluation. *Psychological Review, 67*, 279–300.

Forder, L., Taylor, O., Mankin, H., Scott, R. B., & Franklin, A. (2016). Colour terms affect detection of colour and colour-associated objects suppressed from visual awareness. *PLoS One, 11*(3), e0152212.

Gaillard, R., Del Cul, A., Naccache, L., Vinckier, F., Cohen, L., & Dehaene, S. (2006). Nonconscious semantic processing of emotional words modulates conscious access. *Proceedings of the National Academy of Sciences USA, 103*, 7524–9.

Garrido, L., Duchaine, B., & Nakayama, K. (2008). Face detection in normal and prosopagnosic individuals. *Journal of Neuropsychology, 2*, 119–40.

Gayet, S., & Stein, T. (2017). Between-subject variability in the breaking continuous flash suppression paradigm: Potential causes, consequences, and solutions. *Frontiers in Psychology, 8*, 437.

Gayet, S., Paffen, C. L. E., Belopolsky, A. V., Theeuwes, J., & Van der Stigchel, S. (2016). Visual input signaling threat gains preferential access to awareness in a breaking continuous flash suppression paradigm. *Cognition, 149*, 77–83.

Gayet, S., Paffen, C. L. E., & Van der Stigchel, S. (2013). Information matching the content of visual working memory is prioritized for conscious access. *Psychological Science, 24*, 2472–80.

Gayet, S., Stein, T., & Peelen, M. V. (2019). The danger of interpreting detection differences between image categories: A brief comment on "Mind the snake: Fear detection relies on low spatial frequencies" (Gomes, Soares, Silva, & Silva, 2018). *Emotion.* doi: 10.1037/emo0000550

Gayet, S., Van der Stigchel, S., & Paffen, C. L. E. (2014). Breaking continuous flash suppression: Competing for consciousness on the pre-semantic battlefield. *Frontiers in Psychology, 5*, 450.

Gayet, S., van Maanen, L., Heilbron, M., Paffen, C. L. E., & Van der Stigchel, S. (2016). Visual input that matches the content of visual working memory requires less (not faster) evidence sampling to reach conscious access. *Journal of Vision, 16*(11)26, 1–20.

Getov, S., Kanai, R., Bahrami, B., & Rees, G. (2015). Human brain structure predicts individual differences in preconscious evaluation of facial dominance and trustworthiness. *Social Cognitive and Affective Neuroscience, 10*, 690–9.

Geng, H., Zhang, S., Li, Q., Tao, R., & Xu, S. (2012). Dissociations of subliminal and supraliminal self-face from other-face processing: Behavioral and ERP evidence. *Neuropsychologia, 50*, 2933–42.

Gobbini, M. I., Gors, J. D., Halchenko, Y. O., Hughes, H. C., & Cipolli, C. (2013a). Processing of invisible social cues. *Consciousness and Cognition, 22*, 765–70.

Gobbini, M. I., Gors, J. D., Halchenko, Y. O., Rogers, C., Guntupalli, S., Hughes, H. C., & Cipolli, C. (2013b). Prioritized detection of personally familiar faces. *PLoS One, 8*(6), e66620.

Gomes, N., Silva, S., Silva, C. F., & Soares, S. C. (2017). Beware the serpent: The advantage of ecologically-relevant stimuli in accessing visual awareness. *Evolution and Human Behavior, 38*, 227–34.

Gomes, N., Soares, S. C., Silva. S., & Silva, C. F. (2018). Mind the snake: Fear detection relies on low spatial frequencies. *Emotion, 18*, 886–95.

Gray, K. L. H., Adams, W. J., Hedger, N., Newton, K. E., & Garner, M. (2013). Faces and awareness: Low-level, not emotional factors determine perceptual dominance. *Emotion, 13*, 537–44.

Gray, K. L. H., Haffey, A., Mihaylova, H. L., & Chakrabarti, B. (2018). Lack of privileged access to awareness for rewarding social scenes in autism spectrum disorder. *Journal of Autism and Developmental Disorders*, Epub ahead of print.

Greenwald, A. G., & Draine, S. C. (1998). Distinguishing unconscious from conscious cognition – Reasonable assumptions and replicable findings: Reply to Merikle and Reingold (1998) and Dosher (1998). *Journal of Experimental Psychology: General, 127*, 320–4.

Han, S., & Alais, D. (2018). Strength of continuous flash suppression is optimal when target and masker modulation rates are matched. *Journal of Vision, 18*(3)3, 1–14.

Han S., Blake, R., & Alais, D. (2018). Slow and steady, not fast and furious: Slow temporal modulation strengthens continuous flash suppression. *Consciousness and Cognition, 58*, 10–19.

Han, S., Lunghi, C., & Alais, D. (2016). The temporal frequency tuning of continuous flash suppression reveals peak suppression at very low frequencies. *Scientific Reports, 6*, 35723.

Harris, J. J., Schwarzkopf, D. S., Song, C., Bahrami, B., & Rees, G. (2011). Contextual illusions reveal the limit of unconscious visual processing. *Psychological Science, 22*(3), 399–405. https://doi.org/10.1177/0956797611399293

Hassin, R. R. (2013). Yes it can: On the functional abilities of the human unconscious. *Perspectives on Psychological Science, 8*, 195–207.

Hedger, N., Adams, W. J., & Garner, M. (2015). Fearful faces have a sensory advantage in the competition for awareness. *Journal of Experimental Psychology: Human Perception and Performance, 41*(6), 1748–57.

Hesselmann, G., & Moors, P. (2015). Definitely maybe: Can unconscious processes perform the same functions as conscious processes? *Frontiers in Psychology, 6*, 584.

Hesselmann, G., Hebart, M., & Malach, R. (2011). Differential BOLD activity associated with subjective and objective reports during "blindsight" in normal observers. *Journal of Neuroscience, 31*, 12936–44.

Heyman, T., & Moors, P. (2014). Frequent words do not break continuous flash suppression differently from infrequent or nonexistent words: Implications for semantic processing of words in the absence of awareness. *PLoS One, 9*(8), e104719.

Hochstein, S., & Ahissar, M. (2002). View from the top: Hierarchies and reverse hierarchies in the visual system. *Neuron, 36*, 791–804.

Hong, S. W. (2015). Radial bias for orientation and direction of motion modulates access to visual awareness during continuous flash suppression. *Journal of Vision, 15*(1)3, 1–11.

Hong, S. W., & Blake, R. (2009). Interocular suppression differentially affects achromatic and chromatic mechanisms. *Attention, Perception, and Psychophysics, 71*, 403–11.

Hong, S. W., & Shim, W. M. (2016). When audiovisual correspondence disturbs visual processing. *Experimental Brain Research, 234*, 1325–32.

Hung, S. M., & Hsieh, P. J. (2015). Syntactic processing in the absence of awareness and semantics. *Journal of Experimental Psychology: Human Perception and Performance, 41*, 1376–84.

Hung, S. M., Nieh, C. H., & Hsieh, P. J. (2016). Unconscious processing of facial attractiveness: Invisible attractive faces orient visual attention. *Scientific Reports, 6*, 37117.

Hung, S. M., Styles, S. J., & Hsieh, P. J. (2017). Can a word sound like a shape before you have seen it? Sound-shape mapping prior to conscious awareness. *Psychological Science, 38*, 263–75.

Jiang, Y., Costello, P., & He, S. (2007). Processing of invisible stimuli: Advantage of upright faces and recognizable words in overcoming interocular suppression. *Psychological Science, 18*, 349–55.

Jusyte, A., Mayer, S. V., Künzel, E., Hautzinger, M., & Schönenberg, M. (2015). Unemotional traits predict early processing deficit for fearful expressions in young violent offenders: An investigation using continuous flash suppression. *Psychological Medicine, 45*, 285–97.

Kaiser, D., Stein, T., & Peelen, M. V. (2014). Object grouping based on real-world regularities facilitates perception by reducing competitive interactions in visual cortex. *Proceedings of the National Academy of Sciences USA, 111*, 11217–22.

Kaunitz, L., Fracasso, A., Lingnau, A., & Melcher, D. (2013). Non-conscious processing of motion coherence can boost conscious access. *PLoS One, 8*(4), e60787.

Kaunitz, L., Fracasso, A., Skujevskis, M., & Melcher, D. (2014). Waves of visibility: Probing the depth of inter-ocular suppression with transient and sustained targets. *Frontiers in Psychology, 5*, 804.

Kerr, J. A., Hesselmann, G., Räling, R., Wartenburger, I., & Sterzer, P. (2017). Choice of analysis pathway dramatically affects statistical outcomes in breaking continuous flash suppression. *Scientific Reports, 7*, 3002.

Kobylka, F., Persike, M., & Meinhardt, G. (2017). Object localization does not imply awareness of object category at the break of continuous flash suppression. *Frontiers in Human Neuroscience, 11*, 312.

Korb, S., Osimo, S. A., Suran, T., Goldstein, A., & Rumiati, R. I. (2017). Face proprioception does not modulate access to visual awareness of emotional faces in a continuous flash suppression paradigm. *Consciousness and Cognition, 51*, 166–80.

Kouider, S., & Dehaene, S. (2007). Levels of processing during non-conscious perception: a critical review of visual masking. *Philosophical Transactions of the Royal Society of London B: Biological Sciences, 362*, 857–75.

Kouider, S., & Faivre, N. (2017). Conscious and unconscious perception. In S. Schneider & M. Velmans (eds.), *The Blackwell Companion to Consciousness* (2nd ed., pp. 551–61). Hoboken, NJ: John Wiley & Sons Inc.

Kunimoto, C., Miller, J., & Pashler, H. (2001). Confidence and accuracy of near-threshold discrimination responses. *Consciousness and Cognition, 10*, 294–340.

Li, Y., & Li, S. (2015). Contour integration, attentional cuing, and conscious awareness: An investigation on the processing of collinear and orthogonal contours. *Journal of Vision, 15*(16)10, 1–16.

Liu, D., Wang, L., Wang, Y., & Jiang, Y. (2016). Conscious access to suppressed threatening information is modulated by working memory. *Psychological Science, 27*, 1419–27.

Ludwig, K., Sterzer, P., Kathmann, N., Franz V. H., & Hesselmann, G. (2013). Learning to detect but not to grasp suppressed visual stimuli. *Neuropsychologia, 51*, 2930–8.

Lunghi, C., Lo Verde, L., & Alais, D. (2017). Touch accelerates visual awareness. *i-Perception, 8*(1), 1–14.

Lupyan, G., & Ward, E. J. (2013). Language can boost otherwise unseen objects into visual awareness. *Proceedings of the National Academy of Sciences USA, 110*, 14196–201.

Lykken, D. T. (1957). A study of anxiety in the sociopathic personality. *Journal of Abnormal Psychology, 55*(1), 6–10.

Macrae, C N., Visokomogilski, A., Golubickis, M., Cunningham, W. A., & Sahraie, A. (2017). Self-relevance prioritizes access to visual awareness. *Journal of Experimental Psychology: Human Perception and Performance, 43*, 438–43.

Madipakkam, A. R., Rothkirch, M., Guggenmos, M., Heinz, A., & Sterzer, P. (2015). Gaze direction modulates the relation between neural responses to faces and visual awareness. *Journal of Neuroscience, 35*, 13287–99.

Mastropasqua, T., Tse, P. U., & Turatto, M. (2015). Learning of monocular information facilitates breakthrough to awareness during interocular suppression. *Attention, Perception, and Psychophysics, 77*, 790–803.

Meng, Q., Cui, D., Zhou, K., Chen, L., & Ma, Y. (2012). Advantage of hole stimulus in rivalry competition. *PLoS One, 7*(3), e33053.

Merikle, P. M., Smilek, D., & Eastwood, J. D. (2001). Perception without awareness: Perspectives from cognitive psychology. *Cognition, 79*, 115–34.

Moors, P., Boelens, D., van Overwalle, J., & Wagemans, J. (2016a). Scene integration without awareness: No conclusive evidence for processing scene congruency during continuous flash suppression. *Psychological Science, 27*, 945–56.

Moors, P., Gayet, S., Hedger, N., Stein, T., Sterzer, P., van Ee, R., Wagemans, J., & Hesselmann, G. (2019). Three criteria for evaluating high-level processing in continuous flash suppression. Trends in Cognitive Sciences, 23, 267–269.

Moors, P., Hesselmann, G., Wagemans, J., & van Ee, R. (2017). Continuous flash suppression: Stimulus fractionation rather than integration. *Trends in Cognitive Sciences, 10*, 719–21.

Moors, P., Huygelier, H., Wagemans, J., de-Wit, L., & van Ee, R. (2015). Suppressed visual looming stimuli are not integrated with auditory looming signals: Evidence from continuous flash suppression. *i-Perception, 6*, 48–62.

Moors, P., Wagemans, J., & de-Wit, L. (2014). Moving stimuli are less effectively masked using traditional continuous flash suppression (CFS) compared to a moving Mondrian masks (MMM): A test case for feature-selective suppression and retinotopic adaptation. *PLoS One, 9*(5), e98298.

Moors, P., Wagemans, J., & de-Wit, L. (2016b). Faces in commonly experienced configurations enter awareness faster due to their curvature relative to fixation. *PeerJ, 4*, e1565.

Moors, P., Wagemans, J., & de-Wit, L. (2017). Causal events enter awareness faster than non-causal events. *PeerJ, 5*, e2932.

Moors, P., Wagemans, J., van Ee, R., & de-Wit, L. (2016c). No evidence for surface organization in Kanisza configurations during continuous flash suppression. *Attention, Perception, and Psychophysics. 78*, 902–14.

Moradi, F., Koch, C., & Shimojo, S. (2005). Face adaptation depends on seeing the face. *Neuron, 45*, 169–75.

Mudrik, L., Breska, A., Lamy, D., & Deouell, L. Y. (2011). Integration without awareness: Expanding the limits of unconscious processing. *Psychological Science, 22*, 764–70.

Münkler, P., Rothkirch, M., Dalati, Y., Schmack, K., & Sterzer, P. (2015). Biased recognition of facial affect in patients with major depressive disorder reflects clinical state. *PLoS One, 10*(6), e0129863.

Mustonen, T., Nuutinen, M., Vainio, L., & Häkkinen, J. (2018). Upper nasal hemifield location and nonspatial auditory tones accelerate visual detection during dichoptic viewing. *PLoS One, 13*(7), e0199962.

Nakamura, K., & Kawabata, H. (2018). Preferential access to awareness of attractive faces in a breaking continuous flash suppression paradigm. *Consciousness and Cognition, 65*, 71–82.

Nieuwenhuis, S., & de Kleijn, R. (2011). Consciousness of targets during the attentional blink: A gradual or all-or-none dimension? *Attention, Perception, and Psychophysics, 73*, 364–73.

Noel, J. P., Blanke, O., Serino, A., & Salomon, R. (2017). Interplay between narrative and bodily self in access to consciousness: No difference between self- and non-self attributes. *Frontiers in Psychology, 8*, 72.

Oliver, L. D., Mao, A., & Mitchell, D. G. V. (2015). "Blindsight" and subjective awareness of fearful faces: Inversion reversed the deficits in fear perception associated with core psychopathic traits. *Cognition and Emotion, 29*, 1256–77.

Ostarek, M., & Huettig, F. (2017). Spoken words can make invisible visible: Testing the involvement of low-level visual representations in spoken word processing. *Journal of Experimental Psychology: Human Perception and Performance, 43*, 499–508.

Overgaard, M., Rote, J., Mouridsen, K., & Ramsøy, T. (2006). Is conscious perception gradual or dichotomous? A comparison of report methodologies during a visual task. *Consciousness and Cognition, 15*, 700–8.

Paffen, C. L. E., Gayet, S., Heilbron, M., & Van der Stigchel, S. (2018). Attention-based perceptual learning does not affect access to awareness. *Journal of Vision, 18*(3)7, 1–16.

Pan, Y., Lin, B., Zhao, Y., & Soto, D. (2014). Working memory biasing of visual perception without awareness. *Attention, Perception, and Psychophysics, 76*, 2051–62.

Pessoa, L., & Adolphs, R. (2010). Emotion processing and the amygdala: From a "low road" to "many roads" of evaluating biological significance. *Nature Reviews Neuroscience, 11*, 773–82.

Peters, M. A. K., & Lau, H. (2015). Human observers have optimal introspective access to perceptual processes even for visually masked stimuli. *ELife, 4*, e09651. https://doi.org/10.7554/eLife.09651

Pinto, Y., van Gaal, S., de Lange, F. P., Lamme, V. A. F., & Seth, A. K. (2015). Expectations accelerate entry of visual stimuli into awareness. *Journal of Vision, 15*(8)13, 1–15.

Postman, L., Bronson, W. C., & Gropper, G. L. (1953). Is there a mechanism of perceptual defense? *Journal of Abnormal and Social Psychology, 48*, 215–24.

Prioli, S. C., & Kahan, T. A. (2015). Identifying words that emerge into consciousness: Effects of word valence and unconscious previewing. *Consciousness and Cognition, 35*, 88–97.

Purcell, D. G., & Stewart, A. L. (1988). The face-detection effect: Configuration enhances detection. *Perception and Psychophysics, 43*, 355–66.

Rabagliati, H., Robertson, A., & Carmel, D. (2018). The importance of awareness for understanding language. *Journal of Experimental Psychology: General, 147*, 190–208.

Rabovsky, M., Stein, T., & Rahman, R. A. (2016). Access to awareness for faces during continuous flash suppression is not modulated by affective knowledge. *PLoS One, 11*(4), e0150931.

Rothkirch, M., & Hesselmann, G. (2017). What we talk about when we talk about unconscious processing: A plea for best practices. *Frontiers in Psychology, 8*, 1–6.

Salomon, R., Galli, G., Lukowska, M., Faivre, N., Ruiz, J. B., & Blanke, O. (2016a). An invisible touch: Body-related multisensory conflicts modulate visual consciousness. *Neuropsychologia, 88*, 131–9.

Salomon, R., Kaliuzhna, M., Herbelin, B., & Blanke, O. (2015). Balancing awareness: Vestibular signals modulate visual consciousness in the absence of awareness. *Consciousness and Cognition, 36*, 289–97.

Salomon, R., Lim, M., Herbelin, B., Hesselmann, G., & Blanke, O. (2013). Posing for awareness: Proprioception modulates access to visual consciousness in a continuous flash suppression task. *Journal of Vision, 13*(7)2, 1–8.

Salomon, R., Ronchi, R., Dönz, J., Bello-Ruiz, J., Herbelin, B., Martet, R., Faivre, N., Schaller, J., & Blanke, O. (2016b). The insula mediates access to awareness of visual stimuli presented synchronously to the heartbeat. *Journal of Neuroscience, 26*, 5115–27.

Salomon, R., Ronchi, R., Dönz, J., Bello-Ruiz, J., Herbelin, B., Faivre, N., Schaller, J., & Blanke, O. (2018). Insula mediates heartbeat related effects on visual consciousness. *Cortex, 101*, 87–95.

Schmack, K., Burk, J., Haynes, J.-D., & Sterzer, P. (2016). Predicting subjective affective salience from cortical responses to invisible object stimuli. *Cerebral Cortex, 26*, 3453–60.

Schmidt, T. (2015). Invisible stimuli, implicit thresholds: Why invisibility judgments cannot be interpreted in isolation. *Advances in Cognitive Psychology, 11*, 31–41.

Schmidt, T., & Vorberg, D. (2006). Criteria for unconscious cognition: Three types of dissociation. *Perception and Psychophysics, 68*, 489–504.

Sergent, C., & Dehaene, S. (2004). Is consciousness a gradual phenomenon? *Psychological Science, 15*, 720–8.

Seymour, K., Rhodes, G., Stein, T., & Langdon, R. (2016). Intact unconscious processing of eye contact in schizophrenia. *Schizophrenia Research: Cognition, 3*, 15–19.

Shin, K., Stolte, M., & Chong, S. C. (2009). The effect of spatial attention on invisible stimuli. *Attention, Perception, and Psychophysics, 71*, 1507–13.

Sidis, B. (1898). *The Psychology of Suggestion: A Research into the Subconscious Nature of Man and Society.* New York: Appleton and Co.

Simmons, J. P., Nelson, L. D., & Simonsohn, U. (2011). False-positive psychology: Undisclosed flexibility in data collection and analysis allows presenting anything as significant. *Psychological Science, 22*, 1359–66.

Sklar, A. Y., Deouell, L. Y., & Hassin, R. R. (2018). Integration despite fractionation: Continuous flash suppression. *Trends in Cognitive Sciences, 22*, 956–7.

Sklar, A. Y., Levy, N., Goldstein, A., Mandel, R., Maril, A., & Hassin, R. R. (2012). Reading and doing arithmetic nonconsciously. *Proceedings of the National Academy of Sciences USA, 109*, 19614–19.

Snodgrass, M., Bernat, E., & Shevrin, H. (2004). Unconscious perception: A model-based approach to method and evidence. *Perception and Psychophysics, 66*, 846–67.

Song, C., & Yao, H. (2016). Unconscious processing of invisible visual stimuli. *Scientific Reports, 6*, 38917.

Soto, D., Mäntylä, T., & Silvanto, J. (2011). Working memory without consciousness. *Current Biology, 21*, R912–13.

Stein, T., & Peelen, M. V. (2015). Content-specific expectations enhance stimulus detectability by increasing perceptual sensitivity. *Journal of Experimental Psychology: General, 144*, 1089–1104.

Stein, T., & Sterzer, P. (2011). High-level face shape adaptation depends on visual awareness: Evidence from continuous flash suppression. *Journal of Vision, 11*(8)5, 1–14.

Stein, T., & Sterzer, P. (2012). Not just another face in the crowd: Detecting emotional schematic faces during continuous flash suppression. *Emotion, 12*, 988–96.

Stein, T., & Sterzer, P. (2014). Unconscious processing under interocular suppression: Getting the right measure. *Frontiers in Psychology, 5*, 387.

Stein, T., Awad, D., Gayet, S., & Peelen, M. V. (2018). Unconscious processing of facial dominance: The role of low-level factors in access to awareness. *Journal of Experimental Psychology. General, 147*(11), e1–e13. https://doi.org/10.1037/xge0000521

Stein, T., End, A., & Sterzer, P. (2014). Own-race and own-age biases facilitate visual awareness of faces under interocular suppression. *Frontiers in Human Neuroscience, 8*, 582.

Stein, T., Grubb, C., Bertrand, M., Suh, S. M., & Verosky, S. C. (2017). No impact of affective person knowledge on visual awareness: Evidence from binocular rivalry and continuous flash suppression. *Emotion, 17*(8), 1199–1207. https://doi.org/10.1037/emo0000305

Stein, T., Hebart, M. N., & Sterzer, P. (2011a). Breaking continuous flash suppression: A new measure of unconscious processing during interocular suppression? *Frontiers in Human Neuroscience, 5*, 167.

Stein, T., Kaiser, D., & Hesselmann, G. (2016). Can working memory be non-conscious? *Neuroscience of Consciousness, niv011*, 1–3.

Stein, T., Kaiser, D., & Peelen, M. V. (2015). Interobject grouping facilitates visual awareness. *Journal of Vision, 15*(8)10, 1–11.

Stein, T., Peelen, M. V., & Sterzer, P. (2011b). Adults' awareness of faces follows newborns' looking preferences. *PLoS One, 6*(12), e29361.

Stein, T., Peelen, M. V., & Sterzer, P. (2012a). Eye gaze adaptation under interocular suppression. *Journal of Vision, 12*(7)1, 1–17.

Stein, T., Reeder, R. R., & Peelen, M. V. (2016). Privileged access to awareness for faces and objects of expertise. *Journal of Experimental Psychology: Human Perception and Performance, 42*, 788–9.

Stein, T., Senju, A., Peelen, M. V., & Sterzer, P. (2011c). Eye contact facilitates awareness of faces during interocular suppression. *Cognition, 119*, 307–11.

Stein, T., Seymour, K., Hebart, M. N., & Sterzer, P. (2014). Rapid fear detection relies on high spatial frequencies. *Psychological Science, 25*, 566–74.

Stein, T., Siebold, A., & van Zoest, W. (2016). Testing the idea of privileged awareness of self-relevant information. *Journal of Experimental Psychology: Human Perception and Performance, 42*, 303–7.

Stein, T., Sterzer, P., & Peelen, M. V. (2012b). Privileged detection of conspecifics: evidence from inversion effects during continuous flash suppression. *Cognition, 125*, 64–79.

Stein, T., Thoma, V., & Sterzer, P. (2015). Priming of object detection under continuous flash suppression depends on attention but not on part-whole configuration. *Journal of Vision, 15*(3)15, 1–11.

Sterzer, P., Hilgenfeldt, T., Freudenberg, P., Bermpohl, F., & Adli, M. (2011). Access of emotional information to visual awareness in patients with major depressive disorder. *Psychological Medicine, 41*, 1615–24.

Stewart, L. H., Ajina, S., Getov, S., Bahrami, B., Todorov, A., & Rees, G. (2012). Unconscious evaluation of faces on social dimensions. *Journal of Experimental Psychology: General, 141*, 715–27.

Sun, S. Z., Cant, J. S., & Ferber, S. (2016). A global attentional scope setting prioritizes faces for conscious detection. *Journal of Vision, 16*(6)9, 1–13.

Sun, Y., Cai, Y., & Lu, S. (2015). Hemispheric asymmetry in the influence of language on visual perception. *Consciousness and Cognition, 34*, 16–27.

Sylvers, P. D., Brennan, P. A., & Lilienfeld, S. O. (2011). Psychopathic traits and pretattentive threat processing in children: A novel test of the fearlessness hypothesis. *Psychological Science, 22*, 1280–7.

Tamietto, M., & de Gelder B. (2010). Neural bases of the non-conscious perception of emotional signals. *Nature Reviews Neuroscience, 11*, 697–709.

Tan, J. S., & Yeh, S. L. (2015). Audiovisual integration facilitates unconscious visual scene processing. *Journal of Experimental Psychology: Human Perception and Performance, 41*, 1325–35.

Tsuchiya, N., & Koch, C. (2005). Continuous flash suppression reduces negative afterimages. *Nature Neuroscience, 8*, 1096–1101.

Tsuchiya, N., Moradi, F., Felsen, C., Yamazaki, M., & Adolphs, R. (2009). Intact rapid detection of fearful faces in the absence of the amygdala. *Nature Neuroscience, 12*, 1224–5.

Van den Bussche, E., Van den Noortgate, W., & Reynvoet, B. (2009). Mechanisms of masked priming: A meta-analysis. *Psychological Bulletin, 135*, 452–77.

Van Rullen, R. (2007). The power of the feed-forward sweep. *Advances in Cognitive Psychology, 3*, 167–76.

Vieira, J. B., Wen, S., Oliver, L. D., & Mitchell, D. G. V. (2017). Enhanced conscious processing and blindsight-like detection of fear-conditioned stimuli under continuous flash suppression. *Experimental Brain Research, 235*, 3333–44.

Wang, L., Weng, X., & He, S. (2012). Perceptual grouping without awareness: Superiority of Kanisza triangle in breaking interocular suppression. *PLoS One, 7*(6), e40106.

Weiskrantz, L. (1986). *Blindsight: A Case Study and Implications*. New York: Oxford University Press.

Xu, S., Zhang, S., & Geng, H. (2011). Gaze-induced joint attention persists under high perceptual load and does not depend on awareness. *Vision Research, 51*, 2048–56.

Xu, S., Zhang, S., & Geng, H. (2018). The effect of eye contact is contingent on visual awareness. *Frontiers in Psychology, 9*, 93. https://doi.org/10.3389/fpsyg.2018.00093

Yang, E., & Blake, R. (2012). Deconstructing continuous flash suppression. *Journal of Vision, 12*(3)8, 1–14.

Yang, E., Blake, R., & McDonald, J. E. (2010). A new interocular suppression technique for measuring sensory eye dominance. *Investigative Ophthalmology and Visual Science, 51*, 588–93.

Yang, E., Zald, D. H., & Blake, R. (2007). Fearful expressions gain preferential access to awareness during continuous flash suppression. *Emotion, 7*, 882–6.

Yang, Y.-H., & Yeh, S.-L. (2011). Accessing the meaning of invisible words. *Consciousness and Cognition, 20*(2), 223–33. https://doi.org/10.1016/j.concog.2010.07.005

Yang, Y. H., & Yeh, S. L. (2014). Unmasking the dichoptic mask by sound: Spatial congruency matters. *Experimental Brain Research, 232*, 1109–16.

Yang, E., Brascamp, J., Kang, M.-S., & Blake, R. (2014). On the use of continuous flash suppression for the study of visual processing outside of awareness. *Frontiers in Psychology, 5*, 724. https://doi.org/10.3389/fpsyg.2014.00724

Yang, Y. H., Tien, Y. H., Yang, P. L., & Yeh, S. L. (2017). Role of consciousness in temporal integration of semantic information. *Cognitive, Affective, and Behavioral Neuroscience, 17*, 954–72.

Yokoyama, T., Noguchi, Y., & Kita, S. (2013). Unconscious processing of direct gaze: Evidence from an ERP study. *Neuropsychologia, 51*, 1161–8.

Zhan, M., Engelen, T., & de Gelder, B. (2018). Influence of continuous flash suppression mask frequency on stimulus visibility. *Neuropsychologia*, Epub ahead of print.

Zhan, M., Hortensius, R., & de Gelder, B. (2015). The body as a tool for anger awareness: Differential effects of angry facial and bodily expressions on suppression from awareness. *PLoS One, 10*(10), e01399768.

Zhang, P., Jiang, Y., & He, S. (2012). Voluntary attention modulates processing of eye-specific visual information. *Psychological Science, 23*, 254–60.

Zheng, W., Luo, T., Hu, C. P., & Peng, K. (2018). Glued to which face? Attentional priority effect of female babyface and male mature face. *Frontiers in Psychology, 9*, 286.

Zhou, G., Zhang, L., Liu, J., Yang, J., & Qu, Z. (2010a). Specificity of face processing without visual awareness. *Consciousness and Cognition, 19*, 408–12.

Zhou, W., Jiang, Y., He, S., & Chen, D. (2010b). Olfaction modulates visual perception in binocular rivalry. *Current Biology, 20*, 1356–8.

Zhu, W., Drewes, J., & Melcher, D. (2016). Time for awareness: The influence of temporal properties of the mask on continuous flash suppression effectiveness. *PLoS One, 11*(7), e0159206.

2

WHAT'S UP WITH HIGH-LEVEL PROCESSING DURING CONTINUOUS FLASH SUPPRESSION?

Pieter Moors

LABORATORY OF EXPERIMENTAL PSYCHOLOGY, DEPARTMENT OF BRAIN AND COGNITION, KU LEUVEN

1 Introduction

Every time I wake up from a dark, seemingly dreamless night, something extraordinary happens: I open my eyes, and I *see* (Koenderink, 2012). When I sip from my coffee cup and I look outside my kitchen window, I witness something equally remarkable: "I see a house, trees, sky" (Wertheimer, 1923). I never see brightnesses, spatial frequencies, or orientations. This is fundamental. My visual experience of the world is organized and structured into distinct objects ordered in depth (Wagemans et al., 2012). It seems immediate and effortless. How is such rich conscious experience generated? Can we understand our phenomenology of the visual environment in terms of a complex transformation of the photons hitting the retina to visual awareness, involving several steps in a dynamic, hierarchically organized system entailing multiple feed-forward and feedback loops (Palmer, 1999)?

The mystery of visual awareness, or consciousness in general, has baffled many scientists for decades, if not centuries. The complexity of the problem has generated a rich and diverse literature that approaches consciousness from various angles. Philosophers, psychologists, and neuroscientists alike have provided many extensive, sometimes conflicting views, yielding intense discussions (Cohen, Cavanagh, Chun, & Nakayama, 2012; Cohen & Dennett, 2011; Fahrenfort & Lamme, 2012; Tsuchiya, Block, & Koch, 2012). The inquiries range from formulating theories and models of consciousness (i.e. what constitutes the necessary and sufficient conditions for consciousness to "arise") (Baars, 1993; Cleeremans, 2008; Dennett, 1993; Jackendoff, 1987; Lau & Rosenthal, 2011; Oizumi, Albantakis, & Tononi, 2014; O'Regan & Noë, 2001) to studying states or levels of consciousness (e.g. What is the difference between an individual in a vegetative state versus one who is labelled with having a full conscious experience? Is there some residual – or even full-blown – consciousness left in the individual in the vegetative state?)

(Owen, Coleman, Boly, Davis, Laureys, & Pickard, 2006). Can we pinpoint the neural correlates of consciousness, and if so, how should we interpret these (Crick & Koch, 1998, 2003; Dehaene & Changeux, 2011)? How is consciousness different from processes such as attention and working memory (Koch & Tsuchiya, 2007; Lamme, 2003; Soto, Mäntylä, & Silvanto, 2011; Soto & Silvanto, 2014; Stein, Kaiser, & Hesselmann, 2016a)? Does it even make sense to dissociate these concepts, or are these merely fruitless exercises in taxonomy in which scientists so often indulge?

Although these are all interesting and relevant questions, this chapter does not consider *what* consciousness is or *how* consciousness arises. This is taken for granted and we assume that some states of the visual system will yield conscious experience of a visual stimulus whereas others do not. Rather, we consider the following general question: *which types of stimulus processing can bypass visual awareness, and therefore do not necessarily rely on a conscious experience of the stimulus?* In particular, the focus is on the current evidence for so-called integrated, semantic, high-level processing of invisible stimuli.

Embarking on such an endeavor necessarily entails the choice of a proper paradigm to present observers visual stimuli they cannot see (or rather, fail to report). Let us consider the types of *psychophysical magic* that are at our disposal (Kim & Blake, 2005).

1.1 Rendering a stimulus invisible

A central issue in studying how invisible stimuli are processed is how to render a visual stimulus invisible in the first place (Breitmeyer, 2015; Kim & Blake, 2005). Breitmeyer (2015) recently reviewed all available paradigms, arriving at a list of 24 (sometimes subtly) different methods to render a stimulus invisible (see also the chapter by Breitmeyer and Hesselmann). The choice of a suitable paradigm is by no means a trivial one, and despite their upsides, each also comes with its downsides.

A first possibility is to present stimuli at such an impoverished intensity that they can no longer be discriminated from the background. This method is not frequently used in consciousness research, because degrading stimulus intensity can have the unintended side effect that the stimulus is not processed at all. Thus, a desirable property of a blinding paradigm is that it allows one to present stimuli at intensity levels such that they are detectable when presented independently.

An attractive set of paradigms that fulfills this criterion is visual masking paradigms (forward, backward, sandwich, metacontrast masking) (Breitmeyer & Öğmen, 2006). Here, a stimulus is presented for a very short time (e.g. 16 or 32 milliseconds) and is preceded and/or followed by a masking stimulus. Depending on the asynchrony between the target and masking stimulus, this renders the target stimulus fully invisible. The downside, however, is that stimuli can only be presented for a limited amount of time. Ideally, one would like to present a stimulus for more than some tens of milliseconds to allow for sufficient processing of the stimulus. Two different kinds of paradigms provide a potential solution to this: attention-based paradigms (Mack & Rock, 1998) and those involving dichoptic stimulus presentation (Alais & Blake, 2005). I will limit my discussion to the latter, because the former inevitably involves a manipulation of the attentional state of the observer, which changes the focus of the question in the direction of "can process X occur without attention?" Although blinding paradigms based on attentional manipulations also involve a manipulation of the awareness of the stimulus, the question whether awareness is necessary for processing stimulus property X becomes necessarily confounded with whether attention is necessary. This leads us to a last class of paradigms, in which one stimulus is presented to one eye while a different stimulus is presented to the other eye, at corresponding retinal locations. Although this situation occurs all the time in daily life due to retinal disparity (Arnold, 2011), something remarkable happens when the mismatch between the input to both eyes is sufficiently large. Despite constant retinal input, our phenomenal experience of the input fluctuates in a seemingly stochastic manner between the stimuli presented to both eyes, a phenomenon referred to as binocular rivalry (Blake & Logothetis, 2002; Blake, 1989; Kim & Blake, 2005; Tong, Meng, & Blake, 2006). The advantage of binocular rivalry is that periods of dominance and suppression can last for several seconds, allowing one to render a stimulus invisible for a longer time period. A downside is that it is difficult to control how long a stimulus remains suppressed, but also which stimulus will be suppressed at onset. To control for initial dominance, flash suppression provides a solution (Brascamp, Knapen, Kanai, van Ee, & van den Berg, 2007; van Ee, 2011; Wolfe, 1984). In flash suppression, the stimulus to be suppressed is first presented for a second or so, before presenting the other stimulus to the other eye. This allows the visual system to adapt to this stimulus first, and reliably renders it invisible (suppressed) when the other stimulus is presented to the other eye. However, this is not a desirable situation if it is particularly important that observers are never initially aware of the invisible stimulus. A solution to all of these problems – short stimulus presentation and reliable suppression at trial onset – is offered by a paradigm that was introduced to the field in 2005, continuous flash suppression.

1.2 Continuous flash suppression – a free lunch?

In this chapter, we exclusively focus on studies that have used continuous flash suppression (CFS) to manipulate the contents of visual awareness (Tsuchiya & Koch, 2005; Tsuchiya, Koch, Gilroy, & Blake, 2006). CFS involves a situation of dichoptic stimulation in which a continuously changing mask is presented to one eye, while (most of the time) a static stimulus is presented to the other eye (see Figure 2.1 for an example). In most, if not all, cases this dynamic mask gains initial dominance over the other stimulus. Furthermore, in comparison with binocular rivalry, the CFS mask more strongly and reliably suppresses the other stimulus (Tsuchiya et al., 2006;

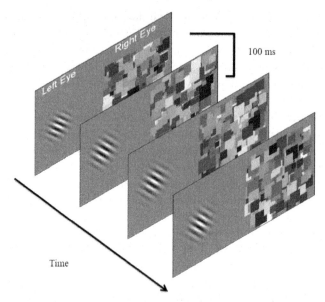

FIGURE 2.1 An example of continuous flash suppression (CFS). Here, an oriented Gabor patch is presented to the left eye, while the typical "Mondrian mask" consisting of squares of random size, position, and color is presented to the right eye. The CFS mask is typically refreshed every 100 ms (i.e. for all individual elements a new random position is generated). Reproduced from Moors et al. 2017 (copyright 2017 Elsevier).

Yang & Blake, 2012). These two attributes, initial dominance and effective suppression, have made CFS an attractive paradigm for consciousness research.

1.3 Studying unconscious processing with CFS

To measure unconscious processing of a stimulus, CFS has largely been used in two different ways, referred to as direct and indirect measures of (unconscious) processing. In the latter case, a stimulus is presented in the absence of awareness and one measures subsequent adaptation aftereffects (Adams, Gray, Garner, & Graf, 2010; Bahrami, Carmel, Walsh, Rees, & Lavie, 2008a, 2008b; Kanai, Tsuchiya, & Verstraten, 2006; Kaunitz, Fracasso, & Melcher, 2011; Maruya, Watanabe, & Watanabe, 2008; Moradi, Koch, & Shimojo, 2005; Stein, Peelen, & Sterzer, 2012; Stein & Sterzer, 2011; Sweeny, Grabowecky, & Suzuki, 2011), attentional shifts elicited by the suppressed stimulus (Jiang, Costello, Fang, Huang, & He, 2006; Palmer & Ramsey, 2012), priming effects (Almeida, Mahon, & Caramazza, 2010; Almeida, Mahon, Nakayama, & Caramazza, 2008; Bahrami et al., 2010; Barbot & Kouider, 2011; Sakuraba, Sakai, Yamanaka, Yokosawa, & Hirayama, 2012), or participants perform a task on the percept elicited by the suppressed stimulus (Harris, Schwarzkopf, Song, Bahrami, & Rees, 2011; Zadbood, Lee, & Blake,

2011). An advantage of these measures is that they follow the classic dissociation logic in that a direct (subjective or objective) measure of stimulus awareness (of the suppressed stimulus) is contrasted with an indirect measure of stimulus processing (i.e. all the measures described above). A particularly tricky aspect of these experiments, however, is how to properly measure awareness of the suppressed stimulus. Traditional "objective" sensitivity measures such as d' have been criticized as a proper measure for assessing stimulus awareness because they are influenced by other factors such as attention, prime-target stimulus-onset asynchrony (SOA), etc. (Vermeiren & Cleeremans, 2012). Furthermore, assessing stimulus awareness often involves accepting the null hypothesis, a question traditional frequentist inference is not able to answer (Amihai, 2012; Sand & Nilsson, 2016). Subjective measures such as the Perceptual Awareness Scale (Ramsøy & Overgaard, 2004), in which participants have to indicate their awareness of the suppressed stimulus on a four-point scale on a trial-by-trial basis, may prove to be a potential solution, but these have their downsides as well. For example, trial-by-trial assessment possibly induces a form of dual tasking that might have unwanted side-effects, both for objective and subjective measures. Furthermore, depending on how effective suppression is, the consequence can be that up to half of the data needs to be removed due to some partial awareness of the stimulus on some trials. These procedures have also been referred to as the "not seen judgments"-only procedures. Schmidt (2015) convincingly argues that paradigms where researchers rely on invisible trials only require specific assumptions about stimulus awareness that are incompatible with the fundamental assumptions of signal detection theory. Instead, he proposes to rely on parametric manipulations of stimulus visibility allowing for the study of qualitative and double dissociations – rather than simple ones.

Partly because of the reasons discussed above, the direct measure to assess unconscious processing during CFS, the breaking CFS (b-CFS) paradigm, has been most popular (Gayet, Van der Stigchel, & Paffen, 2014). In b-CFS, a trial typically starts with presenting a stimulus initially at a low contrast such that it will be perceptually suppressed. Subsequently, the contrast of the suppressed stimulus is gradually increased. The time it takes for the stimulus to break suppression (i.e. become detectable) is used as an index of unconscious processing. The task participants have to perform usually pertains to an aspect of the stimulus orthogonal to the stimulus manipulation (e.g. location detection). The reasoning behind this paradigm is that differential suppression times for different stimuli must be due to some kind of unconscious representation of the stimulus that has been built up during suppression. This, in turn, biases the interocular competition process and yields differential suppression times (Jiang, Costello, & He, 2007). Therefore, these suppression times are taken as an index of unconscious processing. However, b-CFS has been heavily criticized as a paradigm to study unconscious processing. That is, suppression times rely on detecting an aspect of the stimulus as soon as it reaches awareness. Therefore, differences between suppression times might be attributable to criterion differences related to the detection of the stimulus (i.e. different stimuli break suppression at the same time on average, yet have differential detection or decision criteria). To counter this, a binocular control condition in which the target and mask are presented to both eyes has been used. The absence of a difference between "suppression times" in this control condition is then argued to preclude the possibility that differential suppression times in the CFS condition are due to criterion differences in detection. However, because the target and mask are presented to both eyes in this condition, and no interocular suppression is elicited, it has been argued that this condition is too different from the CFS condition to unambiguously provide evidence for unconscious processing (Stein, Hebart, & Sterzer, 2011a; Stein & Sterzer, 2014, see also Chapter 1 by Timo Stein).

1.4 Overview of the chapter

I will focus nearly exclusively on CFS studies as they have been most influential for shaping our understanding of the scope and limits of (unconscious) visual processing over the last ten to fifteen years.[1] First, I will discuss a series of studies that claimed to show the potential of the (b-)CFS paradigm, and provided a renewed interest in showing that there seemingly is no limit to what can be processed unconsciously. Next, a series of studies was published that compellingly challenged many of these initial findings either through failing to replicate them or by showing that the previously observed effects are better explained by low-level stimulus confounds. This set of findings led us to conclude that processing of stimuli suppressed through CFS is most parsimoniously explained through a fractionated representation of the invisible stimulus rather than an integrated one (Moors, Hesselmann, Wagemans, & van Ee, 2017). The term stimulus fractionation was coined previously by Zadbood et al. (2011) whilst the idea of fractionation was advanced by other researchers as well (Hong & Blake, 2009). In the following, I will provide some personal reflections on how I dealt with entering a research field where failing to reproduce previous findings seemed to be the norm rather than the exception.

2 Unconscious high-level processing under CFS

2.1 The first wave of studies

Since its introduction about ten years ago, CFS has been picked up relatively quickly as a potent technique to study unconscious processing of (visual) stimuli. Indeed, CFS has been described as "a more optimal technique for examining preconscious processing mechanisms [compared to binocular rivalry]" (Yang, Zald, & Blake, 2007, p. 882) up to even "a cutting edge masking technique that allows subliminal presentations that last seconds. CFS is a game changer in the study of the unconscious" (Sklar, Levy, Goldstein, Mandel, Maril, & Hassin, 2012, p. 19614). It is probably safe to say that the CFS literature is a very fragmented one, where researchers usually ask whether their stimulus of interest can be processed whilst being suppressed from awareness. It is therefore impossible to simultaneously consider the breadth of the field whilst providing an in-depth discussion of the main findings. Therefore, I aimed to select series of studies on a particular topic which – in my opinion – have shed light on the scope and limits of unconscious visual processing under CFS.

2.1.1 Face stimuli

A landmark study for the development of the field was the study of Jiang et al. (2007) in which b-CFS was introduced for the first time. Here, the authors showed that inverted faces enter awareness more slowly compared to upright faces, a finding that we will see has stood the test of time. In addition, they showed that stimulus familiarity matters for suppression times. Indeed, Chinese characters broke suppression faster compared to Hebrew characters for readers of Chinese, but the opposite effect was obtained for readers of Hebrew. This face inversion effect was quickly corroborated by Yang et al. (2007) by showing that emotional face expressions also showed differential suppression times. In particular, fearful faces entered awareness faster compared to happy or neutral faces, an effect also observed by Tsuchiya, Moradi, Felsen, Yamazaki, and Adolphs (2009). In a similar fashion, eye contact has been shown to influence suppression time – direct gaze stimuli enter awareness faster compared to averted gaze stimuli (Chen & Yeh, 2012; Gobbini, Gors, Halchenko, Hughes, & Cipolli, 2013a; Stein, Senju, Peelen, & Sterzer, 2011b). Furthermore, personally familiar faces seem to be prioritized over the faces of strangers (Geng, Zhang, Li, Tao, & Xu, 2012; Gobbini, Gors, Halchenko, Rogers, et al., 2013b), dominant and untrustworthy faces take longer to emerge compared to neutral faces (Stewart, Ajina, Getov, Bahrami, Todorov, & Rees, 2012), and attractive faces enter awareness faster compared to non-attractive faces (Hung, Nieh, & Hsieh, 2016; Nakamura & Kawabata, 2018). Even more so, presenting an affectively positive or negative stimulus invisibly to observers can influence ratings of a visible, neutral face such that they are rating it as more positive or negative on a particular dimension (Anderson, Siegel, White, & Barrett, 2012; Kring, Siegel, & Barrett, 2014; Siegel, Wormwood, Quigley, & Barrett, 2018). This short summary of CFS studies on processing of invisible face stimuli makes it appealing to interpret the representation of an invisible face stimulus as relatively high-level and complex, at a level in the visual hierarchy where local image features must have been grouped together and are integrated into a coherent, whole stimulus. Further in this chapter, I will critically assess the evidence for this claim.

2.1.2 Word stimuli

The stimulus familiarity effect observed by Jiang et al. (2007) provided a first hint that word stimuli might be processed up to a semantic level during perceptual suppression. Nevertheless, their finding could equally well be explained by some form of heightened sensitivity to shape features an observer frequently encounters throughout daily life. The study by Costello, Jiang, Baartman, McGlennen, and He

(2009) addressed this issue and provided evidence that higher-level word processing might be involved in the familiarity effect as well. The authors used a priming paradigm in which a visible prime was presented first, after which a word was suppressed by CFS and participants had to indicate the word's location as soon as it emerged through the mask. Some of these invisible words were related to the prime word either semantically or at the sub-word level, others were not. The key finding was that suppression times were modulated by the relatedness of the prime. Both semantic as well as sub-word relatedness decreased suppression times relative to unrelated prime words. Yang and Yeh (2011) provided additional evidence on processing of words by showing that negative words took longer to enter awareness compared to neutral words, provided they were presented upright. In contrast to the previous study, Sklar et al. (2012) observed shorter suppression times for short sentences that had an emotionally negative meaning or where the combination of words yielded a semantically incongruent sentence. In line with what one would expect from semantic processing of perceptually suppressed stimuli, Hung and Hsieh (2015) showed that (pseudo-)words that were syntactically congruent with two visibly presented (pseudo-)words (i.e. formed a short, syntactically correct sentence) entered awareness faster than incongruent (pseudo-)words. Zabelina, Guzman-Martinez, Ortega, Grabowecky, Suzuki, & Beeman (2013) asked whether presenting problem words from a compound remote associate problem (e.g. pine-crab-sauce all form a common compound with apple) invisibly to observers (i.e. as a prime stimulus) could accelerate finding the solution when these words would subsequently be presented visibly. The control condition consisted of the same visible target words, yet the prime stimulus consisted of a set of unrelated words. As hypothesized, the authors found that participants solved the associate problem faster when the problem words had already been presented invisibly to them for three seconds and the effect was most pronounced for analytical solutions of the problem. From this set of results, the authors concluded that some form of semantic processing seems to occur for invisible words. On the face of it, this set of studies seems to indicate some form of word processing for perceptually suppressed word stimuli.

2.1.3 Object-scene congruency in natural scenes

The study by Mudrik, Breska, Lamy, and Deouell (2011a) has been particularly influential as evidence for processing of complex visual information during perceptual suppression. In this study, the authors manipulated natural scenes such that they either contained an object that was consistent with the scene content, or contained an object that violated what one could reasonably expect to be present in the scene. For example, a congruent scene would be a basketball player throwing a basketball in the hoop. In the incongruent version, the basketball player would throw a watermelon in the hoop. These images were presented to observers in a b-CFS experiment, and the results indicated that images containing an incongruent object entered awareness faster compared to congruent images. Thus, the results of this study suggested that perceptually suppressed scene stimuli could be processed up to the semantic level and that incongruencies at the semantic level biased the interocular competition process. Interestingly, the same authors previously published a binocular rivalry study in which they showed that incongruent images had longer dominance durations compared to congruent images (Mudrik, Deouell, & Lamy, 2011b. In a later study, they showed that visually masked incongruent images generally slowed down responses to a visible image, also indicating that the semantic content of the images somehow influenced processing of visible images and that these findings generalized across suppression paradigms (Mudrik & Koch, 2013).

2.1.4 Numerical processing and unconscious arithmetic

Three studies reported evidence that numerical information could be processed from invisible stimuli. Bahrami et al. (2010) used a priming paradigm in which one, two, or three sinusoidal gratings (non-symbolic prime) or symbolic primes (arabic digits 1, 2, or 3) were presented invisibly to observers. The task was to enumerate the number of targets presented visibly to observers (also one, two, or three gratings). The authors observed a distance-dependent priming effect where negative target-prime distances interfered with enumeration, whilst positive distance facilitated enumeration. In their conclusion, the authors argued that this distance-dependent priming effect indicates high-level processing of invisible stimuli during interocular suppression. A second study by Sklar et al. (2012) pushed the boundaries of numerical processing of invisible stimuli further by asking whether observers would show congruency priming for naming visible targets when this target was congruent with the result of an invisibly presented addition or subtraction equation (e.g. "$9 - 4 - 3 = $"). Sklar et al. observed congruency priming for subtraction equations only, leading them to conclude that observers could indeed perform arithmetic operations on invisible stimuli, provided these were sufficiently challenging for the duration at which they were presented (i.e. presentation durations of the primes were longer than one second, which might have caused the priming effect of the addition equations to have already dissipated).

2.2 On the appearance of a consistent literature and the a priori likelihood of these findings

The discussion of the studies in the previous section might have given the impression that nearly every stimulus dimension can be processed under CFS. This was the impression I had when starting my PhD in 2012. However, three aspects of the literature rendered that impression more realistic (and maybe slightly more pessimistic). First, when reviewing the literature as a whole (e.g. see the reference list I maintained at www.gestaltrevision.be/s/cfs) it is interesting to note that several of these research lines are happening in parallel without too much interaction or overlap (cf. the fragmented nature of the field mentioned previously). For example, there are studies relying on the assumption that CFS isolates dorsal stream processing (Almeida et al., 2010, 2008). These studies entirely base their premises on a neuroimaging study by Fang and He (2005). A few studies were published in the following years showing that the ventral stream was not completely silent during perceptual suppression, while at the same time a stream-invariant suppression of overall activity was observed (Hesselmann & Malach, 2011; Jiang & He, 2006; Sterzer, Haynes, & Rees, 2008). Second, a wealth of b-CFS studies investigated face processing, but there also exists a series of adaptation studies that show that the locus of adaptation is much earlier in visual processing than would be anticipated from these b-CFS studies (see further in this Chapter). Third, on its own every study seems to present a consistent set of findings. However, when one starts to compare the consistency of these findings across studies, they appear to be less homogeneous than one would initially think. As already alluded to, negative words/sentences have been found to enter awareness faster and slower compared to neutral ones, or unconscious arithmetic has been observed for either addition or subtraction. There might be several reasons for such a pattern of findings. They might indicate genuine processing differences between experimental paradigms (e.g. b-CFS vs. adaptation) or between stimuli (e.g. words vs. sentences). Alternatively, some findings might be flukes whereas others prove to be robust. A particularly pessimistic view is that they might all be flukes and due to publication bias we only see those pop up in the literature that "worked", irrespective of the directionality of the findings.

Based on these observations from the literature, I believe that the initial (and for some researchers, continued) enthusiasm for the potential of CFS to explore uncharted territories in consciousness research is most likely premature and far-fetched. The principal reason for this argument derives from the fact that CFS very likely relies on mechanisms similar to those observed in binocular rivalry (Han & Alais, 2018; Han, Blake, & Alais, 2018; Han, Lunghi, & Alais, 2016; Hong & Blake, 2009; Moors, Stein, Wagemans, & van Ee, 2015; Moors, Wagemans, & de-Wit, 2014; Yang & Blake, 2012). In light of this, the problem with nearly all studies that embark on finding high-level unconscious processing during CFS is that they ignore the representation of the stimulus while it is rendered invisible. Indeed, any paradigm that perceptually suppresses a visual stimulus does so by interfering with the processing of the stimulus in some way (Fogelson, Kohler, Miller, Granger, & Tse, 2014). If not, the stimulus would always be visible to the observer. CFS is closely related to binocular rivalry, of which it is known that the activity related to the perceptually suppressed stimulus is mainly confined to early visual areas (Alais, 2012; Blake & Logothetis, 2002; Logothetis, 1998; Tong et al., 2006). Indeed, rather limited cognitive processing has been observed during binocular rivalry (Blake, 1988; Cave, Blake, & McNamara, 1998; Kang, Blake, & Woodman, 2011; Zimba & Blake, 1983). Therefore, it seems reasonable to adopt the default stance *not* to expect much high-level unconscious processing during CFS (Breitmeyer, 2015). Indeed, recent neuroimaging data suggests that the presence of CFS masks dramatically reduces neural activity related to the suppressed stimulus already in early visual cortex (Yuval-Greenberg & Heeger, 2013). Thus, the representation of the suppressed stimulus is expected to be limited to a loose collection of elemental features that are presumably coded in these early visual areas, despite the fact that the stimulus is presented unbeknownst to the observer for extended periods of time (Gayet et al., 2014).

The reasoning outlined in the previous paragraph can yield two different kinds of attitudes regarding new developments in the field. Either one is skeptical of new findings that seem to counter the available evidence. Alternatively, one embraces the fact that a more powerful paradigm has been developed that (finally) allows researchers to seriously study unconscious visual processing. It is clear that the majority of researchers relying on CFS initially took the latter stance, and saw the studies described in section 2.1 as real progress in the field. Indeed, this latter attitude ignores exactly what we already know about the representation of the stimuli during perceptual suppression. That is, it seems a priori very unlikely that a fractionated stimulus, reduced to its basic features, will evolve into an integrated one, if the processing mechanisms that are usually involved for integrating features of a stimulus never come into play during CFS. Nevertheless, given that one of the first studies using b-CFS showed face inversion and word familiarity effects (Jiang et al., 2007), it became tempting to push the limits of unconscious visual processing further and further, until we can read and do arithmetic unconsciously (Sklar et al., 2012).

A natural question to ask in response is the following: why have so many researchers found evidence for so-called high-level processing of perceptually suppressed stimuli in (b-)CFS experiments? Personally, I believe the majority of positive findings on high-level processing during (b-)CFS are Type 1 errors. However, I cannot provide conclusive proof for this argument, except to let replication speak. For all studies that do not belong to this category of potential Type 1 errors and of which the findings prove to be replicable, I think a simpler explanation more than likely will be found (see further in the chapter for some examples). Lastly, I think the CFS literature severely suffers from a file drawer problem (Rosenthal, 1979). Conferences and workshops have proven an invaluable source of information on this topic, and I know of several (unreported) studies that failed to replicate when tested by other labs. In addition, I also learned about studies starting off with a novel research question but which eventually were not published because they failed to reveal a difference between the experimental conditions – even though they revealed very interesting and important information on stimulus processing during CFS. Although this is a general problem in psychological science, I think CFS studies are a particularly important example of this problem because they can substantially influence contemporary theories on the scope and limits of unconscious visual processing. Personally, I think consciousness research and research on unconscious visual processing in particular would benefit greatly from an attitude change towards embracing null findings showing that this or that paradigm does not allow for this or that type of processing. Such an attitude change is tightly linked to adopting the appropriate statistical methods that allow for such conclusions to be drawn on statistical grounds (e.g. Bayesian methods).

3 The pendulum swings back – sometimes

3.1 Face stimuli

The face inversion effect in b–CFS studies has stood the test of time. More generally, many studies have relied on inversion effects because they appear to be an elegant way to rule out low-level confounds in the observed effects (more on this later). The picture becomes a bit more nuanced when we consider manipulations of face stimuli that go beyond simple inversion. For example, the fear advantage for face stimuli has been shown to primarily be caused by the spatial frequency content of the faces (Gray, Adams, Hedger, Newton, & Garner, 2013; Hedger, Adams, & Garner, 2015b). One study obtained evidence for positive expressions entering awareness faster, yet in control experiments it was shown that this was primarily caused by the curvature of the mouth and face contours (Stein & Sterzer, 2012). Interestingly, this latter finding converges with the one obtained in Moors, Wagemans, and de-Wit (2016b). Here, we investigated whether half-faces in familiar configurations would enter awareness faster – familiarity being defined by presenting the half-face at the location it would naturally occur in the environment. We indeed observed such a familiarity effect, yet it was independent from face inversion. That is, it seemed the most critical factor was the curvature of the face contour relative to fixation, and that convex contours seemed to drive suppression time differences, just like in the study by Stein and Sterzer (2012).

A recent study by Stein, Awad, Gayet, and Peelen (2018) aimed to replicate the b–CFS findings on dominance and trustworthiness of faces reported by Stewart et al. (2012). Specifically, the authors asked whether inverted faces would similarly show dominance-related and untrustworthiness-related slowing. They observed that this was indeed the case, the core effects were not modulated by face inversion whereas the behavioral judgments of perceived dominance and trustworthiness were in fact influenced by face inversion (i.e. they were harder to extract). In further experiments, Stein et al. then pinned down the root cause of differential suppression times. That is, the eye regions seemed to be mostly driving the effects related to slower breakthrough for dominant and untrustworthy faces.

In a related line of research, the claim that personality characteristics of invisible faces can affect the judgments of neutral faces has recently been revised by the same lab that published the initial series of studies (Kleckner et al., 2018). In their study, Kleckner et al. adopted a within-subjects approach where they psychometrically varied stimulus intensity to assess whether the effect of invisible expression on judgment was linked to stimulus awareness or not. Thanks to this fine-grained approach, they were able to reveal that the behavioral judgment effect was observed for awareness levels that significantly differed from chance. It is important to note however that these deviations from chance would not have been detectable according to the common standards in consciousness research, regarding the number of trials per participants. Thus, the authors concluded that facial expressions can indeed influence the perceived expression of a neutral face, but not when they are rendered completely invisible.

As alluded to in section 2.2, a series of visual adaptation studies has also been published – seemingly independently of the b-CFS findings. For example, visual awareness of a face is required for adaptation to complex features such as facial expression (Yang, Hong, & Blake, 2010), face race or gender (Amihai, Deouell, & Bentin, 2011), face identity (Moradi et al., 2005), face shape (Stein & Sterzer, 2011), or eye gaze (Stein et al., 2012). Thus, these studies have mostly shown that invisible face features are processed to a limited extent (i.e. the effects are specific to the adapted size or eye). For example, Stein and Sterzer (2011) observed face shape aftereffects for fully invisible stimuli, yet these aftereffects were only observed if the test stimulus had the same size as the adaptor and was also presented to the same eye as the adaptor. This suggests that the adaptation occurred at a low level of processing, and was specific to simple features such as its exact size and shape. The important implication of this set of studies is not that it invalidates robust findings on invisible face processing that seemingly indicate high-level, integrated representations. To the contrary, these adaptation studies allow calibration as to the level of processing that can be reasonably expected from any type of CFS study. From this perspective, a researcher should consider whether an effect observed in his/her particular study can be reasonably explained by stimulus representations at an early level of visual processing.

In sum, it is clear that follow-up studies have revealed a much more nuanced picture of processing of face stimuli during CFS. Most of these studies are examples where the initial effect proved to be replicable, yet where the root cause of the effect was shown to be due to something much simpler than initially anticipated (e.g. low-level differences, limited awareness of the "invisible" stimulus).

3.2 Word stimuli

For word stimuli, the follow-up studies revealed a somewhat more ambiguous picture. Heyman and Moors (2014) argued that the most basic aspects of word processing which reveal robust and replicable effects for visible words (word frequency, word vs. pseudo-word, word inversion) had been glossed over in all previous studies. In two experiments, they varied word type, inversion, and frequency and observed that it did not influence suppression durations at all. This led them to conclude that the premise on which any study using words and CFS rests is shaky at least. In a related study yet inspired by the approach of Costello et al. (2009), Kerr, Hesselmann, Räling, Wartenburger, and Sterzer (2017) did observe a consistent word inversion effect, yet effects of typicality or prime-target congruency were much less stable when the effect was evaluated against a set of different analytical approaches. In a replication study consisting

52 Pieter Moors

of ten experiments, Rabagliati, Robertson, and Carmel (2018) failed to observe any of the semantic congruency effects in short sentences that were observed in the experiments reported in Sklar et al. (2012). Importantly, the authors also conducted a simulation study in which they observed that typical data-analytic techniques (e.g. repeated measures ANOVA on mean suppression durations) do not have proper Type 1 error rates for typical b-CFS datasets. It is therefore possible that, due to model misspecification, the b-CFS literature suffers from a higher Type 1 error rate compared to other literatures.

Except for the finding of Hung and Hsieh (2015) on syntactic processing which has not yet been the subject of a replication study, it seems most replication studies of behavioral effects on processing of words have yielded null results. However, there are some EEG studies claiming to have found neural correlates derived from processing invisible words, which do not map onto behavioral effects (Eo, Cha, Chong, & Kang, 2016; Lei, Dou, Liu, Zhang, & Li, 2017; Yang, Zhou, Li, Hung, Pegna, & Yeh, 2017), yet the robustness of these EEG results can be questioned (Kang et al., 2011; Yang, Tien, Yang, & Yeh, 2017). Furthermore, one could ask whether such a discrepancy is meaningful in the sense that the neural correlates obtained are reflecting a similar type of processing as would be inferred from a behavioral effect. In sum, follow-up studies on the processing of invisible words during CFS have yielded a situation where more high-powered research seems to be needed to convincingly point us in either direction.

3.3 Object-scene congruency in natural scenes

Three replication experiments reported in Moors, Boelens, van Overwalle, and Wagemans (2016a) consistently failed to replicate the b-CFS findings originally observed in Mudrik et al. (2011a). Rather than invoking an (intense) discussion on the discrepancy between both studies, the original authors decided to revisit one of their own masking studies (Mudrik & Koch, 2013). Interestingly, the core finding of that study failed to replicate as well (Biderman & Mudrik, 2018). This does not imply that object-background relationships in natural scenes cannot be processed unconsciously. Rather, it has been shown that the specific stimuli used in these studies, as well as the paradigms, are not sensitive to any congruency effect that might potentially exist. Thus, at this moment, the field is wide open on this specific topic. Future studies, maybe relying on different paradigms or stimuli, could explore whether the pendulum swings one way or the other.

3.4 Numerical processing and unconscious arithmetic

The distance-dependent priming effect observed by Bahrami et al. (2010) was critically examined by Hesselmann and Knops (2014). They showed it was observed due to a confound in the original experimental design. That is, target numerosity and prime-target distance were not orthogonally manipulated, and response times were influenced by target numerosity. This precluded Bahrami et al. providing a conclusive answer regarding the presence of numerical processing during CFS. In a follow-up study with an improved design, Hesselmann, Darcy, Sterzer, and Knops (2015) obtained evidence only for identity priming, and no conclusive evidence for distance-dependent priming was observed.

The intriguing data obtained by Sklar et al. (2012) were reanalyzed by Moors and Hesselmann (2018) with four considerations in mind: (1) Are the results influenced by analyzing the data using a model selection framework relying on Bayes factors? (2) Sklar et al. claimed an interaction between prime-target congruency and equation type (i.e. a priming effect was observed for subtraction equations only) which was never formally assessed. (3) Do the results show distance-dependent priming, a core feature of numerical processing? (4) Do the data indicate evidence of having unconsciously solved the equation? The core conclusion of these reanalyses was that the evidential value of the original findings was weak, and signatures of numerical processing were not revealed. Karpinski, Briggs, and Yale (2018) performed a replication of the Sklar et al. arithmetic experiment. Their analysis revealed a "borderline significant" interaction between prime-target congruency and equation type, after which a "marginally significant" priming effect for subtraction equations was reported. Thus, the conclusion of this analysis was that there was (at best) weak evidence for unconscious arithmetic. As a follow-up, we decided to conduct a so-called multiverse analysis on the dataset reported in Karpinski et al. (2018). We specified a combination of data exclusion criteria that we considered reasonable, and a full-factorial combination of these resulted in 250 different possible data analysis pipelines (Moors & Hesselmann, 2019). The outcome of these analyses indicated that interaction effect between prime-target congruency and equation type indeed was reliably obtained in 14 percent of the analyses. However, the simple effect that caused it to occur was not the prime-target congruency effect for subtraction equations, but an "equation effect" for congruent trials. That is, it seemed to be the case that participants pronounced the target number faster for congruent subtraction equations compared to congruent addition equations. Inspection of the target numbers indicated that these were smaller for subtraction compared to addition equations. Thus, a stronger representation for smaller numbers might have been the cause of the interaction between prime-target congruency and equation type.

In sum, follow-up studies on numerical processing and arithmetic during CFS all indicated that there is no conclusive evidence for either to happen.

4 What is the most parsimonious summary of the field?

In section 2.2, it seemed pretty straightforward to devise an argument for why high-level processing should not be observed in any kind of CFS study, as well as to discuss evidence backing up this claim. It proves to be much more difficult however to outline a coherent hypothesis about what exactly is driving the differences in suppression times observed in b-CFS studies or the differences in reaction times in priming studies relying on CFS. I preface that, given my reading on the evidence for high-level processing in CFS studies, the discussion outlined here will necessarily be a biased one. Some published findings will fit the proposed hypothesis and others will not.

Our current hypothesis is that CFS reveals the default (or current) sensitivity of early visual cortex to input statistics we have been exposed to throughout our life (e.g. orientation, spatial frequency, etc.), which in turn has shaped the neural representation of these statistical features as well as the strength of their connectivity pattern (Field, 1987; Simoncelli & Olshausen, 2001). Here, it is critical to stress that these sensitivities pertain only to the level at which the stimulus is still represented during CFS. This inevitably implies that some statistical regularities in the environment that are obvious to us might not be revealed through CFS, because the representation of the suppressed stimulus might not yet be sufficiently differentiated at the level of early visual cortex. Alternatively, regularities and statistics that are not obvious to us might be represented in early visual cortex because we are not used to probing exclusively early visual cortex whilst presenting stimuli in a visual experiment. In sum, the to-be-suppressed visual stimulus is fractionated into elemental features at the level of early visual processing, and the distribution of sensitivities at this processing level drives the results we observe in any type of CFS study (Hong & Blake, 2009; Moors et al., 2017; Zadbood et al., 2011). What does this hypothesis imply and, importantly, what does it not imply?

First, as already highlighted, stimuli that require some form of contextual integration relying on iterative feedforward-feedback are not processed as such during CFS. For example, we have shown that the well-known Kanizsa illusory surface stimulus enter awareness faster in a b-CFS context compared to a non-illusory variant because of the difference in low-level image statistics rather than the presence of the illusory surface itself (Moors, Wagemans, van Ee, & de-Wit, 2016c). This conclusion is supported by another study showing that illusory surfaces are not evoked when only the inducing stimuli are suppressed (Harris et al., 2011). Other studies have shown that three-dimensional cast shadows or implied motion are not processed during CFS (Faivre & Koch, 2014; Khuu, Gordon, Balcomb, & Kim, 2014), nor are faces processed holistically (Axelrod & Rees, 2014).

Secondly, simple stimulus features should have a processing benefit during CFS. For example, a radial bias for orientation and motion direction has been observed in suppression times (Hong, 2015), as well as a preference for collinear contours (Li & Li, 2015). Furthermore, suppressed collinear flankers have also been observed to still influence detection of a visible target (Hayashi & Murakami, 2015). Last, for dynamic stimuli, motion coherence also seems to systematically influence suppression times (Chung & Khuu, 2014; Kaunitz, Fracasso, Lingnau, & Melcher, 2013).

Interestingly, a recent set of studies has used CFS as a tool to show that certain visual illusions are processed very early in visual processing. Thus, the motivation to use CFS here is completely the opposite of the initial motivation. That is, the authors needed a paradigm to limit visual processing. Inspired by studies that showed that the Ebbinghaus illusion is primarily processed in monocular channels of early visual cortex whereas the Ponzo illusion is represented somewhat in more upstream areas (Schwarzkopf, Song, & Rees, 2011; Song, Schwarzkopf, & Rees, 2011), Nakashima and Sugita (2018) and Chen, Qiao, Wang, and Jiang (2018) independently reported evidence that the Ebbinghaus illusion still exerts priming effects when presented under perceptual suppression. Moreover, Chen et al. showed that this contrasts with the Ponzo illusion, which does not exert any influence on subsequent processing when it is rendered invisible. To add to this, the early study by Harris et al. (2011) converges with these studies by showing that simultaneous brightness contrast also occurs during perceptual suppression, whereas the Craik-O'Brien-Cornsweet illusion does not (Masuda, Watanabe, Terao, Watanabe, Yagi, & Maruya, 2011).

It is important to stress that this view does not exclude the possibility of modulatory or top-down effects on processing during CFS. Indeed, the contents and load of visual working memory have been shown to influence suppression times (De Loof, Poppe, Cleeremans, Gevers, & Van Opstal, 2015; Gayet, Paffen, & Van der Stigchel, 2013; Pan, Lin, Zhao, & Soto, 2013), as well as expectations (Pinto, van Gaal, de Lange, Lamme, & Seth, 2015; Stein & Peelen, 2015), and the expertise of the observer (Stein, Reeder, & Peelen, 2015). Furthermore, some forms of cross-modal effects can be observed. Invisible scenes presented together with congruent auditory stimuli have been shown to enter awareness faster (Cox & Hong, 2015; Tan & Yeh, 2015). Similar congruency effects have been observed for audiovisual speech (Alsius & Munhall, 2013; Plass, Guzman-Martinez, Ortega, Grabowecky, & Suzuki, 2014). The important point here is that these modulatory or top-down influences play out at the representational level of the suppressed stimulus. Indeed, in an elegant study, Lupyan and Ward (2013) showed that presenting an auditory cue that matched a perceptually suppressed object (e.g. "kangaroo") speeded up the breakthrough of this stimulus compared to incongruent verbal labels. Critically, the authors showed that this facilitatory effect occurred at the perceptual rather than semantic level, implying that effects that "behave like" semantic processing are actually better explained by processing at the early, perceptual level.

A good case in point here is the study of Gelbard-Sagiv, Faivre, Mudrik, and Koch (2016). They showed that repetition priming for famous faces *only* occurred when observers were aware of the color or location of the face (i.e. "low-level awareness") without being aware of its identity. On trials in which suppression was complete, no repetition priming was observed. The authors concluded, however, that low level awareness of the perceptually suppressed face stimulus accompanies "high-level processing" of it. It should be stressed that there is absolutely no principled reason to interpret these results as providing evidence for identity processing of the suppressed face stimulus. What is being shown here is that repeating an invisibly presented face stimulus yields faster responses to the repeated visible face stimulus. This is not a strong test for so-called high-level processing of invisible stimuli. Any perceptual feature the visual system is sensitive to during CFS can yield faster responses. Illustrations of this point are the studies by Almeida and colleagues (Almeida et al., 2010, 2008, 2013). Based on the reasoning that dorsal stream processing would be preserved during CFS (Fang & He, 2005; Ludwig &

Hesselmann, 2015), the authors obtained evidence that perceptually suppressed tools (a supposedly distinct category of objects to which the dorsal stream would be primarily sensitive) could prime other tools, whereas animals (supposedly processed by the ventral stream, which is blocked by CFS) failed to prime other animals. In an attempt to pinpoint what was actually happening during tool priming, Sakuraba et al. (2012) showed that stimulus elongation was the critical factor, independent of whether these stimuli belonged to the tool category or not. Interestingly, this story developed even further, and recently it has been shown that these priming effects are very difficult to robustly replicate, and that the use of anaglyph glasses (which allow for crosstalk between the eyes) might be at the heart of the priming effects that have been observed in the literature (Hesselmann, Darcy, Rothkirch, & Sterzer, 2018; Rothkirch & Hesselmann, 2018). The importance of this sequence of studies should not be underestimated. It shows that it is critical to exclude potential alternative explanations before one advances to an interpretation based on high-level stimulus processing during CFS. Although this issue applies to any experimental study, it again seems particularly important in the context of inferring the scope and limits of unconscious visual processing.

I personally think a particularly strong test of the extent to which perceptually suppressed stimuli are processed is to use a paradigm in which performance on a visible stimulus is measured while invisible stimuli are presented concurrently which, under normal visible conditions, elicit an influence on the visible target stimulus. A good example of a study that used this strategy examined whether flanker interference (i.e. reduced task performance when flanking stimuli are incongruent with respect to the target stimulus on a task-relevant stimulus dimension) would still be elicited by invisible flanker stimuli (Wu, Lo Voi, Lee, Mackie, Wu, & Fan, 2015). The authors presented arrows as flanker stimuli, either visible or suppressed. Participants had to perform a task on a central visible arrow (i.e. indicate its pointing direction). The results revealed that flanker interference was observed in the fully visible trials, whereas no flanker interference was observed on the suppressed trials. This indicates that the representation of the flanking arrows was not sufficiently "arrow-like" to initiate a conflict with the central, visible arrow.

Another prediction that could be derived from framing differences in suppression times as reflecting the sensitivity to "primitive" stimulus features is that, due to the plasticity of the visual system, it should be possible to change representational strength through perceptual learning or through changing stimulus relevance by means of conditioning paradigms. Indeed, it has been shown that stimuli break through faster and more frequently when participants repeatedly perform the same task across different blocks, sessions, or even days (Carmel, 2015; Ludwig, Sterzer, Kathmann, Franz, & Hesselmann, 2013; Mastropasqua, Tse, & Turatto, 2015). Similarly, coupling invisible stimuli with rewards changes their suppression depth (Seitz, Kim, & Watanabe, 2009) or presenting electric shocks together with perceptually suppressed stimuli influences the electrodermal response to those stimuli (Lipp, Kempnich, Jee, & Arnold, 2014; Raio, Carmel, Carrasco, & Phelps, 2012). Furthermore, pairing an initially neutral and visible grating stimulus with electric shocks also influences suppression times such that grating stimuli associated with shocks break suppression faster (Gayet, Paffen, Belopolsky, Theeuwes, & Van der Stigchel, 2016). Interestingly, stimulus-reward coupling for invisible stimuli is monocular (Seitz et al., 2009), whereas triggering the relationship prior to suppression speeds up breakthroughs in both eyes (Gayet, et al., 2016a). Furthermore, Hedger, Adams, and Garner (2015a) showed that threatening stimuli did not elicit differential skin conductance responses compared to neutral stimuli when they were completely suppressed. Only when these stimuli broke suppression during a trial was a differential electrodermal response observed. This provides an important insight as to how threatening or emotional stimuli are represented during suppression.

It should be noted however that not any type of coupling between stimuli can influence processing of perceptually suppressed visual stimuli. For example, associating grating stimuli with the self or the other (i.e. by associating it with the word "you" or "other") did not influence suppression times of the gratings (Stein, Siebold, & van Zoest, 2016b), although recently evidence to the contrary has been reported (Macrae, Visokomogilski, Golubickis, Cunningham, & Sahraie, 2017). Furthermore, associating faces with affective information does not influence subsequent suppression times of these faces (Rabovsky, Stein, & Abdel Rahman, 2016; Stein, Grubb, Bertrand, Suh, & Verosky, 2017).

A final point of discussion pertains to how robust and seemingly high-level effects such as face inversion, body inversion, or the preference for eye gaze can fit in this framework. Indeed, stimulus inversion is generally considered to be an elegant manipulation to control for low-level confounding factors in particular stimuli. However, the point here is that a proper control condition is one that equates processing for early visual cortex, not for mere image characteristics. For face inversion to be tied to more extensive visual processing, we have to make sure inversion cannot be "decoded" from early visual cortex. Goffaux, Duecker, Hausfeld, Schiltz, and Goebel (2016) showed specifically that face inversion can be decoded from primary visual cortex with high accuracy, although *mean* activity does not differ between upright and inverted faces. The critical point here is that, in principle, differential response patterns can be evoked by simple stimulus manipulations that do not change the so-called low-level image properties. Thus, the fact that we are naturally exposed to upright faces might create a pattern of connectivity at the level of early visual cortex which fundamentally differs from the pattern elicited by inverted faces. The same could be true for the processing of eye contact. Here, the studies that have been done using participants with autism spectrum disorder (ASD) might reveal some deeper understanding. First, it has been shown that people with ASD process protofacial stimuli similarly compared to control participants (Akechi et al., 2015). Thus, the general sensitivity for upright face stimuli seems to be preserved. However, the finding that direct gaze enters awareness faster compared to averted gaze (Chen & Yeh, 2012; Stein et al., 2011b) does not seem to be preserved in autism (Akechi et al., 2014). Moreover, the degree to which the preference for direct gaze declines seems to be modulated by autistic traits (Madipakkam, Rothkirch, Dziobek, & Sterzer, 2018). This absence could be explained due to a lack of sampling the eye region within the group of individuals with autism. Indeed, whereas typically developing individuals seem to move their eyes to invisible eye contact stimuli (Rothkirch, Madipakkam, Rehn, & Sterzer, 2015), individuals with autism do not show such behavior, and seem to actively avoid such stimulation (Madipakkam, Rothkirch, Dziobek, & Sterzer, 2017). Thus, the extent to which direct eye contact is sampled in daily life could again shape the connectivity and activity pattern in early visual cortex, resulting in the set of observations discussed above.

Related to the reasoning outlined in the previous paragraph, there is a set of results that potentially reinforces the points made. That is, a few studies have gone beyond the traditional analysis of mean response times and have applied statistical models that provide insight into the full response time distribution. One type of model is the drift-diffusion model, which decomposes the reaction time distribution into a set of parameters that have an interpretation related to information processing. For example, the drift rate parameter indicates information accumulating when the stimulus is being processed, the bias parameter indicates whether one type of response is preferred over another, and the non-decision time parameter indicates the contribution of processes that (supposedly) have nothing to do with information accumulation. Interestingly, each study that has applied this modeling framework has found that experimental manipulations induce differences in the bias parameter, and never in the drift rate parameter (Gayet, van Maanen, Heilbron, Paffen, & Van der Stigchel, 2016b; Macrae et al., 2017). The opposite is commonly observed in cognitive science, where most experimental manipulations elicit differences in the drift rate parameter, rather than the bias parameter. Interestingly, these findings converge with the results obtained from applying event history analysis to a large set of b-CFS data (Moors & Wagemans, 2017). Across several datasets, it was observed that the probability of observing a response during a trial did not differentially evolve over time between experimental conditions. Interpreted together with the results of the drift-diffusion model, this seems to indicate that there is an initial sweep of feed-forward activity when the suppressed stimulus and the CFS mask are presented to the observer. Subsequently, these representations compete with each other without recruiting additional processes that allow them to become more differentiated over time.

To conclude, in this section I have proposed that (differential) processing of stimuli observed in CFS studies reveals the representational strength of the suppressed stimulus at the level of early visual cortex reflecting the image statistics we have been exposed to throughout our life. I discussed what this claim implies, what it does not imply, and the extent to which current evidence within the literature is consistent with it.

5 Reflections on unconscious visual processing and publishing null results

I end this chapter with some considerations and recommendations to young researchers on my view on how studies on unconscious visual processing should proceed to be maximally informative. I should note that I myself have run short on some of these issues. In hindsight, you can always do better, and I am the first to acknowledge that.

First, if you genuinely want to study unconscious visual processing, I think it is of great importance to design experiments that rely on all sorts of different blinding paradigms. Even if these yield conflicting results, this provides crucial information on the level at which certain aspects of invisible stimuli can be processed. In the end, this might yield a more satisfying picture of the hierarchy of processing invisible stimuli. Secondly, you should include the most stringent control conditions imaginable. This might seem an obvious or even redundant consideration, but all too often I came across CFS studies for which I could think of control conditions that could yield an explanation of the data based on much simpler mechanisms. Thirdly, if you fail to find an effect, understand that this might teach you something fundamental about your design or the effect are studying. The published literature is not truth set in stone. If you tweak your design a sufficient number of times based on post hoc rationalizations and based on what is reported in the literature, you have a 100 percent chance of stumbling upon something (something too good to be true, that is). Rather than putting the null finding in your file drawer, think hard about whether it makes sense *not* to expect a difference. As I argued before, in the case of CFS studies it might actually make sense to predict the absence of a difference. I am sure in many other domains of psychology this is also true. Be as open as you can during your research and when you report it. Compared to ten years ago, scientific practice has changed a lot. The Open Science Framework allows you to share your materials, data, experiment, and analysis scripts. Registered reports allow you to get a manuscript accepted in principle, before the data have been collected. The days where a prediction you didn't make before the data were known was put into the introduction of your paper seem to be over. People will understand if not everything is crystal clear in your set of experiments – they probably have experienced that too. Lastly, but maybe most importantly, as Richard Feynman put it so elegantly in 1974: "The first principle is that you must not fool yourself – and you are the easiest person to fool" (Feynman, 1974).

Acknowledgements

Parts of this chapter have been adapted from the Introduction and Discussion section of my PhD dissertation (Moors, 2016).

Note

1 I will limit myself mostly to behavioral studies, although there exist a good deal of studies dealing with the neural correlates of stimuli rendered invisible through CFS. The reasons are partly due to my own expertise as well as the general lack of direct or conceptual replication in this domain, rendering it difficult to gauge the robustness of these findings. For a comprehensive and balanced review on this topic, I refer to Sterzer, Stein, Ludwig, Rothkirch, & Hesselmann (2014).

References

Adams, W. J., Gray, K. L. H., Garner, M., & Graf, E. W. (2010). High-level face adaptation without awareness. *Psychological Science*, *21*(2), 205–10. https://doi.org/10.1177/0956797609359508

Akechi, H., Stein, T., Kikuchi, Y., Tojo, Y., Osanai, H., & Hasegawa, T. (2015). Preferential awareness of protofacial stimuli in autism. *Cognition*, *143*, 129–34. https://doi.org/10.1016/j.cognition.2015.06.016

Akechi, H., Stein, T., Senju, A., Kikuchi, Y., Tojo, Y., Osanai, H., & Hasegawa, T. (2014). Absence of preferential unconscious processing of eye contact in adolescents with autism spectrum disorder. *Autism Research*. https://doi.org/10.1002/aur.1397

Alais, D. (2012). Binocular rivalry: Competition and inhibition in visual perception. *Wiley Interdisciplinary Reviews: Cognitive Science*, *3*(1), 87–103. https://doi.org/10.1002/wcs.151

Alais, D., & Blake, R. (2005). *Binocular Rivalry*. Cambridge, MA: MIT Press.

Almeida, J., Mahon, B. Z., & Caramazza, A. (2010). The role of the dorsal visual processing stream in tool identification. *Psychological Science*, *21*(6), 772–78. https://doi.org/10.1177/0956797610371343

Almeida, J., Mahon, B. Z., Nakayama, K., & Caramazza, A. (2008). Unconscious processing dissociates along categorical lines. *Proceedings of the National Academy of Sciences of the United States of America*, *105*(39), 15214–18. https://doi.org/10.1073/pnas.0805867105

Almeida, J., Mahon, B. Z., Zapater-Raberov, V., Dziuba, A., Cabaço, T., Marques, J. F., & Caramazza, A. (2013). Grasping with the eyes: The role of elongation in visual recognition of manipulable objects. *Cognitive, Affective, and Behavioral Neuroscience*, 1–17. https://doi.org/10.3758/s13415-013-0208-0

Alsius, A., & Munhall, K. G. (2013). Detection of audivisual speech correspondences without visual awareness. *Psychological Science*. https://doi.org/10.1177/0956797612457378

Amihai, I. (2012). Problems in using d' measures to assess subjective awareness. *I-Perception*, *3*(10), 783–85. https://doi.org/10.1068/i0563ic

Amihai, I., Deouell, L., & Bentin, S. (2011). Conscious awareness is necessary for processing race and gender information from faces. *Consciousness and Cognition*, *20*(2), 269–79. https://doi.org/10.1016/j.concog.2010.08.004

Anderson, E., Siegel, E., White, D., & Barrett, L. F. (2012). Out of sight but not out of mind: Unseen affective faces influence evaluations and social impressions. *Emotion*, *12*(6), 1210–221. https://doi.org/10.1037/a0027514

Arnold, D. H. (2011). Why is binocular rivalry uncommon? Discrepant monocular images in the real world. *Frontiers in Human Neuroscience*, *5*, 116. https://doi.org/10.3389/fnhum.2011.00116

Axelrod, V., & Rees, G. (2014). Conscious awareness is required for holistic face processing. *Consciousness and Cognition*, *27*, 233–45. https://doi.org/10.1016/j.concog.2014.05.004

Baars, B. J. (1993). *A Cognitive Theory of Consciousness*. Cambridge: Cambridge University Press.

Bahrami, B., Carmel, D., Walsh, V., Rees, G., & Lavie, N. (2008a). Spatial attention can modulate unconscious orientation processing. *Perception*, *37*(10), 1520–8.

Bahrami, B., Carmel, D., Walsh, V., Rees, G., & Lavie, N. (2008b). Unconscious orientation processing depends on perceptual load. *Journal of Vision*, *8*(3), 1–10. https://doi.org/10.1167/8.3.12

Bahrami, B., Vetter, P., Spolaore, E., Pagano, S., Butterworth, B., & Rees, G. (2010). Unconscious numerical priming despite interocular suppression. *Psychological Science*, *21*(2), 224–33. https://doi.org/10.1177/0956797609360664

Barbot, A., & Kouider, S. (2011). Longer is not better: Nonconscious overstimulation reverses priming influences under interocular suppression. *Attention, Perception and Psychophysics, 74*, 174–84. https://doi.org/10.3758/s13414-011-0226-3

Biderman, N., & Mudrik, L. (2018). Evidence for implicit-but not unconscious-processing of object-scene relations. *Psychological Science, 29*(2), 266–77. https://doi.org/10.1177/0956797617735745

Blake, R. (1988). Dichoptic reading: The role of meaning in binocular rivalry. *Perception and Psychophysics, 44*(2), 133–41.

Blake, R. (1989). A neural theory of binocular rivalry. *Psychological Review, 96*(1), 145–67.

Blake, R., & Logothetis, N. K. (2002). Visual competition. *Nature Reviews Neuroscience, 3*(1), 13–21. https://doi.org/10.1038/nrn701

Brascamp, J. W., Knapen, T. H. J., Kanai, R., van Ee, R., & van den Berg, A. V. (2007). Flash suppression and flash facilitation in binocular rivalry. *Journal of Vision, 7*(12), 1–12. https://doi.org/10.1167/7.12.12

Breitmeyer, B. G. (2015). Psychophysical "blinding" methods reveal a functional hierarchy of unconscious visual processing. *Consciousness and Cognition, 35*, 234–50. https://doi.org/10.1016/j.concog.2015.01.012

Breitmeyer, B. G., & Öğmen, H. (2006). *Visual Masking: Time Slices through Conscious and Unconscious Vision*. Oxford: Oxford University Press.

Carmel, D. (2015). Learning to become aware: Practice promotes a generalised ability to overcome visual suppression. Presented at the 19th Annual Meeting of the Association for the Scientific Study of Consciousness, Paris.

Cave, C. B., Blake, R., & McNamara, T. (1998). Binocular rivalry disrupts visual priming. *Psychological Science, 9*(4), 299–302. https://doi.org/10.1111/1467-9280.00059

Chen, L., Qiao, C., Wang, Y., & Jiang, Y. (2018). Subconscious processing reveals dissociable contextual modulations of visual size perception. *Cognition, 180*, 259–67. https://doi.org/10.1016/j.cognition.2018.07.014

Chen, Y.-C., & Yeh, S.-L. (2012). Look into my eyes and I will see you: Unconscious processing of human gaze. *Consciousness and Cognition, 21*(4), 1703–10. https://doi.org/10.1016/j.concog.2012.10.001

Chung, C. Y. L., & Khuu, S. K. (2014). The processing of coherent global form and motion patterns without visual awareness. *Frontiers in Psychology, 5*, 195. https://doi.org/10.3389/fpsyg.2014.00195

Cleeremans, A. (2008). Consciousness: The radical plasticity thesis. *Progress in Brain Research, 168*, 19–33. https://doi.org/10.1016/S0079-6123(07)68003-0

Cohen, M. A., & Dennett, D. C. (2011). Consciousness cannot be separated from function. *Trends in Cognitive Sciences, 15*(8), 358–64. https://doi.org/10.1016/j.tics.2011.06.008

Cohen, M. A., Cavanagh, P., Chun, M. M., & Nakayama, K. (2012). The attentional requirements of consciousness. *Trends in Cognitive Sciences, 16*(8), 411–17. https://doi.org/10.1016/j.tics.2012.06.013

Costello, P., Jiang, Y., Baartman, B., McGlennen, K., & He, S. (2009). Semantic and subword priming during binocular suppression. *Consciousness and Cognition, 18*(2), 375–82. https://doi.org/10.1016/j.concog.2009.02.003

Cox, D., & Hong, S. W. (2015). Semantic-based crossmodal processing during visual suppression. *Frontiers in Psychology, 6*, 722. https://doi.org/10.3389/fpsyg.2015.00722

Crick, F., & Koch, C. (1998). Consciousness and neuroscience. *Cerebral Cortex, 8*(2), 97–107.

Crick, F., & Koch, C. (2003). A framework for consciousness. *Nature Neuroscience, 6*(2), 119–26. https://doi.org/10.1038/nn0203-119

Dehaene, S., & Changeux, J.-P. (2011). Experimental and theoretical approaches to conscious processing. *Neuron, 70*(2), 200–27. https://doi.org/10.1016/j.neuron.2011.03.018

De Loof, E., Poppe, L., Cleeremans, A., Gevers, W., & Van Opstal, F. (2015). Different effects of executive and visuospatial working memory on visual consciousness. *Attention, Perception and Psychophysics*. https://doi.org/10.3758/s13414-015-1000-8

Dennett, D. C. (1993). *Consciousness Explained*. London: Penguin Adult.

Dienes, Z. (2015). How Bayesian statistics are needed to determine whether mental states are unconscious. In M. Overgaard (ed.), *Behavioural Methods in Consciousness Research* (pp. 199–220). Oxford: Oxford University Press.

Dienes, Z. (2016). How Bayes factors change scientific practice. *Journal of Mathematical Psychology*. https://doi.org/10.1016/j.jmp.2015.10.003

Eo, K., Cha, O., Chong, S. C., & Kang, M.-S. (2016). Less is more: Semantic information survives interocular suppression when attention is diverted. *Journal of Neuroscience*, *36*(20), 5489–97. https://doi.org/10.1523/JNEUROSCI.3018-15.2016

Fahrenfort, J. J., & Lamme, V. A. F. (2012). A true science of consciousness explains phenomenology: Comment on Cohen and Dennett. *Trends in Cognitive Sciences*, *16*(3), 138–9. https://doi.org/10.1016/j.tics.2012.01.004

Faivre, N., & Koch, C. (2014). Inferring the direction of implied motion depends on visual awareness. *Journal of Vision*, *14*(4), 4. https://doi.org/10.1167/14.4.4

Fang, F., & He, S. (2005). Cortical responses to invisible objects in the human dorsal and ventral pathways. *Nature Neuroscience*, *8*(10), 1380–5. https://doi.org/10.1038/nn1537

Feynman, R. (1974). Cargo cult science. *Engineering and Science*, *37*(7), 10–13.

Field, D. J. (1987). Relations between the statistics of natural images and the response properties of cortical cells. *Journal of the Optical Society of America A*, *4*(12), 2379. https://doi.org/10.1364/JOSAA.4.002379

Fogelson, S. V., Kohler, P. J., Miller, K. J., Granger, R., & Tse, P. U. (2014). Unconscious neural processing differs with method used to render stimuli invisible. *Frontiers in Psychology*, *5*, 601. https://doi.org/10.3389/fpsyg.2014.00601

Gayet, S., Paffen, C. L. E., Belopolsky, A. V., Theeuwes, J., & Van der Stigchel, S. (2016a). Visual input signaling threat gains preferential access to awareness in a breaking continuous flash suppression paradigm. *Cognition*, *149*, 77–83. https://doi.org/10.1016/j.cognition.2016.01.009

Gayet, S., Paffen, C. L. E., & Van der Stigchel, S. (2013). Information matching the content of visual working memory is prioritized for conscious access. *Psychological Science*, *24*(12), 2472–80. https://doi.org/10.1177/0956797613495882

Gayet, S., Van der Stigchel, S., & Paffen, C. (2014). Breaking continuous flash suppression: Competing for consciousness on the pre-semantic battlefield. *Frontiers in Psychology*, *5*(460). https://doi.org/10.3389/fpsyg.2014.00460

Gayet, S., van Maanen, L., Heilbron, M., Paffen, C. L. E., & Van der Stigchel, S. (2016b). Visual input that matches the content of visual working memory requires less (not faster) evidence sampling to reach conscious access. *Journal of Vision*, *16*(11), 26. https://doi.org/10.1167/16.11.26

Gelbard-Sagiv, H., Faivre, N., Mudrik, L., & Koch, C. (2016). Low-level awareness accompanies "unconscious" high-level processing during continuous flash suppression. *Journal of Vision*, *16*(1), 3. https://doi.org/10.1167/16.1.3

Geng, H., Zhang, S., Li, Q., Tao, R., & Xu, S. (2012). Dissociations of subliminal and supraliminal self-face from other-face processing: Behavioral and ERP evidence. *Neuropsychologia*, *50*(12), 2933–42. https://doi.org/10.1016/j.neuropsychologia.2012.07.040

Gobbini, M. I., Gors, J. D., Halchenko, Y. O., Hughes, H. C., & Cipolli, C. (2013a). Processing of invisible social cues. *Consciousness and Cognition*, *22*(3), 765–70. https://doi.org/10.1016/j.concog.2013.05.002

Gobbini, M. I., Gors, J. D., Halchenko, Y. O., Rogers, C., Guntupalli, J. S., Hughes, H., & Cipolli, C. (2013b). Prioritized detection of personally familiar faces. *PLoS One, 8*(6), e66620. https://doi.org/10.1371/journal.pone.0066620

Goffaux, V., Duecker, F., Hausfeld, L., Schiltz, C., & Goebel, R. (2016). Horizontal tuning for faces originates in high-level Fusiform Face Area. *Neuropsychologia, 81*, 1–11. https://doi.org/10.1016/j.neuropsychologia.2015.12.004

Gray, K. L. H., Adams, W. J., Hedger, N., Newton, K. E., & Garner, M. (2013). Faces and awareness: Low-level, not emotional factors determine perceptual dominance. *Emotion.* https://doi.org/10.1037/a0031403

Han, S., & Alais, D. (2018). Strength of continuous flash suppression is optimal when target and masker modulation rates are matched. *Journal of Vision, 18*(3), 3–3. https://doi.org/10.1167/18.3.3

Han, S., Blake, R., & Alais, D. (2018). Slow and steady, not fast and furious: Slow temporal modulation strengthens continuous flash suppression. *Consciousness and Cognition, 58*, 10–19. https://doi.org/10.1016/j.concog.2017.12.007

Han, S., Lunghi, C., & Alais, D. (2016). The temporal frequency tuning of continuous flash suppression reveals peak suppression at very low frequencies. *Scientific Reports, 6.* https://doi.org/10.1038/srep35723

Harris, J. J., Schwarzkopf, D. S., Song, C., Bahrami, B., & Rees, G. (2011). Contextual illusions reveal the limit of unconscious visual processing. *Psychological Science, 22*(3), 399–405. https://doi.org/10.1177/0956797611399293

Hayashi, D., & Murakami, I. (2015). Facilitation of contrast detection by flankers without perceived orientation. *Journal of Vision, 15*(15), 15. https://doi.org/10.1167/15.15.15

Hedger, N., Adams, W. J., & Garner, M. (2015a). Autonomic arousal and attentional orienting to visual threat are predicted by awareness. *Journal of Experimental Psychology: Human Perception and Performance, 41*(3), 798–806. https://doi.org/10.1037/xhp0000051

Hedger, N., Adams, W. J., & Garner, M. (2015b). Fearful faces have a sensory advantage in the competition for awareness. *Journal of Experimental Psychology: Human Perception and Performance.* https://doi.org/10.1037/xhp0000127

Hesselmann, G., & Knops, A. (2014). No conclusive evidence for numerical priming under interocular suppression. *Psychological Science.* https://doi.org/10.1177/0956797614548876

Hesselmann, G., & Malach, R. (2011). The link between fMRI-BOLD activation and perceptual awareness is "stream-invariant" in the human visual system. *Cerebral Cortex, 21*(12), 2829–37. https://doi.org/10.1093/cercor/bhr085

Hesselmann, G., Darcy, N., Rothkirch, M., & Sterzer, P. (2018). Investigating masked priming along the "vision-for-perception" and "vision-for-action" dimensions of unconscious processing. *Journal of Experimental Psychology: General.* https://doi.org/10.1037/xge0000420

Hesselmann, G., Darcy, N., Sterzer, P., & Knops, A. (2015). Exploring the boundary conditions of unconscious numerical priming effects with continuous flash suppression. *Consciousness and Cognition, 31*, 60–72. https://doi.org/10.1016/j.concog.2014.10.009

Heyman, T., & Moors, P. (2014). Frequent words do not break continuous flash suppression differently from infrequent or nonexistent words: Implications for semantic processing of words in the absence of awareness. *PLoS One, 9*(8), e104719. https://doi.org/10.1371/journal.pone.0104719

Hong, S. W. (2015). Radial bias for orientation and direction of motion modulates access to visual awareness during continuous flash suppression. *Journal of Vision, 15*(1), 3. https://doi.org/10.1167/15.1.3

Hong, S. W., & Blake, R. (2009). Interocular suppression differentially affects achromatic and chromatic mechanisms. *Attention, Perception and Psychophysics, 71*(2), 403–11. https://doi.org/10.3758/APP.71.2.403

Hung, S.-M., & Hsieh, P.-J. (2015). Syntactic processing in the absence of awareness and semantics. *Journal of Experimental Psychology: Human Perception and Performance.* https://doi.org/10.1037/xhp0000094

Hung, S.-M., Nieh, C.-H., & Hsieh, P.-J. (2016). Unconscious processing of facial attractiveness: Invisible attractive faces orient visual attention. *Scientific Reports, 6.* https://doi.org/10.1038/srep37117

Jackendoff, R. (1987). *Consciousness and the computational mind.* Cambridge, MA: MIT Press.

Jiang, Y., & He, S. (2006). Cortical responses to invisible faces: Dissociating subsystems for facial-information processing. *Current Biology, 16*(20), 2023–9. https://doi.org/10.1016/j.cub.2006.08.084

Jiang, Y., Costello, P., Fang, F., Huang, M., & He, S. (2006). A gender- and sexual orientation-dependent spatial attentional effect of invisible images. *Proceedings of the National Academy of Sciences of the United States of America, 103*(45), 17048–52. https://doi.org/10.1073/pnas.0605678103

Jiang, Y., Costello, P., & He, S. (2007). Processing of invisible stimuli: Advantage of upright faces and recognizable words in overcoming interocular suppression. *Psychological Science, 18*(4), 349–55. https://doi.org/10.1111/j.1467-9280.2007.01902.x

Kanai, R., Tsuchiya, N., & Verstraten, F. A. J. (2006). The scope and limits of top-down attention in unconscious visual processing. *Current Biology, 16*(23), 2332–6. https://doi.org/10.1016/j.cub.2006.10.001

Kang, M.-S., Blake, R., & Woodman, G. (2011). Semantic analysis does not occur in the absence of awareness induced by interocular suppression. *Journal of Neuroscience, 31*(38), 13535–45. https://doi.org/10.1523/JNEUROSCI.1691-11.2011

Karpinski, A., Briggs, J. C., & Yale, M. (2018). A direct replication: Unconscious arithmetic processing. *European Journal of Social Psychology.* https://doi.org/10.1002/ejsp.2390

Kaunitz, L., Fracasso, A., Lingnau, A., & Melcher, D. (2013). Non-conscious processing of motion coherence can boost conscious access. *PLoS One, 8*(4), e60787. https://doi.org/10.1371/journal.pone.0060787

Kaunitz, L., Fracasso, A., & Melcher, D. (2011). Unseen complex motion is modulated by attention and generates a visible aftereffect. *Journal of Vision, 11*(13). https://doi.org/10.1167/11.13.10

Kerr, J. A., Hesselmann, G., Räling, R., Wartenburger, I., & Sterzer, P. (2017). Choice of analysis pathway dramatically affects statistical outcomes in breaking continuous flash suppression. *Scientific Reports, 7,* 3002. https://doi.org/10.1038/s41598-017-03396-3

Khuu, S. K., Gordon, J., Balcomb, K., & Kim, J. (2014). The perception of three-dimensional cast-shadow structure is dependent on visual awareness. *Journal of Vision, 14*(3), 25. https://doi.org/10.1167/14.3.25

Kim, C.-Y., & Blake, R. (2005). Psychophysical magic: Eendering the visible "invisible", *Trends in Cognitive Sciences, 9*(8), 381–8. https://doi.org/10.1016/j.tics.2005.06.012

Kleckner, I. R., Anderson, E. C., Betz, N. J., Wormwood, J. B., Eskew, R. T., & Barrett, L. F. (2018). Conscious awareness is necessary for affective faces to influence social judgments. *Journal of Experimental Social Psychology, 79,* 181–7. https://doi.org/10.1016/j.jesp.2018.07.013

Koch, C., & Tsuchiya, N. (2007). Attention and consciousness: Two distinct brain processes. *Trends in Cognitive Sciences, 11*(1), 16–22. https://doi.org/10.1016/j.tics.2006.10.012

Koenderink, J. J. (2012). *Visual Awareness.* Utrecht: De Clootcrans Press.

Kring, A. M., Siegel, E. H., & Barrett, L. F. (2014). Unseen affective faces influence person perception judgments in schizophrenia. *Clinical Psychological Science, 2*(4), 443–54. https://doi.org/10.1177/2167702614536161

Lamme, V. A. F. (2003). Why visual attention and awareness are different. *Trends in Cognitive Sciences*, 7(1), 12–18.

Lau, H., & Rosenthal, D. (2011). Empirical support for higher-order theories of conscious awareness. *Trends in Cognitive Sciences*, 15(8), 365–73. https://doi.org/10.1016/j.tics.2011.05.009

Lei, Y., Dou, H., Liu, Q., Zhang, W., Zhang, Z., & Li, H. (2017). Automatic processing of emotional words in the absence of awareness: The critical role of P2. *Frontiers in Psychology, 8*. https://doi.org/10.3389/fpsyg.2017.00592

Li, Y., & Li, S. (2015). Contour integration, attentional cuing, and conscious awareness: An investigation on the processing of collinear and orthogonal contours. *Journal of Vision*, 15(16), 10. https://doi.org/10.1167/15.16.10

Lipp, O. V., Kempnich, C., Jee, S. H., & Arnold, D. H. (2014). Fear conditioning to subliminal fear relevant and non fear relevant stimuli. *PLoS One*, 9(9), e99332. https://doi.org/10.1371/journal.pone.0099332

Logothetis, N. K. (1998). Single units and conscious vision. *Philosophical Transactions of the Royal Society of London. Series B, Biological Sciences*, 353(1377), 1801–1818. https://doi.org/10.1098/rstb.1998.0333

Ludwig, K., & Hesselmann, G. (2015). Weighing the evidence for a dorsal processing bias under continuous flash suppression. *Consciousness and Cognition*, 35, 251–9. https://doi.org/10.1016/j.concog.2014.12.010

Ludwig, K., Sterzer, P., Kathmann, N., Franz, V. H., & Hesselmann, G. (2013). Learning to detect but not to grasp suppressed visual stimuli. *Neuropsychologia*, 51(13), 2930–8. https://doi.org/10.1016/j.neuropsychologia.2013.09.035

Lupyan, G., & Ward, E. J. (2013). Language can boost otherwise unseen objects into visual awareness. *Proceedings of the National Academy of Sciences*. https://doi.org/10.1073/pnas.1303312110

Mack, A., & Rock, I. (1998). *Inattentional Blindness*. Cambridge, MA: MIT Press.

Macrae, C. N., Visokomogilski, A., Golubickis, M., Cunningham, W. A., & Sahraie, A. (2017). Self-relevance prioritizes access to visual awareness. *Journal of Experimental Psychology: Human Perception and Performance*, 43(3), 438–43. https://doi.org/10.1037/xhp0000361

Madipakkam, A. R., Rothkirch, M., Dziobek, I., & Sterzer, P. (2017). Unconscious avoidance of eye contact in autism spectrum disorder. *Scientific Reports*, 7(1), 13378. https://doi.org/10.1038/s41598-017-13945-5

Madipakkam, A. R., Rothkirch, M., Dziobek, I., & Sterzer, P. (2018). Access to awareness of direct gaze is related to autistic traits. *Psychological Medicine*, 1–7. https://doi.org/10.1017/S0033291718001630

Maruya, K., Watanabe, H., & Watanabe, M. (2008). Adaptation to invisible motion results in low-level but not high-level aftereffects. *Journal of Vision*, 8(11), 1–11. https://doi.org/10.1167/8.11.7

Mastropasqua, T., Tse, P. U., & Turatto, M. (2015). Learning of monocular information facilitates breakthrough to awareness during interocular suppression. *Attention, Perception, and Psychophysics*, 1–14. https://doi.org/10.3758/s13414-015-0839-z

Masuda, A., Watanabe, J., Terao, M., Watanabe, M., Yagi, A., & Maruya, K. (2011). Awareness of central luminance edge is crucial for the Craik-O'Brien-Cornsweet effect. *Frontiers in Human Neuroscience*, 5(125). https://doi.org/10.3389/fnhum.2011.00125

Moors, P. (2016). *Launching Awareness and Chasing Consciousness: Perceptual Organization and Continuous Flash Suppression* (PhD thesis). KU Leuven, Leuven, Belgium.

Moors, P., & Hesselmann, G. (2018). A critical reexamination of doing arithmetic nonconsciously. *Psychonomic Bulletin & Review*, 25(1), 472–81. https://doi.org/10.3758/s13423-017-1292-x

Moors, P., & Hesselmann, G. (2019) Unconscious arithmetic: Assessing the robustness of the results reported by Karpinski, Briggs, and Yale (2018). *Consciousness and Cognition 68*, 97–106.

Moors, P., & Wagemans, J. (2017). Analyzing the time course of processing invisible stimuli: Applying event history analysis to breaking continuous flash suppression data. *Journal of Vision, 17*(10), 143–143. https://doi.org/10.1167/17.10.143

Moors, P., Boelens, D., van Overwalle, J., & Wagemans, J. (2016a). Scene integration without awareness: No conclusive evidence for processing scene congruency during continuous flash suppression. *Psychological Science, 27*(7), 945–56. https://doi.org/10.1177/0956797616642525

Moors, P., Hesselmann, G., Wagemans, J., & van Ee, R. (2017). Continuous flash suppression: Stimulus fractionation rather than integration. *Trends in Cognitive Sciences, 21*(10), 719–21. https://doi.org/10.1016/j.tics.2017.06.005

Moors, P., Stein, T., Wagemans, J., & van Ee, R. (2015). Serial correlations in continuous flash suppression. *Neuroscience of Consciousness, 2015*(1), niv010. https://doi.org/10.1093/nc/niv010

Moors, P., Wagemans, J., & de-Wit, L. (2014). Moving stimuli are less effectively masked using traditional continuous flash suppression (CFS) compared to a moving mondrian mask (MMM): A test case for feature-selective suppression and retinotopic adaptation. *PLoS One, 9*(5), e98298. https://doi.org/10.1371/journal.pone.0098298

Moors, P., Wagemans, J., & de-Wit, L. (2016b). Faces in commonly experienced configurations enter awareness faster due to their curvature relative to fixation. *PeerJ, 4*. https://doi.org/10.7717/peerj.1565

Moors, P., Wagemans, J., van Ee, R., & de-Wit, L. (2016c). No evidence for surface organization in Kanizsa configurations during continuous flash suppression. *Attention, Perception and Psychophysics, 78*(3), 902–14. https://doi.org/10.3758/s13414-015-1043-x

Moradi, F., Koch, C., & Shimojo, S. (2005). Face adaptation depends on seeing the face. *Neuron, 45*(1), 169–75. https://doi.org/10.1016/j.neuron.2004.12.018

Mudrik, L., & Koch, C. (2013). Differential processing of invisible congruent and incongruent scenes: A case for unconscious integration. *Journal of Vision, 13*(13), 24. https://doi.org/10.1167/13.13.24

Mudrik, L., Breska, A., Lamy, D., & Deouell, L. Y. (2011a). Integration without awareness: Expanding the limits of unconscious processing. *Psychological Science, 22*(6), 764–70. https://doi.org/10.1177/0956797611408736

Mudrik, L., Deouell, L. Y., & Lamy, D. (2011b). Scene congruency biases binocular rivalry. *Consciousness and Cognition, 20*(3), 756–67. https://doi.org/10.1016/j.concog.2011.01.001

Nakamura, K., & Kawabata, H. (2018). Preferential access to awareness of attractive faces in a breaking continuous flash suppression paradigm. *Consciousness and Cognition, 65*, 71–82. https://doi.org/10.1016/j.concog.2018.07.010

Nakashima, Y., & Sugita, Y. (2018). Size-contrast illusion induced by unconscious context. *Journal of Vision, 18*(3), 16–16. https://doi.org/10.1167/18.3.16

Oizumi, M., Albantakis, L., & Tononi, G. (2014). From the phenomenology to the mechanisms of consciousness: Integrated information theory 3.0. *PLoS Computational Biology, 10*(5), e1003588. https://doi.org/10.1371/journal.pcbi.1003588

O'Regan, J. K., & Noë, A. (2001). A sensorimotor account of vision and visual consciousness. *Behavioral and Brain Sciences, 24*(5), 939–73.

Owen, A. M., Coleman, M. R., Boly, M., Davis, M. H., Laureys, S., & Pickard, J. D. (2006). Detecting awareness in the vegetative state. *Science, 313*(5792), 1402. https://doi.org/10.1126/science.1130197

Palmer, S. E. (1999). *Vision Science: Photons to Phenomenology* (1st ed.). Cambridge, MA: MIT Press.

Palmer, T. D., & Ramsey, A. K. (2012). The function of consciousness in multisensory integration. *Cognition, 125*(3), 353–64. https://doi.org/10.1016/j.cognition.2012.08.003

Pan, Y., Lin, B., Zhao, Y., & Soto, D. (2013). Working memory biasing of visual perception without awareness. *Attention, Perception and Psychophysics.* https://doi.org/10.3758/s13414-013-0566-2

Pinto, Y., van Gaal, S., de Lange, F. P., Lamme, V. A. F., & Seth, A. K. (2015). Expectations accelerate entry of visual stimuli into awareness. *Journal of Vision, 15*(8), 13. https://doi.org/10.1167/15.8.13

Plass, J., Guzman-Martinez, E., Ortega, L., Grabowecky, M., & Suzuki, S. (2014). Lip reading without awareness. *Psychological Science.* https://doi.org/10.1177/0956797614542132

Rabagliati, H., Robertson, A., & Carmel, D. (2018). The importance of awareness for understanding language. *Journal of Experimental Psychology: General, 147*(2), 190–208. https://doi.org/10.1037/xge0000348

Rabovsky, M., Stein, T., & Abdel Rahman, R. (2016). Access to awareness for faces during continuous flash suppression is not modulated by affective knowledge. *PLoS One.*

Raio, C. M., Carmel, D., Carrasco, M., & Phelps, E. A. (2012). Nonconscious fear is quickly acquired but swiftly forgotten. *Current Biology, 22*(12), R477–9. https://doi.org/10.1016/j.cub.2012.04.023

Ramsøy, T. Z., & Overgaard, M. (2004). Introspection and subliminal perception. *Phenomenology and the Cognitive Sciences, 3*(1), 1–23. https://doi.org/10.1023/B:PHEN.0000041900.30172.e8

Rosenthal, R. (1979). The file drawer problem and tolerance for null results. *Psychological Bulletin, 86*(3), 638–41. https://doi.org/10.1037/0033-2909.86.3.638

Rothkirch, M., & Hesselmann, G. (2018). No evidence for dorsal-stream-based priming under continuous flash suppression. *Consciousness and Cognition.* https://doi.org/10.1016/j.concog.2018.05.011

Rothkirch, M., Madipakkam, A., Rehn, E., & Sterzer, P. (2015). Making eye contact without awareness. *Cognition, 143*, 108–14. https://doi.org/10.1016/j.cognition.2015.06.012

Sakuraba, S., Sakai, S., Yamanaka, M., Yokosawa, K., & Hirayama, K. (2012). Does the human dorsal stream really process a category for tools? *Journal of Neuroscience, 32*(11), 3949–53. https://doi.org/10.1523/JNEUROSCI.3973-11.2012

Sand, A., & Nilsson, M. E. (2016). Subliminal or not? Comparing null-hypothesis and Bayesian methods for testing subliminal priming. *Consciousness and Cognition, 44*, 29–40. https://doi.org/10.1016/j.concog.2016.06.012

Schmidt, T. (2015). Invisible stimuli, implicit thresholds: Why invisibility judgments cannot be interpreted in isolation. *Advances in Cognitive Psychology, 11*(2), 31–41. https://doi.org/10.5709/acp-0169-3

Schwarzkopf, D. S., Song, C., & Rees, G. (2011). The surface area of human V1 predicts the subjective experience of object size. *Nature Neuroscience, 14*(1), 28–30. https://doi.org/10.1038/nn.2706

Seitz, A. R., Kim, D., & Watanabe, T. (2009). Rewards evoke learning of unconsciously processed visual stimuli in adult humans. *Neuron, 61*(5), 700–7. https://doi.org/10.1016/j.neuron.2009.01.016

Siegel, E. H., Wormwood, J. B., Quigley, K. S., & Barrett, L. F. (2018). Seeing what you feel: Affect drives visual perception of structurally neutral faces. *Psychological Science, 29*(4), 496–503. https://doi.org/10.1177/0956797617741718

Simoncelli, E. P., & Olshausen, B. A. (2001). Natural image statistics and neural representation. *Annual Review of Neuroscience, 24*, 1193–1216. https://doi.org/10.1146/annurev.neuro.24.1.1193

Sklar, A. Y., Levy, N., Goldstein, A., Mandel, R., Maril, A., & Hassin, R. R. (2012). Reading and doing arithmetic nonconsciously. *Proceedings of the National Academy of Sciences*, *109*(48), 19614–19. https://doi.org/10.1073/pnas.1211645109

Song, C., Schwarzkopf, D. S., & Rees, G. (2011). Interocular induction of illusory size perception. *BMC Neuroscience*, *12*(1), 27. https://doi.org/10.1186/1471-2202-12-27

Soto, D., & Silvanto, J. (2014). Reappraising the relationship between working memory and conscious awareness. *Trends in Cognitive Sciences*, *18*(10), 520–5. https://doi.org/10.1016/j.tics.2014.06.005

Soto, D., Mäntylä, T., & Silvanto, J. (2011). Working memory without consciousness. *Current Biology*, *21*(22), R912–13. https://doi.org/10.1016/j.cub.2011.09.049

Stein, T., & Peelen, M. V. (2015). Content-specific expectations enhance stimulus detectability by increasing perceptual sensitivity. *Journal of Experimental Psychology: General*. https://doi.org/10.1037/xge0000109

Stein, T., & Sterzer, P. (2011). High-level face shape adaptation depends on visual awareness: Evidence from continuous flash suppression. *Journal of Vision*, *11*(8), 1–14. https://doi.org/10.1167/11.8.5

Stein, T., & Sterzer, P. (2012). Not just another face in the crowd: Detecting emotional schematic faces during continuous flash suppression. *Emotion*, *12*(5), 988–996.

Stein, T., & Sterzer, P. (2014). Unconscious processing under interocular suppression: Getting the right measure. *Frontiers in Psychology*, *5*:387. https://doi.org/doi: 10.3389/fpsyg.2014.00387

Stein, T., Awad, D., Gayet, S., & Peelen, M. V. (2018). Unconscious processing of facial dominance: The role of low-level factors in access to awareness. *Journal of Experimental Psychology: General*.

Stein, T., Grubb, C., Bertrand, M., Suh, S. M., & Verosky, S. C. (2017). No impact of affective person knowledge on visual awareness: Evidence from binocular rivalry and continuous flash suppression. *Emotion*, *17*(8), 1199–1207. https://doi.org/10.1037/emo0000305

Stein, T., Hebart, M. N., & Sterzer, P. (2011a). Breaking continuous flash suppression: A new measure of unconscious processing during interocular suppression? *Frontiers in Human Neuroscience*, *5*, 167. https://doi.org/10.3389/fnhum.2011.00167

Stein, T., Kaiser, D., & Hesselmann, G. (2016a). Can working memory be non-conscious? *Neuroscience of Consciousness*, *2016*(1), niv011. https://doi.org/10.1093/nc/niv011

Stein, T., Peelen, M. V., & Sterzer, P. (2012). Eye gaze adaptation under interocular suppression. *Journal of Vision*, *12*(7), 1. https://doi.org/10.1167/12.7.1

Stein, T., Reeder, R. R., & Peelen, M. V. (2015). Privileged access to awareness for faces and objects of expertise. *Journal of Experimental Psychology: Human Perception and Performance*. https://doi.org/10.1037/xhp0000188

Stein, T., Senju, A., Peelen, M. V., & Sterzer, P. (2011b). Eye contact facilitates awareness of faces during interocular suppression. *Cognition*, *119*(2), 307–11. https://doi.org/10.1016/j.cognition.2011.01.008

Stein, T., Siebold, A., & van Zoest, W. (2016b). Testing the idea of privileged awareness of self-relevant information. *Journal of Experimental Psychology: Human Perception and Performance*. https://doi.org/10.1037/xhp0000197

Sterzer, P., Haynes, J.-D., & Rees, G. (2008). Fine-scale activity patterns in high-level visual areas encode the category of invisible objects. *Journal of Vision*, *8*(15), 1–12. https://doi.org/10.1167/8.15.10

Sterzer, P., Stein, T., Ludwig, K., Rothkirch, M., & Hesselmann, G. (2014). Neural processing of visual information under interocular suppression: A critical review. *Frontiers in Psychology*, *5*, 453. https://doi.org/10.3389/fpsyg.2014.00453

Stewart, L. H., Ajina, S., Getov, S., Bahrami, B., Todorov, A., & Rees, G. (2012). Unconscious evaluation of faces on social dimensions. *Journal of Experimental Psychology: General, 141*(4), 715–27. https://doi.org/10.1037/a0027950

Sweeny, T. D., Grabowecky, M., & Suzuki, S. (2011). Awareness becomes necessary between adaptive pattern coding of open and closed curvatures. *Psychological Science, 22*(7), 943–50. https://doi.org/10.1177/0956797611413292

Tan, J.-S., & Yeh, S.-L. (2015). Audiovisual integration facilitates unconscious visual scene processing. *Journal of Experimental Psychology: Human Perception and Performance.* https://doi.org/10.1037/xhp0000074

Tong, F., Meng, M., & Blake, R. (2006). Neural bases of binocular rivalry. *Trends in Cognitive Sciences, 10*(11), 502–11. https://doi.org/10.1016/j.tics.2006.09.003

Tsuchiya, N., & Koch, C. (2005). Continuous flash suppression reduces negative afterimages. *Nature Neuroscience, 8*(8), 1096–1101. https://doi.org/10.1038/nn1500

Tsuchiya, N., Block, N., & Koch, C. (2012). Top-down attention and consciousness: comment on Cohen et al. *Trends in Cognitive Sciences, 16*(11), 527. https://doi.org/10.1016/j.tics.2012.09.004

Tsuchiya, N., Koch, C., Gilroy, L. A., & Blake, R. (2006). Depth of interocular suppression associated with continuous flash suppression, flash suppression, and binocular rivalry. *Journal of Vision, 6*(10), 1068–78. https://doi.org/10.1167/6.10.6

Tsuchiya, N., Moradi, F., Felsen, C., Yamazaki, M., & Adolphs, R. (2009). Intact rapid detection of fearful faces in the absence of the amygdala. *Nature Neuroscience, 12*(10), 1224–5. https://doi.org/10.1038/nn.2380

van Ee, R. (2011). Percept-switch nucleation in binocular rivalry reveals local adaptation characteristics of early visual processing. *Journal of Vision, 11*(2). https://doi.org/10.1167/11.2.13

Vermeiren, A., & Cleeremans, A. (2012). The validity of d′ measures. *PLoS One, 7*(2), e31595. https://doi.org/10.1371/journal.pone.0031595

Wagemans, J., Elder, J. H., Kubovy, M., Palmer, S. E., Peterson, M. A., Singh, M., & von der Heydt, R. (2012). A century of Gestalt psychology in visual perception: I. Perceptual grouping and figure-ground organization. *Psychological Bulletin, 138*(6), 1172–1217. https://doi.org/10.1037/a0029333

Wertheimer, M. (1923). Untersuchungen zur Lehre von der Gestalt. II. *Psychologische Forschung, 4*(1), 301–50. https://doi.org/10.1007/BF00410640

Wolfe, J. M. (1984). Reversing ocular dominance and suppression in a single flash. *Vision Research, 24*(5), 471–8.

Wu, Q., Lo Voi, J. T. H., Lee, T. Y., Mackie, M.-A., Wu, Y., & Fan, J. (2015). Interocular suppression prevents interference in a flanker task. *Frontiers in Psychology,* 1110. https://doi.org/10.3389/fpsyg.2015.01110

Yang, E., & Blake, R. (2012). Deconstructing continuous flash suppression. *Journal of Vision, 12*(3), 1–14. https://doi.org/10.1167/12.3.8

Yang, E., Hong, S.-W., & Blake, R. (2010). Adaptation aftereffects to facial expressions suppressed from visual awareness. *Journal of Vision, 10*(12), 1–13. https://doi.org/10.1167/10.12.24

Yang, E., Zald, D. H., & Blake, R. (2007). Fearful expressions gain preferential access to awareness during continuous flash suppression. *Emotion, 7*(4), 882–6. https://doi.org/10.1037/1528-3542.7.4.882

Yang, Y.-H., & Yeh, S.-L. (2011). Accessing the meaning of invisible words. *Consciousness and Cognition, 20*(2), 223–33. https://doi.org/10.1016/j.concog.2010.07.005

Yang, Y.-H., Tien, Y.-H., Yang, P.-L., & Yeh, S.-L. (2017). Role of consciousness in temporal integration of semantic information. *Cognitive, Affective, and Behavioral Neuroscience, 17*(5), 954–72. https://doi.org/10.3758/s13415-017-0525-9

Yang, Y.-H., Zhou, J., Li, K.-A., Hung, T., Pegna, A. J., & Yeh, S.-L. (2017). Opposite ERP effects for conscious and unconscious semantic processing under continuous flash suppression. *Consciousness and Cognition*, *54*, 114–28. https://doi.org/10.1016/j.concog.2017.05.008

Yuval-Greenberg, S., & Heeger, D. J. (2013). Continuous flash suppression modulates cortical activity in early visual cortex. *Journal of Neuroscience*, *33*(23), 9635–43. https://doi.org/10.1523/JNEUROSCI.4612-12.2013

Zabelina, D. L., Guzman-Martinez, E., Ortega, L., Grabowecky, M., Suzuki, S., & Beeman, M. (2013). Suppressed semantic information accelerates analytic problem solving. *Psychonomic Bulletin and Review*. https://doi.org/10.3758/s13423-012-0364-1

Zadbood, A., Lee, S.-H., & Blake, R. (2011). Stimulus fractionation by interocular suppression. *Frontiers in Human Neuroscience*, *5*(135). https://doi.org/10.3389/fnhum.2011.00135

Zimba, L. D., & Blake, R. (1983). Binocular rivalry and semantic processing: Out of sight, out of mind. *Journal of Experimental Psychology. Human Perception and Performance*, *9*(5), 807–15.

3

UNCONSCIOUS VISUAL PROCESSING

How a neuro-functional hierarchy can guide future research

Bruno Breitmeyer

DEPARTMENT OF PSYCHOLOGY, UNIVERSITY OF HOUSTON

Guido Hesselmann

DEPARTMENT OF GENERAL AND BIOLOGICAL PSYCHOLOGY, PSYCHOLOGISCHE
HOCHSCHULE BERLIN

1 Introduction

Numerous noninvasive – mainly psychophysical – methods are available to render visual stimuli invisible, i.e. inaccessible to conscious report. These psychophysical "blinding" methods, together with their strengths and weaknesses, have been comprehensively reviewed elsewhere (Axelrod, Bar, & Rees, 2015; Bachmann, Breitmeyer, & Öğmen 2007; Hesselmann, 2013; Kim & Blake, 2005). One of us (Breitmeyer, 2014, 2015) also presented evidence indicating that the various blinding methods can suppress conscious visual processing at different depths or levels of visual processing. The levels varied from very early ones, presumably occurring as early as striate cortex, or even earlier, to stages higher up in the visual cognition hierarchy, such as those associated with feature integration, object recognition, and selective attention.

Comparing what sorts of visual information could or could not be suppressed by the various blinding methods allows one to infer a psychophysically determined functional hierarchy of nonconscious visual processing. For instance, Kouider and Dehaene (2007) provided an extensive review of how comparison of the effects of several blinding methods can inform us on the levels at which unconscious visual processing of a word's orthographic, lexical, and semantic information can or cannot occur. Their conclusion was that while unconscious orthographic and lexical processing can occur at relatively low cortical levels, unconscious semantic processing becomes increasingly evident at higher ones. Specifically regarding metacontrast and binocular-rivalry suppressions, Breitmeyer, Koç, Öğmen, and Ziegler (2008) demonstrated that the metacontrast masking mechanism occurs functionally at a later level of visual processing than that at which binocular-rivalry is resolved. Since (a) binocular-rivalry can suppress the activity giving rise to metacontrast suppression and since (b) metacontrast itself renders a target stimulus invisible, it follows that the processes giving rise to binocular rivalry functionally reside at unconscious levels lower than those giving rise to metacontrast suppression of visibility. In the following years a host of other studies, using various other blinding methods, have obtained findings which allow a more extensive elaboration of the functional hierarchy of unconscious visual processing (see Breitmeyer, 2015). Other than tying some of these functional levels to what are currently thought to be some of the correlated cortical and subcortical structures, any attempt to tightly relate all functional levels to correspondingly distinct anatomical levels or structures was deemed premature. Moreover, since the empirical basis underlying these levels consists of a large yet, at times, equivocal set of findings, the functional hierarchy of unconscious processing is taken to be tentative and therefore modifiable pending new findings or a resolution of past contradictory ones. For that reason, one can and should view the hierarchy more as a provisional basis for an extensive research program than as a settled conceptual structure.

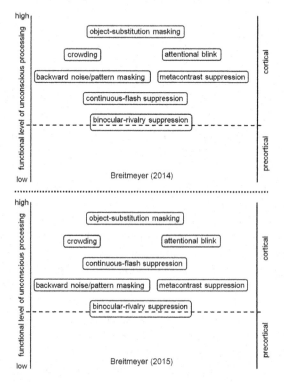

FIGURE 3.1 Tentative neurofunctional hierarchies of several blinding methods proposed, on the top, by Breitmeyer (2014) and, on the bottom, by Breitmeyer (2015). Note that on the top CFS is placed at a level just above binocular-rivalry suppression; whereas on the bottom it is placed higher, at a level just above noise/pattern masking and metacontrast suppression.

To illustrate, Breitmeyer (2014) highlighted the tentative nature of the hierarchy in chapter 5 of his book, *The Visual (Un)conscious and its (Dis)contents*, placing the resolution of binocular-rivalry suppression at a level straddling subcortical, lateral geniculate nucleus (LGN) processing (Haynes, Deichmann, & Rees, 2005; Wunderlich, Schneider, & Kastner, 2005) and early, most probably striate (V1), cortical processing (Lee & Blake, 2004; Tong & Engel, 2001; Tong, Meng, & Blake, 2006). While placing the processes underlying other blinding methods at the cortical level, the cortical sites in which these methods express their suppressive effects were not specified anatomically, although on the basis of extant data some of the sites are more precisely specifiable (see below). One of us (Hesselmann, Darcy, Ludwig, & Sterzer, 2016) then raised the issue, as shown in Figure 3.1, as to why the functional level at which continuous flash suppression (CFS) expresses itself was elevated in the hierarchy depicted in Breitmeyer (2015) relative to the level depicted in Breitmeyer (2014). The provisional – and therefore revisable – nature of the hierarchy noted in Breitmeyer (2014) and reiterated in Breitmeyer (2015) is the reason. In other words, due to findings that were published between the writing of the two publications, revisions regarding the level(s) of processing at which CFS expresses its suppressive effects were appropriately made. As we shall see below, even this revised version of the relative locus of CFS in the functional hierarchy is debatable and subject to even further revision. The same holds for the other higher-level blinding methods covered by Breitmeyer's (2015) review. So as to not revisit all the material in his review, in the present chapter we will focus further analyses on the following blinding methods: CFS, object-substitution masking (OSM), visual crowding, and various attentional blindnesses. Other methods will be discussed when and where they impact relevantly on these selected methods or vice versa.

2 Preliminary thoughts regarding cortical levels of unconscious visual processing

Before proceeding, since structure supports function, some brief comments on the ways a psychophysically determined functional hierarchy relates to cortical anatomy are warranted. This requires consideration of how cortical activity is thought to support unconscious and conscious visual processing. Current approaches such as the global work space model (Baars, 2005; Baars, Franklin, & Ramsoy, 2013; Dehaene & Naccache, 2001; Dehaene, Sergent & Changeux, 2003; Dehaene, Changeux, Naccache, Sackur, & Sergent, 2006) or information integration theory (Tononi, 2004, 2008; Tononi & Koch, 2008) emphasize the complex interactive nature of cortical processing associated with conscious visual processing (see also Edelman, Gally, & Baars, 2011, and Lamme, 2010). Extensive interactions enabled by parallel feedforward and feedback connectivities between lower and higher cortical levels as well as horizontal connectivities between same-level sites are thought to bind the various localized cortical activities that support a unified visual consciousness. Breakdown or weakening of these connectivities, especially those between higher and lower levels of cortical processing, can be produced by psychophysical blinding methods (Godwin, Barry, & Marois, 2015), varying states of sleep (Horovitz, Braun, Carr, Piccioni, Balkin, Fukunaga, & Duyn, 2009) and coma (King, Sitt, Faugeras, Rohaut, El Karoui, Cohen, Naccache, & Dehaene, 2013), as well as drug induced loss of consciousness (Schröter, Spoormaker, Schorer, Wohlschläger, Czisch, Kochs, Claus Zimmer, Hemmer, Schneider, Jordan, & Ilg, 2012). As a consequence, as suggested by the results of Godwin et al. (2015) as well as Dehaene et al.'s (2006) global work space scheme (represented in their figure 2), in visual cortex the effects of psychophysical blinding methods may be differentiable on the basis of localized networks or sites that, while active also in conscious vision, remain active during unconscious vision. We defer discussing this possibility of relating a functional to a cortical hierarchy of unconscious processing until later.

3 Problems regarding localizing the effects of CFS, OSM, crowding, and attentional blindnesses in the functional hierarchy of unconscious visual processing

The core of the functional hierarchy is defined by various types of interocular suppression, various types of visual masking, crowding, OSM, and various types of attentional blindnesses. Even since Breitmeyer's (2015) recent survey of psychophysical blinding methods and the relative position of their expression in the unconscious processing hierarchy, several rereadings of relevant findings indicate that the current state of the hierarchy must be reconsidered, elaborated, and modified. Below we discuss blinding methods and their respective locations in the unconscious processing hierarchy that most need updating.

3.1 Mixed findings obtained with the CFS blinding method

No doubt, since its initial use by Tsuchiya and Koch (2005), CFS has become one of the most frequently used psychophysical blinding methods in recent years. In CFS a random sequence of achromatic or colored Mondrian patterns composed of fragments such as squares or rectangles is presented to one eye at a rate of about 10 frames/s while a prime stimulus is presented, usually with ramped onset and offset, to the other eye. Although CFS is an effective way to render prime stimuli invisible, CFS studies of unconscious priming have yielded mixed results, leading to conclusions and interpretations that are at best questionable (Hesselmann & Knops, 2014; Hesselmann, Darcy, Sterzer & Knops, 2015; Yang, Brascamp, Kang & Blake, 2014). As noted by Yang and Blake (2012), in designing CFS studies, it is important to consider spatiotemporal stimulus properties of the to-be suppressed stimulus as well as the CFS Mondrians. Since visual masking is one way to study the spatiotemporal interactions and properties of visual processing (Öğmen & Breitmeyer, 2006), it also merits, along the lines of Yang et al. (2014), to consider more carefully what sorts of masking mechanisms might contribute to CFS's effectiveness as blinding method. In their study of various blinding techniques, including CSF, Tsuchiya, Koch, Gilroy, & Blake (2006) noted that the first few frames of the Mondrians do not produce strong suppressive effects; the strength of suppression in their study increased to its maximum when five (or more) Mondrian frames were presented.

As noted by Yang et al. (2014), this might offer a reasonable explanation for why suppression may be shallow at shorter presentation durations of the CFS display, a methodological implementation that was adopted in several studies showing unconscious categorical or semantic priming (Almeida, Mahon, Nakayama, & Caramazza, 2008; Almeida, Pajtas, Mahon, Nakayama, & Caramazza, 2013; Eo, Cha, Chong, & Kang, 2016; Sakuraba, Sakai, Yamanaka, Yokosawa, & Hirayama, 2012). One interpretation is that standard visual pattern masking dominates in the initial phase of the Mondrian sequence, followed by a gradual buildup of whatever suppressive processes are responsible for CFS itself. Since semantic priming of responses to a visible target words can be found even though the visibility of the prior prime word is suppressed by pattern masking such as metacontrast and sandwich masking (Kiefer, 2002; Mattler & Wernicke, 2014), it might no longer be surprising that some categorical priming can be found when the prime is suppressed by CFS. However, more recent work did not find evidence for unconscious priming of object categorization by action-relevant features (Hesselmann, Darcy, Rothkirch & Sterzer, 2018; Rothkirch & Hesselmann, 2018), as predicted by the "category priming by stimulus elongation" hypothesis (Almedia, Mahon, Zapater-Raberov, Dziuba, Cabaco, Marques, & Caramazza, 2014). As noted by Tsuchiya et al. (2006), CFS is similar to the standing-wave-of-invisibility (Macknik & Livingstone, 1998), in which a target and mask are sequentially alternated for prolonged durations. Although under these circumstances a mask can serve as both a forward and a backward mask, we think forward pattern masking per se plays no significant role in CFS, since in a single presentation of mask followed by a target, such masking generally is not effective under dichoptic viewing conditions (Breitmeyer, 1984).

We therefore believe that it is the *rate of stimulation at roughly 10 Hz* of the Mondrians that may provide the key to unlocking the effective CFS mechanism. In a study of paracontrast (forward) masking, Breitmeyer, Ziegler, and Hauske (2007) found evidence for two forward masking effects: one was a short-latency and short-lived (~50 ms) suppression, explainable by the spatiotemporal properties of the antagonistic interactions between excitatory center and inhibitory surround surrounds of receptive fields (Breitmeyer, 1984; Öğmen & Breitmeyer, 2006). The other was an inhibitory effect initiated at a longer latency and lasting for long durations of 400 ms or more. We believe that this latter suppressive effect may have its counterpart in the inhibition produced by a single visual stimulus presentation that can last upwards of one second, found in areas 17 and 18 neurons of striate cortex (Berman, Douglas, Martin, & Whitteridge, 1991; Nelson, 1991). As found by Nelson (1991), of interest here is that when the visual stimulus was repeated at rates varying from 1 to 10 Hz, the degree of suppression increased as the repetition rate increased. In fact, at a presentation rate of 10 Hz, also used in most CFS studies, the responsiveness of the cell is all but obliterated after the first few hundred milliseconds of stimulation. Striate neurons are known to be driven binocularly (Cumming & Parker, 1999; Hubel & Wiesel, 1968; Smith, Chino, Ni, & Cheng, 1997), making up a majority of nearly 70 percent of V1 neurons (Crawford, Smith, Harwerth, & von Noorden, 1984). All of this comports well with Tsuchiya et al.'s (2006) finding that the effectiveness of the CFS suppressor increases to its maximum over the initial 400–500 ms of the Mondrians. Reasonably assuming that the results found in cat and monkey visual cortex generalize to human visual cortex, we propose that the CFS sequence presented to one eye, at least after a half to one second of stimulation, produces a profound inhibition of binocularly driven neurons in early visual cortex, specifically V1, that in turns leads to a suppression of visibility of the stimuli presented to the other eye.

The neurofunctional scheme illustrated above in the bottom panel of Figure 3.1 was based on the above cited studies, whose findings showed that semantic and categorical priming survives CFS suppression of the primes. Our analysis of these findings shows that these findings may have been produced by suboptimal effectiveness of the CFS procedure implemented in these studies. For these reasons, we believe (1) that prior studies putatively demonstrating that stimuli whose visibility is suppressed by CFS can produce categorical or semantic priming be viewed skeptically and interpreted with caution and (2) that reversion to the neurofunctional hierarchical scheme originally proposed by Breitmeyer (2014), in which CFS occurs at a low cortical level (see Figure 3.1, upper panel), is currently preferable. Moreover, at least some of the studies on high-level priming under CFS were inspired by the notion that CFS selectively disrupts stimulus identification mediated by the ventral "vision-for-perception" pathway, while preserving stimulus features processed by the dorsal "vision-for-action" pathway (Lin & He, 2009). This notion was mainly based on early functional magnetic resonance imaging (fMRI) work showing that neural activity along the dorsal visual pathway remains largely intact when images of manipulable objects (tools) are rendered invisible by CFS (Fang & He, 2005). The notion that CFS could be used to "isolate" or "bias" dorsal visual processing also seemed to resonate well with the characteristics of the perception-action model (Milner, 2012; Milner & Goodale, 2006), and it has contributed to the method's success by inspiring different lines of behavioral and neuroimaging research (Ludwig & Hesselmann, 2015). However, more recent neuroimaging studies did not confirm this dorsal-ventral dissociation (Hesselmann & Malach, 2011; Fogelson, Kohler, Miller, Granger, & Tse, 2014; Ludwig, Kathmann, Sterzer, & Hesselmann, 2015). One fMRI study parametrically manipulated stimulus visibility, but did not find evidence for a "sweet spot" under CFS, i.e. a level of stimulus visibility that would allow decoding of stimulus-related information in the dorsal stream, while completely suppressing information processing in the ventral stream (Ludwig et al., 2015). Instead, both visual streams were closely linked to visual awareness, such that fully CF-suppressed stimuli were associated with a stream-invariant reduction of neural activity. When recent non-replications and critical reanalyses of published data are also taken into account, one

Unconscious visual processing **77**

plausible scenario emerges in which the representation of CF-suppressed stimuli is fractionated rather than integrated, and restricted to basic features of the visual input (Moors, Hesselmann, Wagemans, & van Ee, 2017).

To highlight our skepticism, below we will present evidence strongly indicating that CFS acts at the striate level of processing.

3.2 Mixed findings obtained with the OSM blinding method

Suppression of unconscious semantic and categorical priming have been found with low-level binocular-rivalry suppression (Blake, 1998; Zimba & Blake, 1983) and have been reported with high-level OSM (Chen & Treisman, 2009; Reiss & Hoffman, 2006). Yet the effects of suppression produced by metacontrast (Mattler & Wernicke, 2014), backward pattern masking (Stenberg, Lindgren, Johansson, Olsson, & Rosen, 2000), crowding (Yeh, He, & Cavanagh, 2012), and the attentional blink (Luck, Vogel, & Shapiro, 1996; Rolke, Heil, Streb, & Hennighausen, 2001; Shapiro, Driver, Ward, & Sorenson, 1997), all of which fall functionally between the low-level effects of binocular-rivalry suppression and the high-level effects of OSM suppression, leave unconscious semantic processing intact. Paradoxically, (i) if these four methods exert their suppressive effects prior to those exerted by OSM and (ii) if as Reiss and Hoffman's (2006) and Chen and Treisman's (2009) results imply, object-substitution masking disrupts or blocks unconscious semantic/categorical processing, then should the former three methods not also disrupt or block such processing? The fact that they do not produce such disruption suggests that either there is something unique about the processes underlying OSM, e.g. they lie outside the functional hierarchy of the processes activated by the above four methods, or the evidence for semantic priming under the OSM regime needs to be reconsidered. Indeed, Goodhew, Visser, Lipp, and Dux (2011) recently did report evidence for such priming.[1] This confirms the maxim that failure to obtain a given effect does not establish the absence of the effect. Since the Goodhew et al. (2011) results are more consistent with the other known properties of the unconscious processing hierarchy, we now grant greater credibility to them than to the results of Reiss and Hoffman (2006) and Chen and Treisman (2009).

3.3 Mixed findings obtained with the crowding blinding method

Visual crowding is the reduction of the visibility of a target stimulus when it is flanked by nearby distractor stimuli. Levi's (2008) review of crowding indicates that both low- and high-level cortical processes contribute to crowding. Recently Breitmeyer, Tripathy, and Brown (2018) presented evidence that the low-level contribution most likely derives from lateral masking thought to occur as early as striate cortex (Polat, 1999; Polat & Sagi, 2006), whereas the high-level contribution derives from feature integrative levels occurring at post-striate sites (Chakravarthi & Cavanagh, 2009; Levi, 2008; Pelli & Tillman, 2008; Tripathy & Cavanagh, 2002), suggested ones being area V2, V3, and V4 (Anderson, Dakin, Schwarzkopf, Rees, & Greenwood, 2012; Bi, Cai, Zhou, & Fang, 2009; Liu, Jiang, Sun, & He, 2009; Motter & Simoni, 2007; Tyler & Likova, 2007). The V2–V4 locations are apt for the following reasons. (1) The findings reported by Chakravarthi and Cavanagh's (2009) indicate that crowding occurs below the level of OSM masking. (2) Carlson, Rauschenberger, and Verstraten's (2007) fMRI study obtained evidence indicating that OSM reduces activity in human lateral occipital cortex (LOC), located after the early visual areas, V2–V4, in the ventral object recognition pathway (Konen & Kastner, 2008). The relative anatomical levels of V2–V4 and LOC therefore comports well with the relative functional levels of crowding and OSM indicated by Chakravarthi and Cavanagh's (2009) findings.

Chakravarthi and Cavanagh (2009) also noted that (at least the high-level contribution to) crowding is due to what they termed "excessive integration" of target and flanker features. We would argue that such excessive integration is due to coarse spatial resolution of the attentional window (He, Cavanagh, & Intriligator, 1996; Intriligator & Cavanagh, 2001). Since feature binding is closely tied to spatial attention (Briand & Klein, 1987; Friedman-Hill, Robertson, & Treisman, 1995; Treisman, 1998), one would expect crowding to result from faulty feature binding when flankers – and of course their features – fall within the attentional window devoted to the target. Since the size of the window of attention increases with retinal eccentricity (Sagi & Julesz, 1986), one finds, as expected, that the spatial extent of crowding increases with eccentricity (Levi, Hariharan & Klein, 2002; Tripathy & Cavanagh, 2002).

In terms of Block's (2011) distinction between a phenomenal and access consciousness, the viewer has phenomenal awareness of the target but cannot attain or access a higher cognitive, categorical level of awareness other than that of "some vague and unidentifiable entity". The result is that in crowding a low-level phenomenal consciousness can register *that* something is present in the visual field but high-level consciousness cannot clearly access *what* that something is. Moreover, if we inspect Figure 3.2, we note that, although we may not be able to clearly identify either of the targets, our ability to perceptually discriminate them from each other may still be intact. So, some discriminable feature or shape information in phenomenal consciousness must also have attained the level of access consciousness, allowing us to report the differences in appearance of the two targets. The upshot is that, strictly speaking, with crowding we are actually dealing with levels of conscious rather than levels of unconscious processing.

Z C K   +   Z H K

FIGURE 3.2 Examples of two extrafoveal target letters, one to the left, the other to the right of fixation, each crowded by four spatially adjacent letters. When fixating the cross, both targets may not be perceptually identifiable; yet they may still be perceptually discriminable from each other.

3.4 A short note on inattentional blinding methods

Similarly relying on Block's (2011) distinction, phenomenal and access consciousness may also apply to the varieties of attentional blindness, including load-induced blindness (Macdonald & Lavie, 2008), distractor-induced blindness (Michael, Hesselmann, Kiefer, & Niedeggen, 2011), inattentional blindness (Mack & Rock, 1998), change blindness (Simons & Rensink, 2005), surprise-induced blindness (Asplund, Todd, Snyder, Gilbert, & Marois, 2010), and the attentional blink (Niedeggen, Hesselmann, Sahraie, Milders, & Blakemore, 2004; Raymond, Shapiro, & Arnell, 1992). It is possible that in all of these blinding methods something was present in phenomenal consciousness but was not able to attain the higher level of access consciousness. For instance, it is generally believed that the attentional blink prevents information about a target — which may be available, if ever so briefly, to phenomenal consciousness — to be encoded into visual working memory, thus in turn preventing its entry into access consciousness necessary for report. Similarly, in demonstrations of Daniel Simons's "invisible gorilla" video (Simons & Chabris, 1999), usually 50 percent of the viewers report not seeing the gorilla, while the remaining viewers report seeing it. In the famous video, a gorilla enters a larger scene in which several actors toss a ball among themselves, while viewers are asked to count the number of tosses. Presumably the viewers are therefore allocating most, if not all, of their attentional resources to the tossing actions and not to other aspects in the larger scene, including the intrusion of the gorilla. Important to note here is that, while it is nearly certain that if a stimulus does not register in the low-level phenomenal consciousness it also will not register in the high-level access consciousness, we cannot legitimately conclude that if a stimulus does not register in access consciousness, thus allowing for conscious report, it also will not have registered in phenomenal consciousness. We can only conclude that if it registered in access consciousness, it must have registered also in phenomenal consciousness. That said, did the gorilla, unlike a crowded target, not register as some vague unidentified thing in the phenomenal consciousness of the viewers in the 50 percent of viewers who were inattentionally "blind"? Remotely possible, but highly improbable. For if their phenomenal visual field did not contain a trace of something vaguely corresponding to the high-contrast retinal stimulation provided by the gorilla and by the other aspects of the larger scene that were not attended to, the functional anatomy of their visual system supporting phenomenal consciousness would be wondrously different from the viewers who did see and therefore can report seeing the gorilla. In other words, it is all but incredible to claim that the only things present in the phenomenal visual fields of viewers who reported not noticing the gorilla were the tossing actions of the actors in the film. On that basis we suggest that, as in the case of crowding, with inattentional blindnesses of this sort it is more likely that we are dealing with levels of conscious processing at the phenomenal and cognitive-assess level rather than with levels of unconscious processing.

4 The role of contrast response functions (CRFs) in assessing functional and cortical levels of unconscious visual processing

Breitmeyer et al. (2018) recently developed a rationale for using CRFs to explore the relative functional and cortical levels of unconscious and conscious visual processing. Their rationale was based on the fact that the response of neural ensembles in striate cortex tends to track physical contrast by increasing nearly linearly with stimulus contrast; while at later, extrastriate regions (e.g. see Figure 3.3) the response of neural ensembles increases in a nonlinear manner, with the response amplified at low Michelson contrasts, where it rises rapidly over the contrast range of 0 to 0.3 and thereafter gradually increases toward maximal (saturated) response (Hall, Holliday, Hillebrand, Furlong, Singh, & Barnes, 2005; Tootell, Hadjikhani, Vanduffel, Liu, Mendola, Sereno, & Dale, 1998). In line with prior suggestions (Avidan, Harel, Hendler, Ben-Bashat, Zohary, & Malach, 2002), this nonlinear amplification at higher, increasingly percept-related sites in extrastriate cortex (Leopold & Logothetis, 1996; Logothetis & Schall, 1989; Sheinberg & Logothetis, 1997) would aid the perception of stimuli, especially those with contrasts ≤ 0.30,

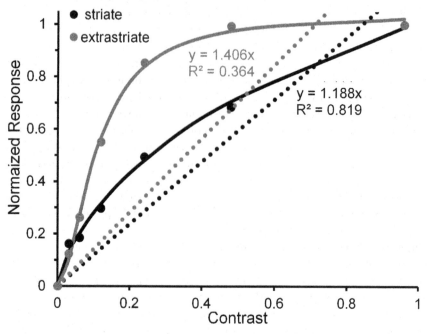

FIGURE 3.3 Normalized neural-ensemble responses in striate and extrastriate cortex. Note that best linear fit found for striate-cortex results accounts for 82% of systematic variability, while for extrastriate results it accounts for only 36% of systematic variability. Solid lines correspond to best fitting Naka-Rushton equations; dotted lines, to best fitting linear equations. Adapted from Breitmeyer et al. (2018), with permission.

Unconscious visual processing **81**

which constitute 70 percent of local contrasts (Chirimuuta & Tolhurst, 2005; Tadmor & Tolhurst, 2000).[2]

This approach to the study of functional levels of processing has already been successfully applied to the comparison of several visual illusions (Brown, Breitmeyer, Hale & Plummer, 2018). For instance, in comparing the simultaneous brightness illusion with the Poggendorff illusion, Brown et al. (2018) found that when the contrast of the illusion inducers was increased, the magnitude of the Poggendorff illusion increased much more steeply over low contrasts ranging from 0.0 to 0.32 than did the simultaneous brightness illusion. This result was expected, since according to theory, and in line with the results of Hall et al. (2005) depicted in Figure 3.3, the Poggendorff illusion is influenced strongly by higher-level, extrastriate percept-related processes (Spehar & Gillam, 2002; Zanuttini, 1976) but only slightly by effects of low-level lateral inhibition (Coren, 1970); whereas on theoretical grounds the simultaneous brightness illusion can be strongly influenced by low-level, even retinal, lateral inhibition (Spillmann, 1971).

While here applied to clearly visible illusory phenomena, the question remains as to whether Breitmeyer et al.'s (2018) CRF-dependent rationale can also be applied to levels of unconscious processing. Indeed it can. Breitmeyer et al. (2018) also presented evidence based on previously reported findings. (1) Pedestal masking increases linearly with the contrast of the pedestal mask not only when it is visible (Greenlee & Heitger, 1998; Watanabe, Paik, & Blake, 2004) but also when rendered invisible by binocular-rivalry suppression (Watanabe et al. 2004). This indicates that the mechanism of conscious and well an unconscious pedestal masking is primarily found in striate cortex. (2) Over an illusion-inducer contrast ranging from 0.0 to 0.5, Pearson and Clifford (2005) found that the strength of the simultaneous tilt illusion increased clearly nonlinearly, rising steeply and attaining maximal strength at an inducer contrast of only 0.1, when the inducer was visible, but linearly over the entire range when the inducer's visibility was suppressed during binocular-rivalry. This indicates that, when visible, the inducer exerted its effects at high, percept-related levels of functional and cortical processing. However, since binocular-rivalry is resolved at an early, most likely striate cortical level (Lee & Blake, 2004; Tong & Engel, 2001; Tong, Meng, & Blake, 2006), one would expect that when the inducer's visibility is suppressed by binocular-rivalry as in Pearson and Clifford's (2005) study, the strength of the illusion is determined by neural interactions at low cortical levels, where the CRF is nearly linear.

Above we proposed that extant evidence already indicates that CFS acts at the striate level of processing. The evidence derives from studies of afterimages. It was thought for some time that afterimages were produced by bleaching of retinal receptors (e.g. Craik, 1940; Sakitt, 1976), although other work was consistent with post-receptor, neural adaptation (Loomis, 1972; Virsu & Laurinen, 1977; Wilson, 1997). Tsuchiya and Koch (2005) demonstrated that the strength of an afterimage produced by an adapting stimulus is reduced when the visibility of the adapting stimulus, presented to one eye, is compromised by CFS stimulation presented to the other eye. The fact that the CFS and the adapting stimulus were presented to separate eyes implies that the generation of afterimages, though involving retinal levels of processing, must involve also cortical sites at which interocular CFS occurs. Following up on a study examining the opposing effects of consciousness and attention on afterimage strength (van Boxtel, Tsuchiya, & Koch, 2010), van Boxtel (2017) recently investigated how afterimage strength, measured by its duration, produced after a 4-s viewing of a Gabor patch was affected as its contrast varied from 0.03 to 1.00. The Gabor patch was presented to one eye, and in one condition a checkerboard pattern flickering in counterphase at 7.5 Hz and presented to the other eye rendered the Gabor patch invisible; whereas in the other condition, rendering the Gabor patch visible, no counterphasing checkerboard was presented to the other eye. In Figure 3.4 are shown the results when the carrier frequency of the Gabor patch was 0.23 c/deg.[3] What is striking about these results is that they bear a strong similarity to the results depicted in Figure 3.3. There the best linear fit to the striate results accounts for 82 percent of systematic variability,

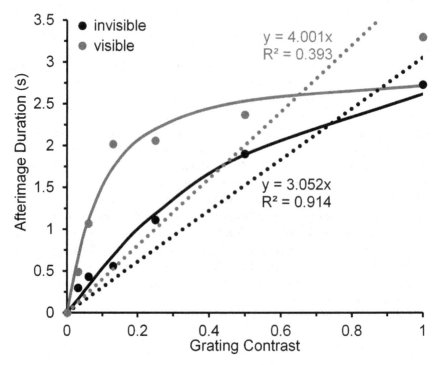

FIGURE 3.4 Duration, in seconds, of Gabor-patch afterimages as a function of adapting Gabor contrast when the Gabor was visible or rendered invisible by CFS. Note that in the invisible condition the results yield a best linear fit that accounts for 91% of systematic variability, while in the visible condition it accounts for only 39%. Solid lines correspond to best fitting Naka-Rushton equations; dotted lines, to best fitting linear equations. Adapted from van Boxtel (2017), with permission.

Unconscious visual processing **83**

whereas the best linear fit to the to the extrastriate results accounts for only 36 percent of systematic variability. In comparison, in the van Boxtel (2017) results depicted in Figure 3.4, the best linear fit to the results in the invisible Gabor patch condition accounts for 91 percent of systematic variability, whereas the best linear fit to the results in the visible Gabor patch condition accounts for only 39 percent of systematic variability. This similarity in the comparison confers confidence to two related claims. (1) In the visible condition, low-level as well as high-level cortical processes, where the CRF is strongly nonlinear, determined the duration of the after-image. (2) When the CFS rendered the Gabor patch invisible it did so at the level of striate cortex, where the CRF is nearly linear.

5 Some recommendations and suggestions for future research

Taken together, all the topics discussed above can provide guidance for future research. Up to now, studies of unconscious processing in which psychophysical blinding methods have been used have been consistent with those blinding methods expressing themselves in early, most likely striate levels of processing. However, one exception is the use of visual crowding as a blinding method. As noted, with crowding one is actually examining (phenomenal and access) levels of conscious processing. Nonetheless, Breitmeyer et al. (2018) showed that even here one can make novel predictions for future research. By eliminating the visibility of the crowding flankers via use of binocular-rivalry suppression or CFS, one should no longer obtain a strong nonlinear CRF relating the magnitude of the crowding effect to the contrast of the flankers, as was found by Pelli et al. (2004). Instead, since the crowding effect is now no longer accessing high-level feature-integrative cortical processes but is restricted to the low, striate level of unconscious processing, the CRF ought to be linear.

In addition, one can apply the above rationale to higher, extrastriate levels of unconscious processing. As an example, supposing that we vary the contrast of backward pattern masks that, though rendering a prime word invisible, allow semantic information to pass and to facilitate the response to semantically related target words (Mattler & Wernicke, 2014), we expect the unconscious processing of the prime word to attain the semantic level. We additionally expect that this level would be higher than that of the unconscious processing in striate cortex. Thus, by varying the contrast of the prime word from 0.0 to 1.0, one would in turn expect, in line with activation of extrastriate visual cortex, that the generated CRF be clearly nonlinear. The rationale of course could apply to a number of other blinding methods such as sandwich masking (Kiefer, 2002) by varying the contrast of the sandwich mask, and OSM (Chakravarthi & Cavanagh, 2006, Goodhew et al., 2012) by varying the contrast of the (typically four) stimuli adjacent to the prime. Moreover, by comparing two such blinding methods, each of which yields a clearly nonlinear CRF, it might also be possible to establish a hierarchy of extrastriate unconscious processing, provided that the two methods yield significantly different nonlinear CRFs.

84 Breitmeyer and Hesselmann

Although psychophysical studies can determine *relative functional* levels of unconscious processing, brain recording and imaging studies are needed to clarify and pinpoint the *actual anatomical* levels of cortical processing associated with psychophysically determined functional levels. Indeed, extant findings which combine psychophysical and neuroimaging already indicate that the two types of studies can converge on the same conclusion regarding the neurofunctional level of unconscious processing. Above we noted that the psychophysically obtained linearity of the CRF relating the effectiveness of the pedestal mask as its contrast increases (Greenlee & Heitger, 1998; Watanabe et al., 2004) indicates that the mechanism of conscious as well as unconscious pedestal masking is localized in striate cortex. Using combined psychophysical and fMRI techniques, Zenger-Landoldt and Heeger (2003), varying the Michelson contrast of the pedestal-mask from 0.1 to 0.8, replicated the linearity of the CRF relating the effectiveness of the pedestal mask as its contrast increases when psychophysical measures were used. Moreover, the fMRI signal obtained from V1 also increased linearly with pedestal-mask contrast and correlated strongly ($r \approx 0.97$) with the psychophysically obtained measures. This convergence of findings using the two measures indicates that similar convergence will likely be found with other visual phenomena such as visual crowding, visual illusions, object recognition that rely on higher levels of cortical processing. Here, however, we would expect both measures to yield increasingly nonlinear CRFs as the implicated level of processing in the ventral (and dorsal) cortical hierarchy increases.

Although applying these pending experimental research strategies could increase our knowledge of the functional and cortical hierarchy of unconscious processing, we believe that it would also behoove us to apply extensive and rather Herculean meta-analytic researches to extant findings. Here one strategy is to perform a thorough meta-analysis of published results obtained with each of the blinding methods, by addressing, among other criterial issues, specifically what types of visual information processing (e.g. chromatic, achromatic, shape, lexical, semantic, etc.) are or else are not suppressed. This would allow one to determine the relative functional and cortical levels of unconscious processing yielded by each blinding method. Once this is accomplished, one could compare the results of the meta-analyses obtained with the different blinding methods to yield a picture, based on already available findings, of possible different levels of unconscious processing.

6 Summary and conclusions

The notion of a functional hierarchy of unconscious processing provides a fruitful program for future empirical and scholarly research. It already has been applied to establish a tentative hierarchy that is revisable as new findings emerge. Moreover, we have presented evidence that the functional hierarchy can also be related to what is known about the anatomical hierarchy of cortical visual processing. Consequently, it could also guide future brain-recording and brain-imaging studies to more clearly delineate the hierarchy of unconscious cortical processing. Combining experimental with meta-analytic research methods promises to yield a more refined and conclusive picture of a functional and cortical hierarchy of unconscious processing (and conscious processing, if one includes the blinding methods of crowding and of inattentional blindness).

Notes

1 In 2014, when the first author wrote his (Breitmeyer, 2015) article on blinding methods and their relation to a functional hierarchy of unconscious processing, he was not aware of the article published by Goodhew et al. (2012).
2 The Naka-Rushton equation is given by $R\left(C\right) = R_{max} \cdot C^{\alpha}/(C_{0.5}^{\alpha} + C^{\alpha})$; where R_{max} is the maximal response magnitude, C is the contrast, $C_{0.5}$ is the contrast at which half of R_{max} is obtained. R_{max}, $C_{0.5}$, and α are free parameters.
3 Van Boxtel (2017) used spatial frequencies, 0.23 and 3.0 c/deg, of the Gabor patch, and the observer's primary task was to provide a measure of the afterimage duration when devoting all attentional resources to that task or else when these resources are at least partially withdrawn from this task by introducing a secondary, distracting task. Moreover, when the 3.0 c/deg Gabor patch was used to produce after images, under the fully attended condition, a floor effect was obtained in that regardless of the contrast of the Gabor patch, very brief, if any, afterimages were obtained. For these reasons, we discuss results, shown in our Figure 3.3, only for the fully attended primary task, since in the other studies of blinding methods covered in our chapter, full attention was directed to whatever experimental task the observers were asked to accomplish.

References

Almeida, J., Mahon, B. Z., Nakayama, K., & Caramazza, A. (2008). Unconscious processing dissociates along categorical lines. *Proceedings of the National Academy of Sciences USA*, *105*, 15214–18.

Almeida, J., Mahon, B. Z., Zapater-Raberov, V., Dziuba, A., Cabaco, T., Marques, J. F., & Caramazza, A. (2014). Grasping with the eyes: The role of elongation in visual recognition of manipulable objects. *Cognitive and Affective Behavioral Neuroscience*, *14*, 319–35. doi:10.3758/s13415-013-0208-0

Almeida, J., Pajtas, P. E., Mahon, B. Z., Nakayama, K., & Caramazza, A. (2013). Affect of the unconscious: Visually suppressed angry faces modulate our decisions. *Cognitive, Affective and Behavioral Neuroscience*, *13*, 94–101.

Anderson, E. J., Dakin, S. C., Schwarzkopf, D. S., Rees, G., & Greenwood, J. A. (2012). The neural correlates of crowding-induced changes in appearance. *Current Biology*, *22*, 1199–1206.

Asplund, C. L., Todd, J. J., Snyder, A. P., Gilbert, C. M., & Marois, R. (2010). Surprise-induced blindness: A stimulus-driven attentional limit to conscious perception. *Journal of Experimental Psychology: Human Perception and Performance*, *36*, 1372–81.

Avidan, G., Harel, M., Hendler, T., Ben-Bashat, D., Zohary, E., & Malach, R. (2002). Contrast sensitivity in human visual areas and its relationship to object recognition. *Journal of Neurophysiology*, *87*, 3102–16.

Axelrod, V., Bar, M., & Rees, G. (2015). Exploring the unconscious using faces. *Trends in Cognitive Sciences*, *19*, 35–45. doi:10.1016/j.tics.2014.11.003

Baars, B. J. (2005). Global workspace theory of consciousness: Toward a cognitive neuroscience of human experience. *Progress in Brain Research*, *150*, 45–53.

Baars, B. J., Franklin, S., & Ramsoy, T. Z. (2013). Global work-space dynamics: Cortical "binding and propagation" enables conscious contents. *Frontiers in Psychology*, *4*, 200. doi: 10.3389/fpsyg.2013.00200.

Bachmann, T., Breitmeyer, B. G., & Öğmen, H. (2007). *The Experimental Phenomena of Consciousness: A Brief Dictionary*. Oxford: Oxford University Press.

Berman, N. J., Douglas, R. J., Martin, K. A., & Whitteridge, D. (1991). Mechanisms of inhibition in cat visual cortex. *Journal of Physiology, 440*, 697–722.

Bi, T., Cai, P., Zhou, T., & Fang, F. (2009). The effect of crowding on orientation-selective adaptation in human early visual cortex. *Journal of Vision, 9*(11)13, 1–10. http://journalofvision.org/9/11/13/, doi:10.1167/9.11.13.

Blake, R. (1998). What can be "perceived" in the absence of visual awareness? *Current Directions in Psychological Science, 6*(6), 157–62.

Block, N. (2011). Perceptual consciousness overflows cognitive access. *Trends in Cognitive Sciences, 15*(12), 567–75. https://doi.org/10.1016/j.tics.2011.11.001

Breitmeyer, B. G. (1984). *Visual Masking: An Integrative Approach*. New York: Oxford University Press.

Breitmeyer, B. G. (2014). *The Visual (Un)conscious and its (Dis)contents*. Oxford: Oxford University Press.

Breitmeyer, B. G. (2015). Psychophysical "blinding" methods reveal a functional hierarchy of unconscious visual processing. *Consciousness and Cognition, 35*, 234–50.

Breitmeyer, B. G., Koç, A., Öğmen, H., & Ziegler, R. (2008). Functional hierarchies of nonconscious visual processing. *Vision Research, 48*(14), 1509–13. https://doi.org/10.1016/j.visres.2008.03.015

Breitmeyer, B. G., Tripathy, S. P., & Brown, J. M. (2018). Can contrast-response functions indicate visual processing levels? *Vision, 2*, 14. doi:10.3390/vision2010014

Breitmeyer, B. G., Ziegler, R., & Hauske, G. (2007). Central factors contributing to para-contrast modulation of contour and brightness perception. *Visual Neuroscience, 24*(2), 191–6. https://doi.org/10.1017/S0952523807070393

Briand, K. A., & Klein, R. M. (1987). Is Posner's "beam" the same as Treisman's "glue"? On the relation between visual orienting and feature integration theory. *Journal of Experimental Psychology: Human Perception and Performance, 13*, 228–41.

Brown, J. M., Breitmeyer, B. G., Hale, R. G., & Plummer, R. W. (2018). Contrast sensitivity indicates processing level of visual illusions. *Journal of Experimental Psychology: Human Perception and Performance, 44*, 1557–66.

Carlson, T. A., Rauschenberger, R., & Verstraten, F. A. J. (2007). No representation without awareness in the lateral occipital cortex. *Psychological Science, 18*, 298–302.

Chakravarthi, R., & Cavanagh, P. (2009). Recovery of a crowded object by masking the flankers: Determining the locus of feature integration. *Journal of Vision, 9*(4), 1–9. doi: 10.1167/9.10.4.

Chen, Z., & Treisman, A. (2009). Implicit perception and level of processing in object-substitution masking. *Psychological Science, 20*(5), 560–7. https://doi.org/10.1111/j.1467-9280.2009.02328.x

Chirimuuta, M., & Tolhurst, D. J. (2005). Does a Bayesian model of V1 contrast coding offer a neurophysiological account of human contrast discrimination? *Vision Research, 45*, 2943–59.

Coren, S. (1970). Lateral inhibition and geometric illusions. *Quarterly Journal of Experimental Psychology, 22*, 274–8.

Craik, K. J. W. (1940). Origin of visual after-images. *Nature, 145*, 512.

Crawford, M. L., Smith, E. L., III, Harwerth, R. S., & von Noorden, G. K. (1984). Stereoblind monkeys have few binocular neurons. *Investigative Ophthalmology and Visual Science, 25*, 779–81.

Cumming, B. G., & Parker, A. J. (1999). Binocular neurons in V1 of awake monkeys are selective for absolute, not relative, disparity. *Journal of Neuroscience, 19*, 5602–18.

Dehaene, S., Changeux, J. P., Naccache, L., Sackur, J., & Sergent, C. (2006). Conscious, preconscious, and subliminal processing: A testable taxonomy. *Trends in Cognitive Science, 10*, 204–11.

Dehaene, S., & Naccache, L. (2001). Towards a cognitive neuroscience of consciousness: Basic evidence and a workspace framework. *Cognition, 79*, 1–37.

Dehaene, S., Sergent, C., & Changeux, J.-P. (2003). A neuronal network model linking subjective reports and objective physiological data during conscious perception. *Proceedings of the National Academy of Sciences USA, 100*, 8520–5.

Edelman, G. M., Gally, J. A., and Baars, B. J. (2011). Biology of consciousness. *Frontiers in Psychology, 2*, 1–7. doi: 10.3389/fpsyg.2011.00004.

Eo, K., Cha, O., Chong, S. C., & Kang, M. S. (2016). Less is more: Semantic information survives interocular suppression when attention is diverted. *Journal of Neuroscience, 36*, 5489–97. doi:10.1523/JNEUROSCI.3018-15.2016

Fang, F., & He, S. (2005). Cortical responses to invisible objects in the human dorsal and ventral pathways. *Nature Neuroscience, 10*, 1380–5.

Fogelson, S. V., Kohler, P. J., Miller, K. J., Granger, R., & Tse, P. U. (2014). Unconscious neural processing differs with method used to render stimuli invisible. *Frontiers in Psychology, 5*, 601. doi: 10.3389/fpsyg.2014.00601

Friedman-Hill, S. R., Robertson, L. C., & Treisman, A. (1995). Parietal contributions to visual feature binding: Evidence from a patient with bilateral lesions. *Science, 269*, 853–5.

Godwin, D., Barry, R. L., & Marois, R. (2015). Breakdown of the brain's functional network modularity with awareness. *Proceedings of the National Academy of Sciences USA, 112*, 3799–3804.

Goodhew, S. C., Visser, T. A. W., Lipp, O. V., & Dux, P. E. (2011). Implicit semantic perception in object substitution masking. *Cognition, 118*, 130–4.

Greenlee, M. W., & Heitger, F. (1998). The functional role of contrast adaptation. *Vision Research, 28*, 791–7.

Hall, S. D., Holliday, I. E., Hillebrand, A., Furlong, P. L., Singh, K. D., & Barnes, G. R. (2005). Distinct contrast response functions in striate and extra-striate regions of visual cortex revealed with magnetoencephalography (MEG). *Clinical Neurophysiology, 116*, 1716–22.

Haynes, J. D., Deichmann, R., & Rees, G. (2005). Eye-specific effects of binocular rivalry in the human lateral geniculate nucleus. *Nature, 438*(7067), 496–9.

He, S., Cavanagh, P., & Intriligator, J. (1996). Attentional resolution and the locus of visual awareness. *Nature, 383*, 334–7.

Hesselmann, G. (2013). Dissecting visual awareness with FMRI. *Neuroscientist, 19*, 495–508. doi:10.1177/1073858413485988

Hesselmann, G., & Knops, A. (2014). No conclusive evidence for numerical priming under interocular suppression. *Psychological Science, 25*(11), 2116–19. https://doi.org/10.1177/0956797614548876

Hesselmann, G., & Malach, R. (2011). The link between fMRI-BOLD activation and perceptual awareness is "stream-invariant" in the human visual system. *Cerebral Cortex, 21*, 2829–37.

Hesselmann, G., Darcy, N., Ludwig, K., & Sterzer, P. (2016). Priming in a shape task but not in a category task under continuous flash suppression. *Journal of Vision, 16*(3). https://doi.org/Artn 17 10.1167/16.3.17

Hesselmann, G., Darcy, N., Rothkirch, M., & Sterzer, P. (2018). Investigating masked priming along the "vision-for-perception" and "vision-for-action" dimensions of unconscious processing. *Journal of Experimental Psychology: General, 147*(11), 1641–59. https://doi.org/10.1037/xge0000420

Hesselmann, G., Darcy, N., Sterzer, P., & Knops, A. (2015). Exploring the boundary conditions of unconscious numerical priming effects with continuous flash suppression. *Consciousness and Cognition, 31*, 60–72. https://doi.org/10.1016/j.concog.2014.10.009

Horovitz, S. G., Braun, A. R., Carr, W. S., Piccioni, D., Balkin, T. J., Fukunaga, M., and Duyn, J. H. (2009). Decoupling the brain's default mode network during deep sleep. *Proceedings of the National Academy of Sciences USA, 106*, 11376–81.

Hubel, D., & Wiesel, T. N. (1968). Receptive fields and functional architecture of the monkey striate cortex. *Journal of Physiology (London), 195*: 215–43.

Intriligator, J., & Cavanagh, P. (2001). The spatial resolution of visual attention. *Cognitive Psychology, 43*, 171–216.

Kiefer, M. (2002). The N400 is modulated by unconsciously perceived masked words: Further evidence for an automatic spreading activation account of N400 priming effects. *Cognitive Brain Research, 13*, 27–39.

Kim, C.-Y., & Blake, R. (2005). Psychophysical magic: Rendering the visible "invisible". *Trends in Cognitive Sciences, 9*, 381–8.

King, J.-R., Sitt, J. D., Faugeras, F., Rohaut, B., El Karoui, I., Cohen, L., Naccache, L., & Dehaene, S. (2013). Information sharing in the brain indexes consciousness in noncommunicative patients. *Current Biology, 23*, 1914–19.

Konen, C. S., & Kastner, S. (2008). Two hierarchically organized neural systems for object information in human visual cortex. *Nature Neuroscience, 11*, 224–31.

Kouider, S., & Dehaene, S. (2007). Levels of processing during non-conscious perception: A critical review of visual masking. *Philosophical Transactions of the Royal Society B, 362*, 857–75.

Lamme, V. A. F. (2010). How neuroscience will change our view on consciousness. *Cognitive Neuroscience, 1*(3), 204–20. https://doi.org/10.1080/17588921003731586

Lee, S.-H., & Blake, R. (2004). A fresh look at interocular grouping during binocular rivalry. *Vision Research, 44*, 983–91.

Leopold, D. A., & Logothetis, N. K. (1996). Activity changes in early visual cortex reflect monkey's percept during binocular rivalry. *Nature, 379*, 549–52.

Levi, D. M. (2008). Crowding – An essential bottleneck for object recognition: A minireview. *Vision Research, 48*, 635–54.

Levi, D. M., Hariharan, S., & Klein, S. A. (2002). Suppressive and facilitatory spatial interactions in peripheral vision: Peripheral crowding is neither size invariant nor simple contrast masking. *Journal of Vision, 2*, 3. doi:10.1167/2.2.3

Lin, Z., & He, S. (2009). Seeing the invisible: The scope and limits of unconscious processing in binocular rivalry. *Progress in Neurobiology, 87*, 195–211. doi:10.1016/j.pneurobio.2008.09.002

Liu, T., Jiang, Y., Sun, X., & He. S. (2009). Reduction of the crowding effect in spatially adjacent but cortically remote visual stimuli. *Current Biology, 19*, 127–32.

Logothetis, N., & Schall, J. D. (1989). Neuronal correlates of subjective visual perception. *Science, 245*, 761–3.

Loomis, J. M. (1972). The photopigment bleaching hypothesis of complementary afterimages: A psychophysical test. *Vision Research, 12*, 1587–94.

Luck, S. J., Vogel, E. K., & Shapiro, K. L. (1996). Word meanings can be accessed but not reported during the attentional blink. *Nature, 383*, 616–18.

Ludwig, K., & Hesselmann, G. (2015). Weighing the evidence for a dorsal processing bias under continuous flash suppression. *Consciousness and Cognition, 35*, 251–259. https://doi.org/10.1016/j.concog.2014.12.010

Ludwig, K., Kathmann, N., Sterzer, P., & Hesselmann, G. (2015). Investigating category- and shape-selective neural processing in ventral and dorsal visual stream under interocular suppression. *Human Brain Mapping, 36*, 137–49. http://dx.doi.org/10.1002/hbm.22618

Macdonald, J. S. P., & Lavie, N. (2008). Load induced blindness. *Journal of Experimental Psychology: Human Perception and Performance, 34*, 1078–91.

Mack, A., & Rock, I. (1998). *Inattentional Blindness.* Cambridge, MA: MIT Press.

Macknik, S. L., & Livingstone, M. S. (1998). Neuronal correlates of visibility and invisibility in the primate visual system. *Nature Neuroscience, 1*(2), 144–9. https://doi.org/10.1038/393

Mattler, U., & Wernicke, M. (2014). Paper presented at the 2nd international workshop "Neuro-Cognitive Mechanisms of Conscious and Unconscious Visual Perception", Hanse-Wissenschaftskolleg, Delmenhosrt, Germany, June 30–July 2.

Michael, L., Hesselmann, G., Kiefer, M., & Niedeggen, M. (2011). Distractor-induced blindness for orientation changes and coherent motion. *Vision Research, 51*, 1781–7.

Milner, A. D. (2012). Is visual processing in the dorsal stream accessible to consciousness? *Proceedings of Biological Sciences, 279*, 2289–98. doi:10.1098/rspb.2011.2663

Milner, A. D., & Goodale, M. A. (2006). *The Visual Brain in Action* (2nd ed.). Oxford: Oxford University Press.

Moors, P., Hesselmann, G., Wagemans, J., & van Ee, R. (2017). Continuous flash Suppression: Stimulus fractionation rather than integration. *Trends in Cognitive Sciences, 21*, 719–21. doi:10.1016/j.tics.2017.06.005

Motter, B.C., & Simoni, D.A. (2007). The roles of cortical image separation and size in active visual search performance *Journal of Vision, 7*(6), 1–15. doi: 10.1167/7.2.6.

Niedeggen, M., Hesselmann, G., Sahraie, A., Milders, M., & Blakemore, C. (2004). Probing the prerequisites for motion blindness. *Journal of Cognitive Neuroscience, 16*, 584–97. doi:10.1162/089892904323057317

Nelson, S. B. (1991). Temporal interactions in the cat visual system. I. Orientation-selective suppression in the visual cortex. *Journal of Neuroscience, 11*, 344–56.

Öğmen, H., & Breitmeyer, B. G. (eds). (2006). *The First Half Second: The Microgenesis and Temporal Dynamics of Unconscious and Conscious Visual Processes.* Cambridge, MA: MIT Press.

Pearson, J., & Clifford, C. W. G. (2005). Suppressed patterns alter vision during binocular rivalry. *Current Biology, 15*, 2142–8.

Pelli, D. G., & Tillman, K. A. (2008). The uncrowded window of object recognition. *Nature Neuroscience, 11*(10), 1129–35.

Pelli, D. G., Palomares, M., & Majaj, N. J. (2004). Crowding is unlike ordinary masking: distinguishing feature integration from detection. *Journal of Vision, 4*(12), 1136–69. https://doi.org/10.1167/4.12.12

Polat, U. (1999). Functional architecture of long-range perceptual interactions. *Spatial Vision, 12*, 143–62.

Polat, U., & Sagi, D. (2006) Temporal asymmetry of collinear lateral interactions. *Vision Research, 46*, 953–60.

Raymond, J. E., Shapiro, K. L., & Arnell, K. M. (1992). Temporary suppression of visual processing in an RSVP task: An attentional blink? *Journal of Experimental Psychology: Human Perception and Performance, 18*, 849–60.

Reiss, J. E., & Hoffman, J. E. (2006). Object substitution masking interferes with semantic processing: evidence from event-related potentials. *Psychological Science, 17*(12), 1015–20. https://doi.org/10.1111/j.1467-9280.2006.01820.x

Rolke, B., Heil, M., Streb, J., & Hennighausen, E. (2001). Missed prime words within the attentional blink evoke an N400 semantic priming effect. *Psychophysiology, 38*, 165–74.

Rothkirch, M., & Hesselmann, G. (2018). No evidence for dorsal-stream-based priming under continuous flash suppression. *Consciousness and Cognition, 2*. pii: S1053-8100(18)30108-9. doi: 10.1016/j.concog.2018.05.011. [Epub ahead of print]

Sagi, D., & Julesz, B. (1986). Enhanced detection in the aperture of focal attention during simple discrimination tasks. *Nature, 321,* 693–5.

Sakitt, B. (1976). Psychophysical correlates of photoreceptor activity. *Vision Research, 16,* 129–40.

Sakuraba, S., Sakai, S., Yamanaka, M., Yokosawa, K., & Hirayama, K. (2012). Does the human dorsal stream really process a category for tools? *Journal of Neuroscience, 32,* 3949–53.

Schröter, M. S., Spoormaker, V. I., Schorer, A., Wohlschläger, A., Czisch, M., Kochs, Claus Zimmer, E. F., Hemmer, B., Schneider, G., Jordan, D., & Ilg, R. (2012). Spatiotemporal reconfiguration of large-scale brain functional networks during propofol-induced loss of consciousness. *Journal of Neuroscience, 32,* 12832–40.

Shapiro, K. L., Driver, J., Ward, R., & Sorenson, R. E. (1997). Priming from the attentional blink: A failure to extract visual tokens but not visual types. *Psychological Science, 8,* 95–100.

Sheinberg, D. L., & Logothetis, N. K. (1997). The role of temporal cortical areas in perceptual organization. *Proceedings of the National Academy of Sciences USA, 94,* 3408–13.

Simons, D. J., & Rensink, R. A. (2005). Change blindness: Past, present, and future. *Trends in Cognitive Sciences, 9,* 16–20.

Simons, D. J., & Chabris, C. F. (1999). Gorillas in our midst: Sustained inattentional blindness for dynamic events. *Perception, 28,* 1059–74.

Smith, E. L., III, Chino, Y., Ni, J., & Cheng, H. (1997). Binocular combination of contrast signals by striate cortical neurons in the monkey. *Journal of Neurophysiology, 78,* 366–82.

Spehar, B., & Gillam, B. (2002). Modal completion in the Poggendorff illusion: Support for the depth processng theory. *Psychological Science, 13,* 306–12.

Spillmann, L. (1971). Foveal perceptive fields in the human visual system measured with simultaneous contrast in grids and bars. *Pflügers Archiv, 326,* 281–99.

Stenberg, G., Lindgren, M., Johansson, M., Olsson, A., & Rosen, I. (2000). Semantic processing without conscious identification: Evidence from event-related potentials. *Journal of Experimental Psychology: Learning, Memory, and Cognition, 26,* 973–1004.

Tadmor, Y., & Tolhurst, D. J. (2000). Calculating the contrasts that retinal ganglion cells and LGN neurones encounter in natural scenes. *Vision Research, 40,* 3145–57.

Tong, F., & Engel, S. A. (2001). Interocular rivalry revealed in the human cortical blindspot representation. *Nature, 411,* 195–9.

Tong, F., Meng, M., & Blake, R. (2006). Neural bases of binocular rivalry. *Trends in Cognitive Sciences, 10,* 502–11.

Tononi, G. (2004). An information integration theory of consciousness. *BMC Neuroscience, 5,* 42.

Tononi G. (2008). Consciousness as integrated information: A provisional manifesto. *Biological Bulletin, 215,* 216–42.

Tononi, G., & Koch, C. (2008). The neural correlates of consciousness: An update. *Annals of the New York Academy of Science, 1124,* 239–61.

Tootell, R. B. H., Hadjikhani, N. K., Vanduffel, W., Liu, A. K., Mendola, J. D., Sereno, M. I., & Dale, A.M. (1998). Functional analysis of primary visual cortex (V1) in humans. *Proceedings of the National Academy of Sciences USA, 95,* 811–17.

Treisman, A. (1998). Feature binding, attention and object perception. *Philosophical Transactions of the Royal Society B, 353,* 1295–1306.

Tripathy, S. P., & Cavanagh, P. (2002). The extent of crowding in peripheral vision does not scale with target size. *Vision Research, 42,* 2357–69.

Tsuchiya, N., & Koch, C. (2005). Continuous flash suppression reduces negative afterimages, *Nature Neuroscience, 8,* 1096–1101.

Tsuchiya, N., Koch, C., Gilroy, L. A., & Blake, R. (2006). Depth of interocular suppression associated with continuous flash suppression, flash suppression, and binocular rivalry. *Journal of Vision, 6*, 1068–78. doi:10.1167/6.10.6

Tyler, C. W., & Likova, L. T. (2007). Crowding: A neuroanalytic approach. *Journal of Vision, 7*(2)16, 1–9, http://journalofvision.org/7/2/16/, doi:10.1167/7.2.16.

van Boxtel, J. J. A. (2017). Different signal enhancement pathways of attention and consciousness underlie perception in humans. *Journal of Neuroscience, 37*, 5912–22.

van Boxtel, J. J. A., Tsuchiya, N., & Koch, C. (2010). Opposing effects of attention and consciousness on afterimages. *Proceedings of the National Academy of Sciences USA, 107*, 8883–8.

van Gaal, S., & Lamme, V. A. F. (2012). Unconscious high-level information processing: Implication for neurobiological theories of consciousness. *Neuroscientist, 18*, 287–301.

Virsu, V., & Laurinen, P. (1977). Long-lasting afterimages caused by neural adaptation. *Vision Research, 17*, 853–60.

Watanabe, K., Paik, Y., & Blake, R. (2004). Preserved gain control for luminance contrast during binocular rivalry suppression. *Vision Research, 44*, 3065–71.

Wilson, H. R. (1997). A neural model of foveal light adaptation and afterimage formation. *Visual Neuroscience, 14*, 403–23.

Wunderlich, K., Schneider, K. A., & Kastner, S. (2005). Neural correlates of binocular rivalry in the human lateral geniculate nucleus. *Nature Neuroscience, 8*(11), 1595–1602. https://doi.org/nn1554 [pii] 10.1038/nn1554

Yang, E., & Blake, R. (2012). Deconstructing continuous flash suppression. *Journal of Vision, 12*(3)8, 1–14. http://www.journalofvision.org/content/12/3/8, doi:10.1167/12.3.8.

Yang, E., Brascamp, J., Kang, M.-S., & Blake, R. (2014). On the use of continuous flash suppression for the study of visual processing outside of awareness. *Frontiers in Psychology, 5*, 724. http://dx.doi.org/10.3389/fpsyg.2014.00724.

Yeh, S.-L., He, S., & Cavanagh, P. (2012). Semantic priming from crowded words. *Psychological Science, 23*, 608–16.

Zanuttini, L. (1976). A new explanation for the Poggendorff illusion. *Perception and Psychophysics, 20*, 29–32.

Zenger-Landoldt, B., & Heeger, D. J. (2003). Response suppression in V1 agrees with psychohysics of surround masking. *Journal of Neuroscience, 23*, 6884–93.

Zimba, L. D., & Blake, R. (1983). Binocular rivalry and semantic processing: Out of sight, out of mind. *Journal of Experimental Psychology: Human Perception and Performance, 9*(5), 807–15.

4

THE UNCONSCIOUS PROCESSING OF SOCIAL INFORMATION

Apoorva Rajiv Madipakkam

UNIVERSITY OF LÜBECK

Marcus Rothkirch

CHARITÉ – UNIVERSITÄTSMEDIZIN BERLIN

1 Introduction

The English poet John Donne said, "No man is an island". Human beings are social animals and the precise processing of social information is critical for successful interactions and normal development. In fact, the proper processing of social information is so crucial that deficits in correctly recognizing such cues are the characteristics of many psychiatric and neurodevelopmental disorders. Given this high relevance, in this chapter, we focus on the extent to which social information can be processed outside of visual awareness and can influence one's own behavior in the absence of awareness. Our review of this topic covers two lines of research. First, we discuss studies in which social stimuli were entirely suppressed from observers' awareness. Secondly, we include studies in which social stimuli that were initially suppressed from awareness were presented until they overcame suppression. In the latter case, suppression times are usually seen as a marker for un- or preconscious processing, though the exact relation between unconscious processes and suppression times is still a matter of discussion. In particular, we focus on the significance of facial expressions and facial features in communication and the previously popular but now hotly debated "low-road" pathway for the processing of social information outside of awareness. The chapter concludes with the importance of the unconscious processing of social information in psychiatric disorders and the promise of new therapeutic interventions using unconscious neural reinforcement or Decoded Neurofeedback. By the end of this chapter, we hope that the reader not only has a clear overview of what kind of social information can be processed unconsciously, but also a deeper understanding of the specific role of the amygdala in processing social information and the methodological pitfalls that plague studies investigating unconscious processing.

2 What's in a face? The many roads of face processing

The expression of facial emotions as well as their perception and interpretation is a vital part of human communication. Not only do emotional expressions enrich verbal communication but they can also immediately signal one's own emotional state to others. It is thus unsurprising that the notion that emotional expressions have preferential access to visual awareness and that they can even be processed without the observer's conscious knowledge has spawned a multitude of studies, if not even initiated an individual branch of empirical research. Empirical findings, especially in the last two decades, suggest that facial emotions have profound influences on a vast variety of human behavior – unfolding in the true absence or the brink of visual awareness. In this context, especially the influence of faces expressing fear has been extensively studied. Fearful faces have been found to enter awareness earlier than faces with neutral expressions (Milders, Sahraie, Logan, & Donnellon, 2006; Yang, Zald, & Blake, 2007), to attract spatial attention in the absence of awareness (Carlson & Reinke, 2008), and to unconsciously improve visual discrimination for other supraliminal stimuli (Tamietto & de Gelder, 2008). Such findings are not limited to fearful faces, as also other subliminally presented emotional expressions appear to affect behavioral and neural responses. For instance, the impression of a supraliminal face, in terms of its pleasantness, attractiveness, emotional expression et cetera, is affected by the antecedent or simultaneous presentation of a subliminal emotional face (Adams, Gray, Garner, & Graf, 2010; Anderson, Siegel, White, & Barrett, 2012; Harris & Ciaramitaro, 2016; Mumenthaler & Sander, 2015; Ye, He, Hu, Yu, & Wang, 2014). Subliminal faces with emotional expressions influence the likeability of abstract items (Almeida, Pajtas, Mahon, Nakayama, & Caramazza, 2013; Kouider, Berthet, & Faivre, 2011), which also triggers physiological responses (Chiesa, Liuzza, Acciarino, & Aglioti, 2015). Furthermore, observers can also mimic facial expressions that they are unconsciously exposed to (Kaiser, Davey, Parkhouse, Meeres, & Scott, 2016; Tamietto, Castelli, Vighetti, Perozzo, Geminiani, Weiskrantz, & de Gelder, 2009). Even "higher-level" cognitive operations such as learning (Watanabe & Haruno, 2015) or food consumption (Winkielman & Berridge, 2004) are biased by the subliminal appearance of emotional faces. In addition, even subtle facial information that signifies the dominance or trustworthiness of another person is related to the time until the face overcomes suppression (Stewart, Ajina, Getov, Bahrami, Todorov, & Rees, 2012). This could indicate that also more abstract threats, like a person's potential to be untrustworthy, impacts pre- and unconscious stages of visual processing. Finally, the speed with which a face emerges into consciousness appears to depend on its level of attractiveness (Hung, Nieh, & Hsieh, 2016; Nakamura & Kawabata, 2018).

Naturally, this raises the question of whether there is a special processing unit or network in the brain that enables the processing of emotional expressions and the initiation of appropriate responses despite the individual's unawareness of the faces. In this context, the idea that visual input containing behaviorally relevant emotional information can be processed via a subcortical route (also termed "low road")

94 Madipakkam and Rothkirch

enjoys popularity. This theory, which was introduced by LeDoux (1998), posits that visual stimuli are not only processed along a cortical pathway via the visual cortex. Instead, a second pathway exists that is purported to deliver a coarse but fast analysis of visual input in order to trigger appropriate reactions, especially in situations in which a fast response is desirable, for instance in cases of imminent danger. This second pathway processes visual information through the superior colliculus, pulvinar, and, as the most essential component, the amygdala, bypassing cortical visual areas. Observations of increased neural responses in the amygdala (Whalen, Rauch, Etcoff, McInerney, Lee, & Jenike, 1998; Williams, Morris, McGlone, Abbott, & Mattingley, 2004) or an increased functional connectivity between the amygdala, superior colliculus, and pulvinar (Morris, Ohman, & Dolan, 1999) for subliminally presented fearful faces resonate well with this theory. Likewise, social information like the trustworthiness of a subliminal face also seems to be encoded in the amygdala as the central relay station of the subcortical pathway (Freeman, Stolier, Ingbretsen, & Hehman, 2014). Further support for this view comes from a meta-analysis showing robust activation in the amygdala, among other cortical and subcortical sites, for the subliminal presentation of emotional faces (Brooks, Savov, Allzén, Benedict, Fredriksson, & Schiöth, 2012).

All in all, this suggests that the human brain is tuned to the fast and unconscious processing of others' emotions, which can influence the individual's behavior despite the lack of conscious knowledge. What is especially remarkable is the multifaceted nature of these unconscious influences: even "higher-level" cognitive operations involved in decision-making and affective evaluations seem to be affected by a simple manipulation – the masked presentation of an emotional face. This has obviously deeper implications, as the affected person not only lacks introspection into these processes but is also unable to resist such influences that are taking place outside their conscious knowledge. Formulated in an exaggerated way, this turns the affected person into a passive plaything of external events. In the following, we will view this matter from a different angle and try to illustrate why the concept of such a widespread and profound unconscious impact of emotional expressions should not be uncritically adopted.

In general, the empirical research focusing on the unconscious processing of visual stimuli has come under fire more than once, especially because of the often insufficient assessment of observers' level of awareness (Eriksen, 1960; Holender, 1986; Kunimoto, Miller, & Pashler, 2001). Besides, there are also, mostly methodological, concerns specifically related to the study of unconscious emotions. We will only touch upon the more general critical aspects of the appropriate measure of observers' awareness in those cases where they have been investigated in the context of subliminal facial expressions.

It is usually implicitly assumed that the presentation of a particular emotion has a more or less uniform effect. For instance, a fearful face should be recognized as fearful or threatening by different observers and should trigger a certain kind of response. However, humans are fairly poor at accurately discriminating emotions from photographs taken from real-life situations (Aviezer, Trope, & Todorov,

2012; Fernández-Dols & Crivelli, 2013; Landis, 1929). From an evolutionary perspective, it is thus questionable how a neural system that is supposedly adapted to the fast and unconscious recognition of affective information performs poorly under natural conditions. It is further implicitly presupposed that a specific facial expression evokes a respective emotional state. Again, fearful faces are extensively studied because they activate threat-related responses. It is, however, often overlooked that fearful expressions are ambiguous as they offer several interpretations. The person expressing the fear could be afraid of the observer, but also of another external person or event. In the first case, the observer does not need to feel threatened, as the observer is the threat. One could even wonder why it is usually fearful faces that are associated with threat and not, say, angry faces, which seem to pose a clearer threat to the observer. Instead, angry expressions seem to rather delay than accelerate the access of faces to visual awareness (Gray, Adams, Hedger, Newton, & Garner, 2013). What is more, the idea of a privileged unconscious processing of threat-related visual input is thwarted by consistent findings of a prioritized processing of neutral faces in comparison to dominant and untrustworthy faces (Hedger, Gray, Garner, & Adams, 2016). In this context, Whalen (1998) offers the interpretation that the observation of neural responses to masked fearful faces may be more closely linked to the ambiguity of biologically relevant stimuli, instead of being a clear-cut response to the fear-inducing input. One of the most challenging aspects, however, is the inherent correlation between different facial expressions and their low-level stimulus characteristics. This entails that variations in emotional expressions are confounded with stimulus properties like contrast, luminance, and spatial frequency. Such confounds bear the risk that behavioral or neural differences caused by low-level stimulus features may be falsely attributed to the emotional category of the face. Indeed, fearful faces not only markedly differ in their low-level properties from other facial expressions, these differences also largely account for variations in suppression times, especially due to the greater exposure to the iris and the sclera (Gray et al., 2013; Hedger, Adams, & Garner, 2015; Hedger et al., 2016). Similar observations have been made for facial dominance and trustworthiness (Stein, Awad, Gayet, & Peelen, 2018), indicating that the preferential awareness of faces with respect to these characteristics is also largely dependent on low-level stimulus features. What makes matters even more complicated is the fact that the successful suppression of a visual stimulus is dependent on the low-level characteristics of the stimulus and the mask (Han, Lunghi, & Alais, 2016). Consequently, when the same masking procedure (i.e. same masking stimuli, same stimulus durations, etc.) is applied to stimuli with different emotional expressions, differences in the outcome measure may not necessarily index the absence vs. presence of the unconscious processing of a particular emotion. Instead, this could indicate that suppression was more effective for one and suboptimal for the other emotion due to the underlying low-level characteristics (Maxwell & Davidson, 2004; Milders, Sahraie, & Logan, 2008). Nevertheless, the registration of observers' awareness is indispensable and nontrivial, as observers are often capable of reliably detecting even only very briefly presented fearful faces (Pessoa, Japee, & Ungerleider, 2005; Szczepanowski & Pessoa, 2007). In this context, it is noteworthy that studies that provide a rigorous implementation and control of the stimulus masking procedure and observers' awareness often fail to find clear evidence in favor of the processing of facial emotions in the absence of awareness. In this sense, "null effects" have been reported for a range of phenomena that previously were supposed to demonstrate the almost unlimited potential of unconsciously processed emotional faces. That the influence of emotional faces is abolished when they are presented outside of awareness has been shown for phenomena like affective priming (Lähteenmäki, Hyönä, Koivisto, & Nummenmaa, 2015; Lohse & Overgaard, 2017), adaptation aftereffects (Yang, Hong, & Blake, 2010), affective blindsight (Rajananda, Zhu, & Peters, 2018), the influence on social judgments (Kleckner, Anderson, Betz, Wormwood, Eskew, & Barrett, 2018), facial mimicry (Korb, Osimo, Suran, Goldstein, & Rumiati, 2017), and physiological responses (Tsikandilakis & Chapman, 2018).

Given the inextricable association between low-level features and high-level affective content, a refinement of the dual-pathway account of emotion processing states that the preferential processing of fearful faces is based on the projection of lower spatial frequencies via magnocellular channels connecting the subcortical regions in the brain (Vuilleumier, Armony, Driver, & Dolan, 2003). Obviously, this would indicate that the subcortical pathway is not directly attuned to the prioritization of emotional faces, but that a rapid processing of facial emotions is only indirectly mediated by a prioritization of low spatial frequencies. Yet, it is even questionable whether such a preference is the basis for the processing of emotional faces in the absence of awareness. Stein, Seymour, Hebart, and Sterzer (2014) observed that, in opposition to the dual-pathway model, faster awareness of fearful faces is reliant on high spatial frequencies (but see also Willenbockel, Lepore, Nguyen, Bouthillier, & Gosselin (2012), for empirical support of the notion that unconscious emotion processing is dependent on low frequencies). In a similar vein, critics of the notion of an independent subcortical route for the fast and unconscious processing of fearful expressions have pointed out that this theory stands on shaky grounds (Cauchoix & Crouzet, 2013; Pessoa & Adolphs, 2010). According to them, neural responses in subcortical areas do not precede responses in cortical areas. As Palermo and Rhodes (2007) show, neural responses to faces in occipital cortex have latencies of at least 80 ms, while responses to faces in the amygdala exhibit latencies of at least 100 ms. Furthermore, lesions of the amygdala do not necessarily seem to impair the fast recognition of and attentional capture by fearful faces (Piech, McHugo, Smith, Dukic, Van der Meer, Abou-Khalil . . . & Zald, 2011; Tsuchiya, Moradi, Felsen, Yamazaki, & Adolphs, 2009). Mirroring the situation for the research on the behavioral consequences of the subliminal presentation of emotional expressions, a stricter control of participants' level of awareness is also often accompanied by an absence of amygdala responses to masked fearful faces (Pessoa, Japee, Sturman, & Ungerleider, 2006; Phillips, Williams, Heining, Herba, Russell, Andrew . . . & Gray, 2004). This is not to say that subcortical areas are completely irrelevant for the recognition of emotional expressions. However,

Social information processing **97**

their supposedly unique role of providing a fast and coarse evaluation of emotional information that is independent of cortical input is likely oversimplified. As concisely put by Pessoa & Adolphs (2011): "Multiple roads are better than one."

3 Neutral today, fearful tomorrow: learning of social information

As we have outlined in the previous section, the inherent confound between low-level features of emotional faces and their affective content impedes the study of the unconscious processing of emotional expressions. A promising avenue to circumvent such deficiencies is to ascribe social relevance to face stimuli in a systematically and controlled way by pairing them with external affective events. One widely used approach to achieve this is by means of conditioning. In contrast to emotional expressions, where the social relevance of the face is already emitted by the face itself, in the context of conditioning the observer learns over time that a particular face or a certain behavior is associated with a positive or negative outcome. For classical fear conditioning, for example, a particular stimulus, in our case a face stimulus, is systematically paired with an unconditioned stimulus (US), which is often an aversive white noise burst or an electrical shock. Through this systematic association, the face stimulus becomes a conditioned stimulus (usually referred to as CS+). Another stimulus (CS-) that is not associated with the US serves as the control condition. For another observer the association between the face stimuli and the outcome can be reversed so that the low-level features of the face can be disentangled from its affective content. Such a rigorous experimental control of the social relevance of a face is undoubtedly beneficial for the investigation of unconscious effects.

However, there is also a downside to this approach. The unconscious processing of emotional expressions is, at least according to the underlying theoretical concept, rather straightforward, in that it is expected that a masked face stimulus with a particular emotional expression triggers a certain behavioral and neural response. How unconscious effects of learned affective values of faces would unfold, is, in contrast, more ambiguous. In conditioning studies, the face stimuli are usually first paired with the US during a conditioning phase. In a subsequent stage, the CS+ and CS- stimuli are presented again without the US and the critical response measure is assessed. In most classical conditioning studies focusing on unconscious processes, the conditioning phase is conducted with supraliminal faces, while the effects of interest are later assessed during the subliminal presentation of the conditioned faces. In a series of studies following this design, skin conductance responses (SCRs) to the subliminal faces were enhanced for the CS+ in comparison to the CS- face (Olsson & Phelps, 2004; Parra, Esteves, Flykt, & Öhman, 1997; Saban & Hugdahl, 1999; Vieira, Wen, Oliver, & Mitchell, 2017). In contrast, for other studies the conditioning procedure was performed with subliminal faces, while SCRs have then been recorded in response to the supraliminal stimuli. Albeit, similar findings have been reported for this approach (Esteves, Parra, Dimberg, & Ohman, 1994). Raio, Carmel, Carrasco, and Phelps (2012) even showed differences in SCRs to conditioned face stimuli that were presented subliminally throughout the whole experiment. Other physiological measures, like startle reflex (Golkar & Öhman, 2012) and facial muscle contractions (Bunce, Bernat, Wong, & Shevrin, 1999) exhibit analogous response patterns. Though the mentioned empirical work appears to converge at similar effects of conditioned subliminal face stimuli, namely increased responses to the CS+ versus CS- stimuli, it should be kept in mind that these results are essentially based on different research lines. We will discuss the implications of this aspect below.

How is the information about faces rendered socially relevant through conditioning relayed in the brain, such that it leads to differential physiological responses when the faces are presented subliminally? The idea is that the underlying neural circuitry is in principle the same as that involved in the unconscious processing of facial emotions. According to this notion, the subcortical pathway automatically and rapidly detects fear-relevant stimuli in the environment (Ohman & Mineka, 2001). The amygdala constitutes the core of this pathway (Olsson & Phelps, 2007), as we have outlined in more detail in the preceding section. Although there is empirical evidence supporting this concept (Morris, Ohman, & Dolan, 1998), we would like to recall that caution is warranted when referring to the subcortical pathway of emotion processing. In studies measuring event-related potentials during the subliminal presentation of the CS+, neural signatures of the CS+ (Wong, Bernat, Bunce, & Shevrin, 1997) as well as of the expected US (Wong, Shevrin, & Williams, 1994) have been primarily identified over parietal and occipital areas. However, these findings should also be taken with a grain of salt. Lovibond and Shanks (2002) have pointed out that the counterbalancing of conditions was insufficient, and no measure was reported to validate the effectiveness of conditioning (for instance, SCRs) in these studies.

It is somewhat surprising that the work on the unconscious effects of conditioned faces has almost exclusively focused on physiological variables, mainly the recording of SCRs, as outcome measure. Beyond this, it has remained largely unclear whether and to what extent subliminal conditioned faces impact behavior. Madipakkam, Rothkirch, Wilbertz, and Sterzer (2016) recorded eye movements as a measure of attentional bias in response to subliminally presented conditioned faces, but did not observe such a bias towards one of the face stimuli. Until further evidence is gathered one might thus conclude that the unconscious effects of conditioned faces are restricted to physiological responses but are not observable at the behavioral level. Indeed, according to a recent meta-analysis, which did not exclusively focus on face stimuli, a systematic increase in physiological responses to subliminal fear-conditioned stimuli is reported in the scientific literature (van der Ploeg, Brosschot, Versluis, & Verkuil, 2017). However, this is only one piece of the puzzle. Notwithstanding the report of unconscious effects of fear conditioning across studies, the authors of this meta-analysis propose to remain wary regarding a premature affirmation of such effects. Skepticism seems to be advisable especially due to the substantial heterogeneity between studies. For instance, most studies employed fearful or angry faces, presumably because it is argued that stimuli already possessing an affective value are easier to associate with other affective events and are more resistant to extinction (Ohman & Mineka, 2001). Yet, also neutral (Vieira et al., 2017) and even schematic faces (Wong et al., 1994) have been used. How the effectiveness of conditioning might interact with the facial expression is largely unclear and awaits further research. Another aspect that we briefly brought up earlier are the different approaches to studying unconscious effects of conditioning. When the conditioning procedure is carried out with supraliminal stimuli, observers are – or at least have the possibility of being – fully aware of the contingencies, that is the pairing between CS and US. On the other hand, for those studies where stimuli are presented subliminally only during the conditioning phase, observers not only lack awareness of the stimuli but also of contingencies, given that visual masking was effective. As a consequence, these different experimental designs likely target distinct underlying processes. The influence of observers' contingency awareness on the outcome of the conditioning process further seems to depend on whether delay or trace conditioning is applied, that is on the temporal relation between CS and US (Clark, Manns, & Squire, 2002), which adds a further level of complexity. Finally, and as comprehensively discussed by Lovibond & Shanks (2002), the measures that are used to evaluate participants' awareness are often inadequate. This is especially problematic because it can bring about an overestimation of unconscious processes, since participants that are judged unaware of a stimulus might still have residual awareness. We will turn towards this issue again in the concluding section, as it concerns not only conditioning studies, but is a general predicament in consciousness research. Likewise, the meta-analysis by Hedger et al. (2016) identified a marked variation in effect sizes related to subliminal stimuli that gained relevance through fear conditioning across studies. For evaluative conditioning, a form of conditioning that specifically refers to the change of the affective evaluation of the CS, effects are statistically indistinguishable from zero when the CS or US is presented subliminally (Hofmann, De Houwer, Perugini, Baeyens, & Crombez, 2010; Stahl, Haaf, & Corneille, 2016). In light of this heterogeneity between studies and the shortcomings of previous research, an international research network on fear conditioning has recently expressed the need for an open debate of methodological questions (Lonsdorf, Menz, Andreatta, Fullana, Golkar, Haaker . . . & Merz, 2017). With their contribution, this consortium hopes to initiate a movement towards methodological coherence in order to allow for a better comparability between studies.

While fear conditioning is the predominant technique to equip faces with social relevance, there are also other ways to do this. Anderson, Siegel, Bliss-Moreau, & Barrett (2011) chose a more "naturalistic" approach by pairing faces with brief biographic descriptions in the form of positive, negative, or neutral gossip. Faces linked to negative gossip dominated visual awareness in comparison to the other conditions. However, attempts at replicating this effect have been unsuccessful so far (Rabovsky, Stein, & Abdel Rahman, 2016; Stein, Grubb, Bertrand, Suh, & Verosky, 2017). It might well be that such a manipulation is less powerful in changing the affective content of a face than in the case of classical conditioning. Given the mixed results of studies on the processing of subliminal classically conditioned faces and the raised criticism of these studies, one can conclude that the evidence for the unconscious processing of learned affective values of faces is rather limited. Zooming into the face, in the next section, we will introduce the topic of unconscious processing of facial features, focusing on the eyes.

4 Eye see, therefore I am

The eyes speak a language of their own. While emotional expressions convey information about others' current affective state, the direction of eye gaze reveals the person's intentions and their focus of attention. Although this seems like an understated cue compared to facial emotions, it is important to note that most of the information of an emotional expression comes from the eyes. Furthermore, in interpersonal situations, the focus of the interaction partner primarily lies on the eye region of the other person. A plethora of research is available on the processing of eye gaze to fully visible stimuli (Kleinke, 1986; Macrae, Hood, Milne, Rowe, & Mason, 2002; Senju & Johnson, 2009b). The well-established 'stare-in-the crowd' effect, the phenomenon that attention is captured more strongly by people looking directly at another person (direct gaze) compared to an averted gaze, has been replicated several times (Senju & Hasegawa, 2006; von Grünau & Anston, 1995). More than a century ago, in 1898, the psychologist Edward Titchener, reported on the "feeling of being stared at", the "prickling" at the nape of the neck that is a consequence of a person's gaze being directed at us (Titchener, 1898). Thus, it seems as though humans are perceptive to the gaze of another person even before becoming completely aware of it. This next section will discuss work that has been done on the unconscious processing of single facial features, specifically eye gaze.

Humans are very sensitive to the information conveyed by the eyes of another person. This sensitivity seems to begin very early in development with already 7-month-old infants showing discriminatory responses to fearful and non-fearful eyes and to direct and averted gaze stimuli presented below the perceptual threshold (Jessen & Grossmann, 2014). These discriminatory effects also persist later in development with adults showing similar responses, i.e. a privileged access to awareness for faces with direct in comparison to averted gaze (Chen & Yeh, 2012; Stein, Senju, Peelen, & Sterzer, 2011). Interestingly, not only do faces with direct gaze gain privileged access to awareness, they also capture attention and bias eye movements outside of awareness (Rothkirch, Madipakkam, Rehn, & Sterzer, 2015). This bias to direct gaze is not restricted to behavior but is also observed at the neural level. For example, Burra and colleagues showed amygdala activation to direct gaze in a cortically blind patient (Burra, Hervais-Adelman, Kerzel, Tamietto, de Gelder, & Pegna, 2013). Similarly, direct gaze elicited larger neural responses than an averted gaze when suppressed from awareness (Yokoyama, Noguchi, & Kita, 2013). More recently, it was shown that faces with direct gaze required less neural activity to enter awareness than faces with an averted gaze,

Social information processing **101**

suggesting a more efficient neural coding of direct gaze (Madipakkam, Rothkirch, Guggenmos, Heinz, & Sterzer, 2015).

While direct gaze indicates that the receiver (observer) of the gaze is the focus of interest for the sender, an averted gaze on the other hand indicates to the observer that there is interesting information somewhere else in the environment. Following the gaze of another person results in shifts in attention that are thought to be automatic and reflexive (Driver, Davis, Ricciardelli, Kidd, Maxwell, & Baron-Cohen, 1999; Langton, Watt, & Bruce, 2000). This gaze-evoked shift in attention or joint attention is pivotal for typical social development and is well investigated with fully visible gaze cues in infants and adults alike (Frischen, Bayliss, & Tipper, 2007). Using schematic faces that were presented subliminally with the help of backward masking, Sato, Okada, and Toichi (2007) showed that participants were faster to respond to targets appearing congruent to the subliminally presented gaze cue, suggesting that the gaze cues triggered shifts in attention without awareness. Since then, a number of studies have followed, providing evidence for an unconscious processing of averted gaze. For example, objects looked at by subliminal gaze cues were detected faster and more preferred than those that were not looked at by the gaze cue (Mitsuda & Masaki, 2018) and such unconscious shifts in attention were present even under high perceptual load (Xu, Zhang, & Geng, 2011). These unconscious attentional shifts were also investigated at the neural level and were found to activate bilateral subcortical structures, including the superior colliculus and amygdala, and the middle temporal and inferior frontal gyri in the right hemisphere (Sato, Kochiyama, Uono, & Toichi, 2016).

The anatomical areas involved in processing eye gaze are well known and include a core system consisting of occipitotemporal lobe regions like the fusiform face area (FFA), superior temporal sulcus (STS), and the intraparietal sulcus (IPS), as well as an extended system which includes the amygdala (Haxby, Hoffman, & Gobbini, 2002; Nummenmaa & Calder, 2009). However, the exact role of the amygdala in processing gaze direction is still debated. While a study in patients with amygdala lesions showed reduced attentional orienting to gaze cues (Akiyama, Kato, Muramatsu, Umeda, Saito, & Kashima, 2007), a single cell recording study reported that the amygdala neurons encoded face identity rather than gaze direction itself (Mormann, Niediek, Tudusciuc, Quesada, Coenen, Elger, & Adolphs, 2015). Furthermore, what is even less clear is the way in which these anatomical areas respond to a specific gaze direction. Some studies report an increased neural activity to direct vs. averted gaze (Burra et al., 2013; George, Driver, & Dolan, 2001; Pelphrey, Viola, & McCarthy, 2004) whereas others report an enhanced neural activity in these same regions to an averted gaze (Sato et al., 2016). Thus, it is evident that, when comparing or summarizing results from different studies, several factors that could influence the results need to be accounted for. First, the stimuli used play an important role in determining what exactly is being processed. Some studies use only images of the eyes (Jessen & Grossmann, 2014), some use schematic faces (Chen & Yeh, 2012), some use full face images (Rothkirch et al., 2015; Stein et al., 2011; Yokoyama et al., 2013) or even dynamic face stimuli (Pelphrey et al., 2004; Schilbach, Wohlschlaeger,

Kraemer, Newen, Shah, Fink, & Vogeley, 2006). However, even between the studies using face images, there is another confound, namely the eye white. The human eye is unique with its prominent white sclera that facilitates social interactions (Tomasello, Hare, Lehmann, & Call, 2007). In studies that do not control for the low-level confounds like contrast or the eye whites between the conditions, it remains unknown what exactly is being processed outside of awareness and becomes difficult to interpret the results. One elegant way of overcoming the confound between eye whites and gaze direction is by rotating the head. These head-rotated stimuli then differ only in the direction of their eye gaze by shifting only the pupils in the iris of the eye. Such stimuli were first used in studies investigating responses to direct gaze in consciously presented stimuli (Senju & Hasegawa, 2006) but have also been increasingly used in a number of studies investigating the unconscious processing of gaze direction (Madipakkam et al., 2015; Rothkirch et al., 2015; Stein et al., 2011). Secondly, a common and more general concern in all studies investigating unconscious processing is the kind of masking used and the interaction between the mask and the stimuli. For example, Straube, Dietrich, Mothes-Lasch, Mentzel, and Miltner (2010) observed an increased activation of the amygdala to subliminally presented fearful vs. happy eyes but only when the masks used were also faces, suggesting that the increased activations could be an interaction between the fearful eyes and the masks or parts of the mask rather than to the eyes alone. Lastly, the task of the participant, i.e. whether gaze directions are task relevant or whether participants perform an independent task, could also play a role in the extent to which the information is processed and contribute to a discrepancy between studies.

Given the factors discussed above, the important question is to what extent the results observed in the lab regarding social attention can be generalized to a real-world context. Although this is particularly hard to investigate for unconscious processing, progress has been made in experiments using fully visible stimuli. The biggest criticism of lab-based experiments investigating social attention is that they are performed in isolation without any real context and with preselected stimuli. For instance, the perception of eye gaze can interact with the perception of the emotional expression, biasing the interpretation of these social cues, or at least rendering them less ambiguous (Lobmaier, Tiddeman, & Perrett, 2008; Milders, Hietanen, Leppänen, & Braun, 2011). Furthermore, in a typical social interaction, the eyes simultaneously act as signals (provide information to the observer) and channels (collect information from the observer) (Argyle & Cook, 1976). Recently, Hayward and colleagues showed that while the overall results between a real-world social attention task and a lab-based task were similar, the congruence between the two environments was low in single individuals. These results suggest that what is measured during the cuing procedure in a lab is indeed vastly different from the corresponding measure of social attention in a real-world interaction, probably due to the lack of a larger social context and the presence of a live agent (Hayward, Voorhies, Morris, Capozzi, & Ristic, 2017). Thus, in order to bring about comparable, generalizable results, future lab-based studies should keep in mind the type of stimuli used, the context, and the possibility to involve both the encoding

Social information processing **103**

and signaling functions of social attention by manipulating the potential for social interaction in the absence of a live agent (Nussenbaum & Amso, 2016; Pfeiffer, Schilbach, Timmermans, Kuzmanovic, Georgescu, Bente, & Vogeley, 2014).

Finally, while the eye region can be seen as the most relevant and defining feature of a face, there are also other features that play a role for the transmission of social signals. Especially for the recognition of emotions or verbal communication, attention to the mouth region is equally important. There is evidence that the congruence between lip movements and spoken words facilitates awareness of a face (Alsius & Munhall, 2013) or can even be processed unconsciously (Plass, Guzman-Martinez, Ortega, Grabowecky, & Suzuki, 2014), suggesting some form of audiovisual integration without awareness. However, research specifically focusing on the unconscious processing of the mouth region is still nascent. Moreover, what has to be taken into account is that the visual masking of dynamic stimuli, as in the case of lip movements, poses a greater challenge than masking static stimuli (Moors, Wagemans, & de-Wit, 2014).

5 A beautiful mind

Thus far, the chapter has focused on the extent to which social information is processed outside of awareness in neurotypical individuals. This next section will focus on the relevance of unconscious social information processing in psychiatry. The literature is rich with studies investigating the unconscious processing of social information in a range of psychiatric and neurodevelopmental disorders including autism spectrum disorder (ASD), anxiety, major depressive disorder, antisocial personality disorder, and schizophrenia, to name a few (see review: Taschereau-Dumouchel, Liu, & Lau, 2018b). Given that these disorders manifest themselves differently, they also affect the processing of social stimuli outside of awareness in different ways. The important question however is how do abnormalities in the unconscious processing in patients with psychiatric disorders lead to a better understanding of these disorders?

Broadly speaking, we could say that there are two ways in which the unconscious processing in patients with psychiatric disorders could aid the understanding of these diseases. For some disorders, impairments in responses to social signals are a "by-product" of the disorder. For example, in major depressive disorder (MDD), cognitive theories suggest that negative biases affect most cognitive processes including perception. In line with this, Sterzer, Hilgenfeldt, Freudenberg, Bermpohl, and Adli, (2011) showed that participants with MDD required less time to process sad faces that were initially suppressed compared to happy faces suppressed from awareness, suggesting altered emotion processing at automatic processing stages (but see Münkler, Rothkirch, Dalati, Schmack, & Sterzer, 2015). Similarly, people with schizophrenia suffer from a range of social-cognitive deficits including disturbances in the processing of affective and eye gaze information (see review Green & Horan, 2010). Specifically with respect to the processing of affective information, people with schizophrenia are capable of appropriately contracting their facial muscles in response to emotional stimuli (Kring, Kerr, & Earnst, 1999; Varcin, Bailey, & Henry, 2010), yet on their own do not outwardly exhibit many emotional expressions (Kring & Moran, 2008). Regarding the processing of eye gaze information, individuals with schizophrenia spend less time spontaneously scanning the eye region of others' faces (Green & Phillips, 2004) and tend to incorrectly judge an averted gaze as being direct (Hooker & Park, 2005; Rosse, Kendrick, Wyatt, Isaac, & Deutsch, 1994). Quite surprisingly, despite these deficits at the conscious level and in explicit judgement tasks, people with schizophrenia have an intact unconscious processing of eye gaze information (Seymour, Rhodes, Stein, & Langdon, 2016). In other words, the preferential processing of direct gaze compared to an averted gaze outside of awareness, commonly observed in neurotypical individuals, was also observed in patients with schizophrenia. Furthermore, both neurotypicals and individuals with schizophrenia rated neutral faces presented simultaneously with a subliminal smiling face as more warm and trustworthy than when presented with a subliminal scowling face (Kring, Siegel, & Barrett, 2014) and rated Chinese ideographs as more negative when primed subliminally with a sad face than with a neutral face (Suslow, Roestel, & Arolt, 2003). Together, these studies suggest intact early information processing in people with schizophrenia. Thus, in contrast to MDD, social cognitive deficits in schizophrenia are more a deficit in integrating information with the semantic context rather than a deficit in perception per se.

While on the one hand, impairments in responses to social signals may be a consequence of the disorder, on the other, psychiatric disorders like autism spectrum disorder (ASD), social phobia, and antisocial personality disorder are characterized by dysfunctional social responses. For instance, the atypical responses to eye contact which manifest as an avoidance of direct gaze and difficulties in social interactions are the key defining characteristics of autism spectrum disorder. These atypical responses to eye contact in ASD seem to be affected at the early stages of information processing. While typically developed adults preferentially process direct in comparison to averted gaze outside of awareness (Rothkirch et al., 2015; Stein et al., 2011), adults with ASD show no such preference towards unconsciously presented faces with direct gaze (Akechi, Stein, Senju, Kikuchi, Tojo, Osanai, & Hasegawa, 2014; Madipakkam, Rothkirch, Dziobek, & Sterzer, 2017). These atypical responses extend to consciously presented face stimuli as well (Senju & Johnson, 2009a). It is interesting to note however that, like TD individuals, individuals with ASD also showed shorter suppression durations for upright "proto face" stimuli (Akechi, Stein, Kikuchi, Tojo, Osanai, & Hasegawa, 2015). Consequently, the non-typical responses seem to arise with more natural and complex social stimuli. It is plausible that "proto face" stimuli therefore do not activate the social network that is impaired in ASD. Like ASD, antisocial personality disorder is also characterized by impaired social responses. It manifests as persistent antisocial behavior and impaired empathy. In contrast to neurotypical individuals, antisocial violent offenders do not show the typical prioritized processing of fearful faces presented outside of awareness (Jusyte, Mayer, Künzel, Hautzinger, & Schönenberg, 2015).

Thus, the social and emotional processing deficits are present at very early stages of information processing.

Independent of what the atypical response is, in order to understand the disorder better, the goal is to understand the underlying neural mechanism. According to one theory, most unconscious processing is thought to rely on lower-level brain circuits involving the subcortical structures via magnocellular channels (Tamietto & de Gelder, 2010). Whether subcortical input alone is sufficient in processing unconscious stimuli is still a matter of debate (as already noted). With several studies showing an activation of subcortical structures to social stimuli in the absence of awareness in neurotypical adults (Burra et al., 2013; Whalen et al., 1998), and a failure to activate the same structures to subliminally presented face stimuli in ASD participants (Kleinhans, Richards, Johnson, Weaver, Greenson, Dawson, & Aylward, 2011), this argument is not without its support. However, accumulating competing evidence of cortical contributions to unconscious processing also exists (Lin & He, 2009; Hesselmann, Hebart, & Malach, 2011). One way to distinguish between the cortical and subcortical pathway is spatial frequency. While cortical structures like the fusiform face area favor high spatial frequency information regardless of the emotion of the face stimulus, the amygdala, a subcortical structure, favors low spatial frequency information (Johnson, 2005; Lin & He, 2009). Specifically, the magnocellular pathway is crucial in this transfer of low spatial frequency to the amygdala (Adolphs & Spezio, 2006; Gamer & Büchel, 2009). In typical development, the sensitivity to social cues develops rapidly through the magnocellular system (Nation & Penny, 2008). In ASD however, neurodevelopmental abnormalities in the magnocellular cells lead to disruptions in the brain networks involved in social information processing which could result in the decreased saliency to eye gaze information and social cues (Senju & Johnson, 2009a). Thus, the observed atypical responses to eye gaze and social information presented outside of awareness in ASD could reflect a basic deficit in the magnocellular pathway. In schizophrenia, however, while on the one hand evidence suggests that low spatial frequency information (magnocellular processing) may be affected (Butler, Zemon, Schechter, Saperstein, Hoptman, Lim, . . . & Javitt, 2005; Martínez, Hillyard, Dias, Hagler, Butler, Guilfoyle, . . . Javitt, 2008), on the other, early affective information processing is intact (Kring et al., 2014). This seems to suggest that there are conditions under which magnocellular processing may indeed be intact in schizophrenia. Affective processing deficits in schizophrenia are therefore more likely to be a deficit in high level processing, i.e. integrating information with respect to the context, rather than a deficit in early processing pathways.

Insofar as research in diagnosed clinical populations can provide insights into the early processing mechanisms and deficits in these populations, most psychiatric disorders are a spectrum, with traits extending into the typical population. In this context, an interesting question is to what extent automatic, atypical responses to social information presented outside of awareness (which are not under cognitive control of the individual) may even contribute to the development or manifestation of the disease. There are several studies in neurotypicals investigating different traits that show a relationship between the processing of information outside of awareness and the strength of the trait. For example, increasing autistic-like traits were associated with an increased time to process suppressed faces with direct gaze in neurotypical adults (Madipakkam, Rothkirch, Dziobek, & Sterzer, 2019). Similar results were also found in anxiety (Capitão, Underdown, Vile, Yang, Harmer, & Murphy, 2014) and psychopathy (Sylvers, Brennan, & Lilienfeld, 2011; Viding, Sebastian, Dadds, Lockwood, Cecil, De Brito, & McCrory, 2012). In anxiety, participants with an increased trait anxiety score had a faster processing of threat stimuli (Capitão et al., 2014; Sylvers et al., 2011; Viding et al., 2012). In psychopathy, impairments in recognizing danger (fear) are characteristic of the callous-unemotional trait. In support of this fearlessness hypothesis, neurotypical children with higher callous-unemotional scores also took longer to process fearful faces that were suppressed from awareness (Sylvers et al., 2011). Furthermore, boys with high callousness-unemotional traits compared with low callous-unemotional traits showed a hypoactivation of the amygdala to backward masked fearful vs. calm faces (Viding et al., 2012). Thus, the extent to which the early processing of social information is influenced by such traits could be relevant for the development of appropriate therapeutic interventions and could lead to the early detection of these disorders in individuals with high risk. For example, a recent study by Elsabbagh, Mercure, Hudry, Chandler, Pasco, Charman, . . . & BASIS Team (2012) demonstrated that the neural responses to eye gaze in typically developing infants predicted the later development of autism. On a related note, Taschereau-Dumouchel and colleagues have developed a promising new treatment option for anxiety disorders using unconscious neural reinforcement or Decoded Neurofeedback (DecNef) which could be extended to other psychiatric disorders (Taschereau-Dumouchel et al., 2018b; Watanabe, Sasaki, Shibata, & Kawato, 2017). In this method, participants' neural patterns representing specific content, for example, spiders for spider phobic individuals is paired simultaneously with reward. Thus, the valence of the negative stimulus is reduced via associative learning (Koizumi, Amano, Cortese, Shibata, Yoshida, Seymour, . . . & Lau, 2016; Taschereau-Dumouchel, Cortese, Chiba, Knotts, Kawato, & Lau, 2018a). The major advantage of such a fully unconscious intervention is its potential use in double-blind placebo-controlled studies and the lower number of dropouts as participants are exposed to stimuli that they might consciously find stressful. However, such an unconscious presentation of aversive stimuli necessitates clear ethical standards.

6 Conclusion

While a face in itself is already a salient stimulus, facial characteristics like an emotional expression or the direction of eye gaze additionally convey information so that the observer can immediately judge whether, for instance, the counterpart is hostile or sympathetic. The unconscious processing of such information could save valuable time in preparing a suitable reaction. In the preceding sections, we have discussed to what extent the processing of socially relevant information in a face can indeed occur in the absence of awareness. In the following, we will draw a conclusion by integrating these findings and point out further methodological considerations.

6.1 Which social information is processed unconsciously?

The depth of face processing that is required to recognize social information depends on the type of information. The affective value of faces acquired through conditioning, for instance, can only be discriminated based on the identity of the faces. For the discrimination of direct versus averted gaze, in contrast, the processing of the eye region suffices. This implies that the influence of subliminal facial features, like eye gaze, can take effect based on unconscious processes operating on a smaller spatial scale. As holistic face processing, like the processing of one's identity, at least partly rests on the processing of the different facial parts (Piepers & Robbins, 2012), the different types of social information can be ordered according to their complexity. Based on the evidence that we have reviewed in the previous sections, it is reasonable to assume that the effects of the unconscious processing of social information decrease with an increasing level of complexity. This view is bolstered by ample evidence showing that holistic face processing is virtually abolished under unawareness (Amihai, Deouell, & Bentin, 2011; Axelrod & Rees, 2014; Moradi, Koch, & Shimojo, 2005; Stein & Sterzer, 2011). In Figure 4.1, we present a graphical depiction of this view.

6.2 The role of the amygdala

As we have seen in the previous sections, the amygdala is deeply involved in the processing of social information, including emotional expressions and eye gaze. However, there are opposing views on the role of this region in situations where the social information does not reach consciousness. It is rather questionable whether the amygdala is indeed the primary detector of unconsciously presented socially relevant information (see the section on the unconscious processing of emotional information for further details). Palermo and Rhodes (2007) provide an alternative view that be might help to reconcile the inconsistent findings in the literature regarding the importance of this region. The amygdala might not

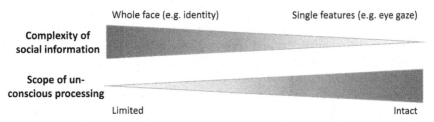

FIGURE 4.1 Possible relation between the complexity of social information and the scope of unconscious processing.

be responsible for the initial detection and discrimination of social information. Instead, it might "tag" visual input that has already been processed by other regions as relevant for the individual, so that further processing resources can be made available for a deeper analysis of this information. It has yet to be clarified which other regions could be responsible for the initial detection of unconscious social information in the environment, but the FFA might be a candidate region for this (Ludwig, Kathmann, Sterzer, & Hesselmann, 2015; Sterzer, Haynes, & Rees, 2008). This notion also fits nicely with an interesting observation in a patient with bilateral amygdala damage (Adolphs, Gosselin, Buchanan, Tranel, Schyns, & Damasio, 2005) who showed an impairment in her recognition of facial expressions. However, after clear verbal instructions to focus on the eyes, her recognition performance improved. This case demonstrates that the social information was still processed despite the damage to the amygdala, but that a part of this information, that is the eyes, was not automatically recognized as relevant any more.

6.3 Methodological considerations

From a methodological point of view, the investigation of unconscious processes is a minefield, especially with respect to the efforts that have to be made to ensure that participants are truly unaware of the critical stimuli. This becomes apparent from the large heterogeneity of approaches to measure awareness and the criticism of these measures (Rothkirch & Hesselmann, 2017). Although the prevailing opinion is that bias-free measures of awareness are essential to make claims about participants' unawareness, another important aspect is the way these measures are used. As pointed out by several authors (Lovibond & Shanks, 2002; Sterzer, Stein, Ludwig, Rothkirch, & Hesselmann, 2014), awareness measures should be tailored to the stimulus feature that is investigated. If, for instance, participants are unable to discriminate the gender of masked faces, they are not necessarily unaware of the emotional expression of these faces. Admittedly, the way awareness measures can be implemented can be limited by the experimental design. Nevertheless, one should be aware that a certain proportion of the differences in the outcomes between studies could likely be traced back to variations in the use of awareness measures.

Another methodological aspect that should be considered for the interpretation of the findings reported in this chapter is the technique used to suppress stimuli from awareness. The most popular techniques are backward masking, continuous flash suppression, and crowding, which should not be seen as interchangeable. Instead, it has been proposed that such techniques form a functional hierarchy regarding the type of visual information that is unconsciously processed (Breitmeyer, 2015; Breitmeyer & Hesselmann, Chapter 3 in this volume). As has been demonstrated, such differences between masking techniques also specifically exist for the unconscious processing of faces (Faivre, Berthet, & Kouider, 2012; Izatt, Dubois, Faivre, & Koch, 2014).

6.4 The essence is in the details

In sum, a lot of progress has been made in the last decade with respect to the investigation of the unconscious processing of social stimuli. One important point to keep in mind when comparing studies is that small sample sizes lead to underpowered studies with low reproducibility of results, a crisis in research for well over a decade (Button, Ioannidis, Mokrysz, Nosek, Flint, Robinson, & Munafò, 2013; Maxwell, 2004). Furthermore, in clinical studies, most participants are under the influence of psychotropic medication, which could affect their performance in the investigated tasks. Lastly, given that most psychiatric disorders lie on a spectrum, the severity of the disorder and the number of years a person has had the disorder could also influence the way they process social information. With modern cognitive neuroscience methods and the fascinating possibility of using an unconscious intervention in anxiety, hope for new therapy options for other psychiatric disorders do not seem so far away.

References

Adams, W. J., Gray, K. L. H., Garner, M., & Graf, E. W. (2010). High-level face adaptation without awareness. *Psychological Science, 21*(2), 205–10.

Adolphs, R., Gosselin, F., Buchanan, T. W., Tranel, D., Schyns, P., & Damasio, A. R. (2005). A mechanism for impaired fear recognition after amygdala damage. *Nature, 433*(7021), 68–72.

Adolphs, R., & Spezio, M. (2006). Role of the amygdala in processing visual social stimuli. *Progress in Brain Research, 156*, 363–78.

Akechi, H., Stein, T., Kikuchi, Y., Tojo, Y., Osanai, H., & Hasegawa, T. (2015). Preferential awareness of protofacial stimuli in autism. *Cognition, 143*, 129–34.

Akechi, H., Stein, T., Senju, A., Kikuchi, Y., Tojo, Y., Osanai, H., & Hasegawa, T. (2014). Absence of preferential unconscious processing of eye contact in adolescents with autism spectrum disorder. *Autism Research, 7*(5), 590–7.

Akiyama, T., Kato, M., Muramatsu, T., Umeda, S., Saito, F., & Kashima, H. (2007). Unilateral amygdala lesions hamper attentional orienting triggered by gaze direction. *Cerebral Cortex, 17*(11), 2593–2600.

Almeida, J., Pajtas, P. E., Mahon, B. Z., Nakayama, K., & Caramazza, A. (2013). Affect of the unconscious: Visually suppressed angry faces modulate our decisions. *Cognitive, Affective and Behavioral Neuroscience, 13*(1), 94–101.

Alsius, A., & Munhall, K. G. (2013). Detection of audiovisual speech correspondences without visual awareness. *Psychological Science, 24*(4), 423–31.

Amihai, I., Deouell, L., & Bentin, S. (2011). Conscious awareness is necessary for processing race and gender information from faces. *Consciousness and Cognition, 20*(2), 269–79.

Anderson, E., Siegel, E. H., Bliss-Moreau, E., & Barrett, L. F. (2011). The visual impact of gossip. *Science, 332*(6036), 1446–8.

Anderson, E., Siegel, E., White, D., & Barrett, L. F. (2012). Out of sight but not out of mind: Unseen affective faces influence evaluations and social impressions. *Emotion, 12*(6), 1210–21.

Argyle, M., & Cook, M. (1976). *Gaze and Mutual Gaze*. Cambridge: Cambridge University Press.

Aviezer, H., Trope, Y., & Todorov, A. (2012). Body cues, not facial expressions, discriminate between intense positive and negative emotions. *Science, 338*(6111), 1225–9.

Axelrod, V., & Rees, G. (2014). Conscious awareness is required for holistic face processing. *Consciousness and Cognition, 27*, 233–45.

Breitmeyer, B. G. (2015). Psychophysical "blinding" methods reveal a functional hierarchy of unconscious visual processing. *Consciousness and Cognition, 35*, 234–50.

Brooks, S. J., Savov, V., Allzén, E., Benedict, C., Fredriksson, R., & Schiöth, H. B. (2012). Exposure to subliminal arousing stimuli induces robust activation in the amygdala, hippocampus, anterior cingulate, insular cortex and primary visual cortex: A systematic meta-analysis of fMRI studies. *NeuroImage, 59*(3), 2962–73.

Bunce, S. C., Bernat, E., Wong, P. S., & Shevrin, H. (1999). Further evidence for unconscious learning: Preliminary support for the conditioning of facial EMG to subliminal stimuli. *Journal of Psychiatric Research, 33*(4), 341–7.

Burra, N., Hervais-Adelman, A., Kerzel, D., Tamietto, M., de Gelder, B., & Pegna, A. J. (2013). Amygdala activation for eye contact despite complete cortical blindness. *Journal of Neuroscience, 33*(25), 10483–9.

Butler, P. D., Zemon, V., Schechter, I., Saperstein, A. M., Hoptman, M. J., Lim, K. O., . . . Javitt, D. C. (2005). Early-stage visual processing and cortical amplification deficits in schizophrenia. *Archives of General Psychiatry, 62*(5), 495–504.

Button, K. S., Ioannidis, J. P. A., Mokrysz, C., Nosek, B. A., Flint, J., Robinson, E. S. J., & Munafò, M. R. (2013). Power failure: Why small sample size undermines the reliability of neuroscience. *Nature Reviews Neuroscience, 14*(5), 365–76.

Capitão, L. P., Underdown, S. J. V., Vile, S., Yang, E., Harmer, C. J., & Murphy, S. E. (2014). Anxiety increases breakthrough of threat stimuli in continuous flash suppression. *Emotion, 14*(6), 1027–36.

Carlson, J. M., & Reinke, K. S. (2008). Masked fearful faces modulate the orienting of covert spatial attention. *Emotion, 8*(4), 522–9.

Cauchoix, M., & Crouzet, S. M. (2013). How plausible is a subcortical account of rapid visual recognition? *Frontiers in Human Neuroscience, 7*, 39.

Chen, Y.-C., & Yeh, S.-L. (2012). Look into my eyes and I will see you: Unconscious processing of human gaze. *Consciousness and Cognition, 21*(4), 1703–10.

Chiesa, P. A., Liuzza, M. T., Acciarino, A., & Aglioti, S. M. (2015). Subliminal perception of others' physical pain and pleasure. *Experimental Brain Research, 233*(8), 2373–82.

Clark, R. E., Manns, J. R., & Squire, L. R. (2002). Classical conditioning, awareness, and brain systems. *Trends in Cognitive Sciences, 6*(12), 524–31.

Driver, J., IV, Davis, G., Ricciardelli, P., Kidd, P., Maxwell, E., & Baron-Cohen, S. (1999). Gaze perception triggers reflexive visuospatial orienting. *Visual Cognition, 6*(5), 509–40.

Elsabbagh, M., Mercure, E., Hudry, K., Chandler, S., Pasco, G., Charman, T., . . . BASIS Team (2012). Infant neural sensitivity to dynamic eye gaze is associated with later emerging autism. *Current Biology, 22*(4), 338–42.

Eriksen, C. W. (1960). Discrimination and learning without awareness: A methodological survey and evaluation. *Psychological Review, 67*, 279–300.

Esteves, F., Parra, C., Dimberg, U., & Ohman, A. (1994). Nonconscious associative learning: Pavlovian conditioning of skin conductance responses to masked fear-relevant facial stimuli. *Psychophysiology, 31*(4), 375–85.

Faivre, N., Berthet, V., & Kouider, S. (2012). Nonconscious influences from emotional faces: A comparison of visual crowding, masking, and continuous flash suppression. *Frontiers in Psychology, 3*, 129.

Fernández-Dols, J.-M., & Crivelli, C. (2013). Emotion and expression: Naturalistic studies. *Emotion Review, 5*(1), 24–9.

Freeman, J. B., Stolier, R. M., Ingbretsen, Z. A., & Hehman, E. A. (2014). Amygdala responsivity to high-level social information from unseen faces. *Journal of Neuroscience, 34*(32), 10573–81.

Frischen, A., Bayliss, A. P., & Tipper, S. P. (2007). Gaze cueing of attention: Visual attention, social cognition, and individual differences. *Psychological Bulletin, 133*(4), 694–724.

Gamer, M., & Büchel, C. (2009). Amygdala activation predicts gaze toward fearful eyes. *Journal of Neuroscience, 29*(28), 9123–6.

George, N., Driver, J., & Dolan, R. J. (2001). Seen gaze-direction modulates fusiform activity and its coupling with other brain areas during face processing. *NeuroImage, 13*(6/1), 1102–12.

Golkar, A., & Öhman, A. (2012). Fear extinction in humans: Effects of acquisition-extinction delay and masked stimulus presentations. *Biological Psychology, 91*(2), 292–301.

Gray, K. L. H., Adams, W. J., Hedger, N., Newton, K. E., & Garner, M. (2013). Faces and awareness: Low-level, not emotional factors determine perceptual dominance. *Emotion, 13*(3), 537–44.

Green, M. F., & Horan, W. P. (2010). Social Cognition in Schizophrenia. *Current Directions in Psychological Science, 19*(4), 243–8.

Green, M. J., & Phillips, M. L. (2004). Social threat perception and the evolution of paranoia. *Neuroscience and Biobehavioral Reviews, 28*(3), 333–42.

Han, S., Lunghi, C., & Alais, D. (2016). The temporal frequency tuning of continuous flash suppression reveals peak suppression at very low frequencies. *Scientific Reports, 6*, 35723.

Harris, D. A., & Ciaramitaro, V. M. (2016). Interdependent mechanisms for processing gender and emotion: The special status of angry male faces. *Frontiers in Psychology, 7*.

Haxby, J. V., Hoffman, E. A., & Gobbini, M. I. (2002). Human neural systems for face recognition and social communication. *Biological Psychiatry, 51*(1), 59–67.

Hayward, D. A., Voorhies, W., Morris, J. L., Capozzi, F., & Ristic, J. (2017). Staring reality in the face: A comparison of social attention across laboratory and real world measures suggests little common ground. *Canadian Journal of Experimental Psychology, 71*(3), 212–25.

Hedger, N., Adams, W. J., & Garner, M. (2015). Fearful faces have a sensory advantage in the competition for awareness. *Journal of Experimental Psychology: Human Perception and Performance, 41*(6), 1748–57.

Hedger, N., Gray, K. L. H., Garner, M., & Adams, W. J. (2016). Are visual threats prioritized without awareness? A critical review and meta-analysis involving 3 behavioral paradigms and 2696 observers. *Psychological Bulletin, 142*(9), 934–68.

Hesselmann, G., Hebart, M., & Malach, R. (2011). Differential BOLD activity associated with subjective and objective reports during "blindsight" in normal observers. *Journal of Neuroscience, 31*(36), 12936–44.

Hofmann, W., De Houwer, J., Perugini, M., Baeyens, F., & Crombez, G. (2010). Evaluative conditioning in humans: A meta-analysis. *Psychological Bulletin, 136*(3), 390–421.

Holender, D. (1986). Semantic activation without conscious identification in dichotic listening, parafoveal vision, and visual masking: A survey and appraisal. *Behavioral and Brain Sciences, 9*(1), 1–23.

Hooker, C., & Park, S. (2005). You must be looking at me: The nature of gaze perception in schizophrenia patients. *Cognitive Neuropsychiatry, 10*(5), 327–45.

Hung, S.-M., Nieh, C.-H., & Hsieh, P.-J. (2016). Unconscious processing of facial attractiveness: Invisible attractive faces orient visual attention. *Scientific Reports, 6*, 37117.

Izatt, G., Dubois, J., Faivre, N., & Koch, C. (2014). A direct comparison of unconscious face processing under masking and interocular suppression. *Frontiers in Psychology, 5*, 659.

Jessen, S., & Grossmann, T. (2014). Unconscious discrimination of social cues from eye whites in infants. *Proceedings of the National Academy of Sciences USA, 111*(45), 16208–13.

Johnson, M. H. (2005). Subcortical face processing. *Nature Reviews. Neuroscience, 6*(10), 766–74.

Jusyte, A., Mayer, S. V., Künzel, E., Hautzinger, M., & Schönenberg, M. (2015). Unemotional traits predict early processing deficit for fearful expressions in young violent offenders: An investigation using continuous flash suppression. *Psychological Medicine, 45*(2), 285–97.

Kaiser, J., Davey, G. C. L., Parkhouse, T., Meeres, J., & Scott, R. B. (2016). Emotional facial activation induced by unconsciously perceived dynamic facial expressions. *International Journal of Psychophysiology, 110*, 207–11.

Kleckner, I. R., Anderson, E. C., Betz, N. J., Wormwood, J. B., Eskew, R. T., & Barrett, L. F. (2018). Conscious awareness is necessary for affective faces to influence social judgments. *Journal of Experimental Social Psychology, 79*, 181–7.

Kleinhans, N. M., Richards, T., Johnson, L. C., Weaver, K. E., Greenson, J., Dawson, G., & Aylward, E. (2011). fMRI evidence of neural abnormalities in the subcortical face processing system in ASD. *NeuroImage, 54*(1), 697–704.

Kleinke, C. L. (1986). Gaze and eye contact: A research review. *Psychological Bulletin, 100*(1), 78–100.

Koizumi, A., Amano, K., Cortese, A., Shibata, K., Yoshida, W., Seymour, B., . . . & Lau, H. (2016). Fear reduction without fear through reinforcement of neural activity that bypasses conscious exposure. *Nature Human Behaviour, 1*.

Korb, S., Osimo, S. A., Suran, T., Goldstein, A., & Rumiati, R. I. (2017). Face proprioception does not modulate access to visual awareness of emotional faces in a continuous flash suppression paradigm. *Consciousness and Cognition, 51*, 166–80.

Kouider, S., Berthet, V., & Faivre, N. (2011). Preference is biased by crowded facial expressions. *Psychological Science, 22*(2), 184–9.

Kring, A. M., Kerr, S. L., & Earnst, K. S. (1999). Schizophrenic patients show facial reactions to emotional facial expressions. *Psychophysiology, 36*(2), 186–92.

Kring, A. M., & Moran, E. K. (2008). Emotional response deficits in schizophrenia: Insights from affective science. *Schizophrenia Bulletin, 34*(5), 819–34.

Kring, A. M., Siegel, E. H., & Barrett, L. F. (2014). Unseen affective faces influence person perception judgments in schizophrenia. *Clinical Psychological Science, 2*(4), 443–54.

Kunimoto, C., Miller, J., & Pashler, H. (2001). Confidence and accuracy of near-threshold discrimination responses. *Consciousness and Cognition, 10*(3), 294–340.

Lähteenmäki, M., Hyönä, J., Koivisto, M., & Nummenmaa, L. (2015). Affective processing requires awareness. *Journal of Experimental Psychology: General, 144*(2), 339–65.

Landis, C. (1929). The interpretation of facial expression in emotion. *Journal of General Psychology, 2*(1), 59–72.

Langton, S. R., Watt, R. J., & Bruce, V. (2000). Do the eyes have it? Cues to the direction of social attention. *Trends in Cognitive Sciences, 4*(2), 50–9.

LeDoux, J. (1998). *The Emotional Brain: The Mysterious Underpinnings of Emotional Life.* New York: Simon & Schuster.

Lin, Z., & He, S. (2009). Seeing the invisible: The scope and limits of unconscious processing in binocular rivalry. *Progress in Neurobiology, 87*(4), 195–211.

Lobmaier, J. S., Tiddeman, B. P., & Perrett, D. I. (2008). Emotional expression modulates perceived gaze direction. *Emotion, 8*(4), 573–7.

Lohse, M., & Overgaard, M. (2017). Emotional priming depends on the degree of conscious experience. *Neuropsychologia.*Online first. www.ncbi.nlm.nih.gov/pubmed/29129593

Lonsdorf, T. B., Menz, M. M., Andreatta, M., Fullana, M. A., Golkar, A., Haaker, J., . . . & Merz, C. J. (2017). Don't fear "fear conditioning": Methodological considerations for the design and analysis of studies on human fear acquisition, extinction, and return of fear. *Neuroscience and Biobehavioral Reviews*, 77, 247–85.

Lovibond, P. F., & Shanks, D. R. (2002). The role of awareness in Pavlovian conditioning: Empirical evidence and theoretical implications. *Journal of Experimental Psychology: Animal Behavior Processes*, 28(1), 3–26.

Ludwig, K., Kathmann, N., Sterzer, P., & Hesselmann, G. (2015). Investigating category- and shape-selective neural processing in ventral and dorsal visual stream under interocular suppression. *Human Brain Mapping*, 36(1), 137–49.

Macrae, C. N., Hood, B. M., Milne, A. B., Rowe, A. C., & Mason, M. F. (2002). Are you looking at me? Eye gaze and person perception. *Psychological Science*, 13(5), 460–4.

Madipakkam, A. R., Rothkirch, M., Dziobek, I., & Sterzer, P. (2017). Unconscious avoidance of eye contact in autism spectrum disorder. *Scientific Reports*, 7(1), 13378.

Madipakkam, A. R., Rothkirch, M., Dziobek, I., & Sterzer, P. (2019). Access to awareness of direct gaze is related to autistic traits. *Psychological Medicine*, 49(6), 980–6.

Madipakkam, A. R., Rothkirch, M., Guggenmos, M., Heinz, A., & Sterzer, P. (2015). Gaze Direction Modulates the Relation between Neural Responses to Faces and Visual Awareness. *Journal of Neuroscience*, 35(39), 13287–99.

Madipakkam, A. R., Rothkirch, M., Wilbertz, G., & Sterzer, P. (2016). Probing the influence of unconscious fear-conditioned visual stimuli on eye movements. *Consciousness and Cognition*, 46, 60–70.

Martínez, A., Hillyard, S. A., Dias, E. C., Hagler, D. J., Butler, P. D., Guilfoyle, D. N., . . . Javitt, D. C. (2008). Magnocellular pathway impairment in schizophrenia: evidence from functional magnetic resonance imaging. *Journal of Neuroscience*, 28(30), 7492–7500.

Maxwell, J., & Davidson, R. (2004). Unequally masked: Indexing differences in the perceptual salience of "unseen" facial expressions. *Cognition and Emotion*, 18(8), 1009–26.

Maxwell, S. E. (2004). The persistence of underpowered studies in psychological research: Causes, consequences, and remedies. *Psychological Methods*, 9(2), 147–63.

Milders, M., Hietanen, J. K., Leppänen, J. M., & Braun, M. (2011). Detection of emotional faces is modulated by the direction of eye gaze. *Emotion*, 11(6), 1456–61.

Milders, M., Sahraie, A., & Logan, S. (2008). Minimum presentation time for masked facial expression discrimination. *Cognition and Emotion*, 22(1), 63–82.

Milders, M., Sahraie, A., Logan, S., & Donnellon, N. (2006). Awareness of faces is modulated by their emotional meaning. *Emotion*, 6(1), 10–17.

Mitsuda, T., & Masaki, S. (2018). Subliminal gaze cues increase preference levels for items in the gaze direction. *Cognition and Emotion*, 32(5), 1146–51.

Moors, P., Wagemans, J., & de Wit, L. (2014). Moving stimuli are less effectively masked using traditional continuous flash suppression (CFS) compared to a moving Mondrian mask (MMM): A test case for feature-selective suppression and retinotopic adaptation. *PLoS One*, 9(5), e98298.

Moradi, F., Koch, C., & Shimojo, S. (2005). Face adaptation depends on seeing the face. *Neuron*, 45(1), 169–75.

Mormann, F., Niediek, J., Tudusciuc, O., Quesada, C. M., Coenen, V. A., Elger, C. E., & Adolphs, R. (2015). Neurons in the human amygdala encode face identity, but not gaze direction. *Nature Neuroscience*, 18(11), 1568–70.

Morris, J. S., Ohman, A., & Dolan, R. J. (1998). Conscious and unconscious emotional learning in the human amygdala. *Nature*, 393(6684), 467–70.

Morris, J. S., Ohman, A., & Dolan, R. J. (1999). A subcortical pathway to the right amygdala mediating "unseen" fear. *Proceedings of the National Academy of Sciences USA, 96*(4), 1680–5.

Mumenthaler, C., & Sander, D. (2015). Automatic integration of social information in emotion recognition. *Journal of Experimental Psychology: General, 144*(2), 392–9.

Münkler, P., Rothkirch, M., Dalati, Y., Schmack, K., & Sterzer, P. (2015). Biased recognition of facial affect in patients with major depressive disorder reflects clinical state. *PLoS One, 10*(6), e0129863.

Nakamura, K., & Kawabata, H. (2018). Preferential access to awareness of attractive faces in a breaking continuous flash suppression paradigm. *Consciousness and Cognition, 65,* 71–82.

Nation, K., & Penny, S. (2008). Sensitivity to eye gaze in autism: Is it normal? Is it automatic? Is it social? *Development and Psychopathology, 20*(1), 79–97.

Nummenmaa, L., & Calder, A. J. (2009). Neural mechanisms of social attention. *Trends in Cognitive Sciences, 13*(3), 135–43.

Nussenbaum, K., & Amso, D. (2016). An attentional Goldilocks effect: An optimal amount of social interactivity promotes word learning from video. *Journal of Cognition and Development, 17*(1), 30–40.

Ohman, A., & Mineka, S. (2001). Fears, phobias, and preparedness: Toward an evolved module of fear and fear learning. *Psychological Review, 108*(3), 483–522.

Olsson, A., & Phelps, E. A. (2004). Learned fear of "unseen" faces after Pavlovian, observational, and instructed fear. *Psychological Science, 15*(12), 822–8.

Olsson, A., & Phelps, E. A. (2007). Social learning of fear. *Nature Neuroscience, 10*(9), 1095–1102.

Palermo, R., & Rhodes, G. (2007). Are you always on my mind? A review of how face perception and attention interact. *Neuropsychologia, 45*(1), 75–92.

Parra, C., Esteves, F., Flykt, A., & Öhman, A. (1997). Pavlovian conditioning to social stimuli. *European Psychologist, 2*(2), 106–17.

Pelphrey, K. A., Viola, R. J., & McCarthy, G. (2004). When strangers pass: Processing of mutual and averted social gaze in the superior temporal sulcus. *Psychological Science, 15*(9), 598–603.

Pessoa, L., & Adolphs, R. (2010). Emotion processing and the amygdala: From a "low road" to "many roads" of evaluating biological significance. *Nature Reviews Neuroscience, 11*(11), 773–83.

Pessoa, L., & Adolphs, R. (2011). Emotion and the brain: Multiple roads are better than one. *Nature Reviews Neuroscience, 12*(7), 425.

Pessoa, L., Japee, S., Sturman, D., & Ungerleider, L. G. (2006). Target visibility and visual awareness modulate amygdala responses to fearful faces. *Cerebral Cortex, 16*(3), 366–75.

Pessoa, L., Japee, S., & Ungerleider, L. G. (2005). Visual awareness and the detection of fearful faces. *Emotion, 5*(2), 243–7.

Pfeiffer, U. J., Schilbach, L., Timmermans, B., Kuzmanovic, B., Georgescu, A. L., Bente, G., & Vogeley, K. (2014). Why we interact: On the functional role of the striatum in the subjective experience of social interaction. *NeuroImage, 101,* 124–37.

Phillips, M. L., Williams, L. M., Heining, M., Herba, C. M., Russell, T., Andrew, C., . . . Gray, J. A. (2004). Differential neural responses to overt and covert presentations of facial expressions of fear and disgust. *NeuroImage, 21*(4), 1484–96.

Piech, R. M., McHugo, M., Smith, S. D., Dukic, M. S., Van der Meer, J., Abou-Khalil, B., . . . Zald, D. H. (2011). Attentional capture by emotional stimuli is preserved in patients with amygdala lesions. *Neuropsychologia, 49*(12), 3314–19.

Piepers, D. W., & Robbins, R. A. (2012). A review and clarification of the terms "holistic," "configural," and "relational" in the face perception literature. *Frontiers in Psychology, 3*, 559.

Plass, J., Guzman-Martinez, E., Ortega, L., Grabowecky, M., & Suzuki, S. (2014). Lip reading without awareness. *Psychological Science, 25*(9), 1835–7.

Rabovsky, M., Stein, T., & Abdel Rahman, R. (2016). Access to awareness for faces during continuous flash suppression is not modulated by affective knowledge. *PLoS One, 11*(4), e0150931.

Raio, C. M., Carmel, D., Carrasco, M., & Phelps, E. A. (2012). Nonconscious fear is quickly acquired but swiftly forgotten. *Current Biology, 22*(12), R477–9.

Rajananda, S., Zhu, J., & Peters, M. A. K. (2018). Normal observers show no evidence for blindsight in facial emotion perception. *BioR, xiv*, 314906. https://www.biorxiv.org/content/10.1101/314906v1

Rosse, R. B., Kendrick, K., Wyatt, R. J., Isaac, A., & Deutsch, S. I. (1994). Gaze discrimination in patients with schizophrenia: preliminary report. *American Journal of Psychiatry, 151*(6), 919–21.

Rothkirch, M., & Hesselmann, G. (2017). What we talk about when we talk about unconscious processing: A plea for best practices. *Frontiers in Psychology, 8*, 835.

Rothkirch, M., Madipakkam, A. R., Rehn, E., & Sterzer, P. (2015). Making eye contact without awareness. *Cognition, 143*, 108–14.

Saban, S., & Hugdahl, K. (1999). Nonaware classical conditioning to pictorial facial stimuli in a between-groups paradigm. *Integrative Physiological and Behavioral Science, 34*(1), 19–29.

Sato, W., Kochiyama, T., Uono, S., & Toichi, M. (2016). Neural mechanisms underlying conscious and unconscious attentional shifts triggered by eye gaze. *NeuroImage, 124*(A), 118–26.

Sato, W., Okada, T., & Toichi, M. (2007). Attentional shift by gaze is triggered without awareness. *Experimental Brain Research, 183*(1), 87–94.

Schilbach, L., Wohlschlaeger, A. M., Kraemer, N. C., Newen, A., Shah, N. J., Fink, G. R., & Vogeley, K. (2006). Being with virtual others: Neural correlates of social interaction. *Neuropsychologia, 44*(5), 718–30.

Senju, A., & Hasegawa, T. (2006). Do the upright eyes have it? *Psychonomic Bulletin and Review, 13*(2), 223–8.

Senju, A., & Johnson, M. H. (2009a). Atypical eye contact in autism: Models, mechanisms and development. *Neuroscience and Biobehavioral Reviews, 33*(8), 1204–14.

Senju, A., & Johnson, M. H. (2009b). The eye contact effect: Mechanisms and development. *Trends in Cognitive Sciences, 13*(3), 127–34.

Seymour, K., Rhodes, G., Stein, T., & Langdon, R. (2016). Intact unconscious processing of eye contact in schizophrenia. *Schizophrenia Research: Cognition, 3*, 15–19.

Stahl, C., Haaf, J., & Corneille, O. (2016). Subliminal evaluative conditioning? Above-chance CS identification may be necessary and insufficient for attitude learning. *Journal of Experimental Psychology: General, 145*(9), 1107–31.

Stein, T., & Sterzer, P. (2011). High-level face shape adaptation depends on visual awareness: Evidence from continuous flash suppression. *Journal of Vision, 11*(8), 5.

Stein, T., Awad, D., Gayet, S., & Peelen, M. (2018). Unconscious processing of facial dominance: The role of low-level factors in access to awareness. *Journal of Experimental Psychology: General, 147*(11), e1–13.

Stein, T., Grubb, C., Bertrand, M., Suh, S. M., & Verosky, S. C. (2017). No impact of affective person knowledge on visual awareness: Evidence from binocular rivalry and continuous flash suppression. *Emotion, 17*(8), 1199–1207.

Stein, T., Senju, A., Peelen, M. V., & Sterzer, P. (2011). Eye contact facilitates awareness of faces during interocular suppression. *Cognition, 119*(2), 307–11.

Stein, T., Seymour, K., Hebart, M. N., & Sterzer, P. (2014). Rapid fear detection relies on high spatial frequencies. *Psychological Science, 25*(2), 566–74.

Sterzer, P., Hilgenfeldt, T., Freudenberg, P., Bermpohl, F., & Adli, M. (2011). Access of emotional information to visual awareness in patients with major depressive disorder. *Psychological Medicine, 41*(8), 1615–24.

Sterzer, Philipp, Haynes, J.-D., & Rees, G. (2008). Fine-scale activity patterns in high-level visual areas encode the category of invisible objects. *Journal of Vision, 8*(15)10, 1–12.

Sterzer, Philipp, Stein, T., Ludwig, K., Rothkirch, M., & Hesselmann, G. (2014). Neural processing of visual information under interocular suppression: A critical review. *Frontiers in Psychology, 5*, 453.

Stewart, L. H., Ajina, S., Getov, S., Bahrami, B., Todorov, A., & Rees, G. (2012). Unconscious evaluation of faces on social dimensions. *Journal of Experimental Psychology: General, 141*(4), 715–27.

Straube, T., Dietrich, C., Mothes-Lasch, M., Mentzel, H.-J., & Miltner, W. H. R. (2010). The volatility of the amygdala response to masked fearful eyes. *Human Brain Mapping, 31*(10), 1601–8.

Suslow, T., Roestel, C., & Arolt, V. (2003). Affective priming in schizophrenia with and without affective negative symptoms. *European Archives of Psychiatry and Clinical Neuroscience, 253*(6), 292–300.

Sylvers, P. D., Brennan, P. A., & Lilienfeld, S. O. (2011). Psychopathic traits and preattentive threat processing in children: A novel test of the fearlessness hypothesis. *Psychological Science, 22*(10), 1280–7.

Szczepanowski, R., & Pessoa, L. (2007). Fear perception: Can objective and subjective awareness measures be dissociated? *Journal of Vision, 7*(4), 10.

Tamietto, M., & de Gelder, B. (2008). Affective blindsight in the intact brain: Neural interhemispheric summation for unseen fearful expressions. *Neuropsychologia, 46*(3), 820–8.

Tamietto, M., & de Gelder, B. (2010). Neural bases of the non-conscious perception of emotional signals. *Nature Reviews. Neuroscience, 11*(10), 697–709.

Tamietto, M., Castelli, L., Vighetti, S., Perozzo, P., Geminiani, G., Weiskrantz, L., & de Gelder, B. (2009). Unseen facial and bodily expressions trigger fast emotional reactions. *Proceedings of the National Academy of Sciences USA, 106*(42), 17661–6.

Taschereau-Dumouchel, V., Cortese, A., Chiba, T., Knotts, J. D., Kawato, M., & Lau, H. (2018a). Towards an unconscious neural reinforcement intervention for common fears. *Proceedings of the National Academy of Sciences USA, 115*(13), 3470–5.

Taschereau-Dumouchel, V., Liu, K.-Y., & Lau, H. (2018b). Unconscious psychological treatments for physiological survival circuits. *Current Opinion in Behavioral Sciences, 24*, 62–8.

Titchener, E. B. (1898). The "feeling of being stared at." *Science, 8*(208), 895–7.

Tomasello, M., Hare, B., Lehmann, H., & Call, J. (2007). Reliance on head versus eyes in the gaze following of great apes and human infants: The cooperative eye hypothesis. *Journal of Human Evolution, 52*(3), 314–20.

Tsikandilakis, M., & Chapman, P. (2018). Skin conductance responses to masked emotional faces are modulated by hit rate but not signal detection theory adjustments for subjective differences in the detection threshold. *Perception, 47*(4), 432–50.

Tsuchiya, N., Moradi, F., Felsen, C., Yamazaki, M., & Adolphs, R. (2009). Intact rapid detection of fearful faces in the absence of the amygdala. *Nature Neuroscience, 12*(10), 1224–5.

van der Ploeg, M. M., Brosschot, J. F., Versluis, A., & Verkuil, B. (2017). Peripheral physiological responses to subliminally presented negative affective stimuli: A systematic review. *Biological Psychology, 129*, 131–53.

Varcin, K. J., Bailey, P. E., & Henry, J. D. (2010). Empathic deficits in schizophrenia: The potential role of rapid facial mimicry. *Journal of the International Neuropsychological Society*, *16*(4), 621–9.

Viding, E., Sebastian, C. L., Dadds, M. R., Lockwood, P. L., Cecil, C. A. M., De Brito, S. A., & McCrory, E. J. (2012). Amygdala response to preattentive masked fear in children with conduct problems: The role of callous-unemotional traits. *American Journal of Psychiatry*, *169*(10), 1109–16.

Vieira, J. B., Wen, S., Oliver, L. D., & Mitchell, D. G. V. (2017). Enhanced conscious processing and blindsight-like detection of fear-conditioned stimuli under continuous flash suppression. *Experimental Brain Research*, *235*(11), 3333–44.

von Grünau, M., & Anston, C. (1995). The detection of gaze direction: A stare-in-the-crowd effect. *Perception*, *24*(11), 1297–1313.

Vuilleumier, P., Armony, J. L., Driver, J., & Dolan, R. J. (2003). Distinct spatial frequency sensitivities for processing faces and emotional expressions. *Nature Neuroscience*, *6*(6), 624–31.

Watanabe, N., & Haruno, M. (2015). Effects of subconscious and conscious emotions on human cue-reward association learning. *Scientific Reports*, *5*, 8478.

Watanabe, T., Sasaki, Y., Shibata, K., & Kawato, M. (2017). Advances in fMRI real-time neurofeedback. *Trends in Cognitive Sciences*, *21*(12), 997–1010.

Whalen, P. J., Rauch, S. L., Etcoff, N. L., McInerney, S. C., Lee, M. B., & Jenike, M. A. (1998). Masked presentations of emotional facial expressions modulate amygdala activity without explicit knowledge. *Journal of Neuroscience*, *18*(1), 411–18.

Whalen, P. J. (1998). Fear, vigilance, and ambiguity: Initial neuroimaging studies of the human amygdala. *Current Directions in Psychological Science*, *7*(6), 177–88.

Willenbockel, V., Lepore, F., Nguyen, D. K., Bouthillier, A., & Gosselin, F. (2012). Spatial frequency tuning during the conscious and non-conscious perception of emotional facial expressions: An intracranial ERP study. *Frontiers in Psychology*, *3*, 237.

Williams, M. A., Morris, A. P., McGlone, F., Abbott, D. F., & Mattingley, J. B. (2004). Amygdala responses to fearful and happy facial expressions under conditions of binocular suppression. *Journal of Neuroscience*, *24*(12), 2898–2904.

Winkielman, P., & Berridge, K. C. (2004). Unconscious emotion. *Current Directions in Psychological Science*, *13*(3), 120–3.

Wong, P. S., Bernat, E., Bunce, S., & Shevrin, H. (1997). Brain indices of nonconscious associative learning. *Consciousness and Cognition*, *6*(4), 519–44.

Wong, P. S., Shevrin, H., & Williams, W. J. (1994). Conscious and nonconscious processes: An ERP index of an anticipatory response in a conditioning paradigm using visually masked stimuli. *Psychophysiology*, *31*(1), 87–101.

Xu, S., Zhang, S., & Geng, H. (2011). Gaze-induced joint attention persists under high perceptual load and does not depend on awareness. *Vision Research*, *51*(18), 2048–56.

Yang, E., Hong, S.-W., & Blake, R. (2010). Adaptation aftereffects to facial expressions suppressed from visual awareness. *Journal of Vision*, *10*(12), 24.

Yang, E., Zald, D. H., & Blake, R. (2007). Fearful expressions gain preferential access to awareness during continuous flash suppression. *Emotion*, *7*(4), 882–6.

Ye, X., He, S., Hu, Y., Yu, Y. Q., & Wang, K. (2014). Interference between conscious and unconscious facial expression information. *PLoS One*, *9*(8), e105156.

Yokoyama, T., Noguchi, Y., & Kita, S. (2013). Unconscious processing of direct gaze: Evidence from an ERP study. *Neuropsychologia*, *51*(7), 1161–8.

5

STUDYING THE BENEFITS AND COSTS OF CONSCIOUS PERCEPTION WITH THE LIMINAL-PRIME PARADIGM

Dominique Lamy, Eyal A. Ophir, and Maayan Avneon

TEL AVIV UNIVERSITY

1 Introduction

Heated controversies over what counts as conscious perception have burdened the study of unconscious processing throughout its history and have not abated to this day (e.g. Cheesman & Merikle, 1986; Erdelyi, 1986; Eriksen, 1960; Holender, 1986; Peters, Ro, & Lau, 2016; Reingold, 2004; Sand, 2016; Schmidt, 2015; Shanks, 2017; Vermeiren & Cleeremans, 2012; Wierzchoń, Asanowicz, Paulewicz, & Cleeremans, 2012). The main dividing line has been and remains whether conscious perception should be indexed by subjective reports or by objective performance on tasks that measure perceptual discriminations. The steady stream of papers reviewing the pros and cons of subjective and objective measures over the years (e.g. Dehaene & Changeux, 2011; Hannula, Simons & Cohen, 2005; Kouider & Dehaene, 2007; Merikle, Smilek & Eastwood, 2001; Overgaard, 2015; Rothkirch & Hesselmann, 2017; Snodgrass, Bernat, & Shevrin, 2004; Persuh, 2018; Timmermans & Cleeremans, 2015) attests that neither of the two approaches has yet reached consensus.

1.1 The subliminal-prime paradigm

The standard paradigm currently used in order to investigate unconscious processing with objective measures of conscious perception (henceforth, the standard subliminal-prime paradigm) consists of two experimental phases: a priming phase and a prime-awareness phase. In the first (priming) phase, unconscious processing is assessed as the degree to which a subliminal prime influences the response to a visible target. The second (prime-awareness-test) phase is similar to the priming phase, except that observers are required to discriminate some property of the prime. Chance performance on this discrimination task is held to attest to the subliminality of the prime in the priming phase (e.g. Ansorge, Kiss, & Eimer, 2009; Ansorge,

Kiefer, Khalid, Grassl, & König, 2010; Almeida, Pajtas, Mahon, Nakayama & Caramazza, 2013; Dehaene, Naccache, Le Clec'H, Koechlin, Mueller, Dehaene-Lambertz, Van de Moortele, & Le Bihan, 1998; Hsieh, Colas, & Kanwisher, 2011; Jiang, Costello, Fang, Huang, & He, 2006; Frings & Wentura, 2008; Heinemann, Kunde, & Kiesel, 2009; Kiefer & Brendel, 2006; Klinger, Burton, & Pitts, 2000; Kunde, Kiesel & Hoffmann, 2003; Manly, Fish. Griffiths, Molenveld, Zhou, & Davis, 2014; Naccache & Dehaene, 2001; Van Gaal, Lamme, & Ridderinkhof, 2010; Van Opstal, de Lange, & Dehaene, 2011).

This paradigm remains very much in use (e.g. Greenwald & De Houwer, 2017; Kiefer, 2018; Stein, Utz, & Van Opstal, 2018; Yang & Yeh, 2018) despite a long history of criticisms mainly pointing out problems of exhaustiveness (the measured discrimination performance may not index all the consciously experienced information about the critical stimulus), exclusiveness (discrimination performance may be determined by both consciously and unconsciously processed information), null sensitivity (demonstrating null sensitivity requires many more trials than are usually used in the prime-awareness phase), and task comparability (discrimination performance and priming are measured under different task conditions; for recent versions of this criticism see Lin & Murray, 2014; Pratte & Rouder, 2009).

The task comparability problem (Merikle & Reingold, 1998) mostly results from the two measures being collected in different phases of the experiment (e.g. Atas, Desender, Gevers & Cleeremans, 2016; Kouider, Eger, Dolan & Henson, 2008; Naccache, Blandin, & Dehaene, 2002; Van den Bussche & Reynvoet, 2007; Van Gaal, Ridderinkhof, Fahrenfort, Scholte, & Lamme, 2008; Van Opstal et al., 2011). Several authors have attempted to resolve this problem by measuring target and prime discrimination responses in the same blocks of trials. Accordingly, participants were either required to provide two responses, a speeded discrimination response relative to the target and a similar yet non-speeded discrimination response relative to the prime, either on each trial (e.g. Faivre, Mudrik, Schwartz, & Koch, 2014b; Haase & Fisk, 2015; Koivisto & Rientamo, 2016) or on different trials, unpredictably (e.g. Schlossmacher, Junghöfer, Straube, & Bruchmann, 2017). For instance, in Koivisto and Rientamo's (2016) study, participants were asked to indicate whether the target was an animal or not, as fast as possible, and then to make the same discrimination with a non-speeded response relative to the prime. However, with this procedure, the response associated with the target is most likely to contaminate the response to the prime: as the correct responses on the two tasks are uncorrelated, such contamination lowers prime discrimination performance and therefore leads to an underestimation of conscious perception (e.g. Peremen & Lamy, 2014a, Exp.1).

1.2 Renewed interest in subjective measures of conscious perception

These criticisms have spurred renewed interest in subjective measures and promoted the development of graded scales that capture subtler variations in conscious experience than did earlier dichotomic subjective measures (for reviews, see Overgaard,

Timmermans, Sandberg, & Cleeremans, 2010; Sandberg, Timmermans, Overgaard, & Cleeremans, 2010; Timmermans & Cleeremans, 2015). The Perceptual Awareness Scale (PAS), developed by Ramsøy and Overgaard (2004), requires participants to rate the clarity of their experience of a stimulus. It includes four levels – "no experience", "brief glimpse", "almost clear image", or "absolutely clear image", that were derived from participants' spontaneous ratings. Additional subjective scales require participants to either report how confident they are that their answer on a forced-choice discrimination task is correct (confidence ratings (CR), e.g. Armstrong & Dienes, 2013; Cheesman & Merikle, 1986; Dienes, Altmann, Kwan, & Goode, 1995) or place a wager on that decision (post-decision wagering (PDW), e.g. Persaud, McLeod, & Cowey, 2007). It is noteworthy that only PAS directly indexes the quality of the participants' conscious experience, while CR and PDW index meta-cognitive judgments on the participants' discrimination performance (see Wierzchoń, Paulewicz, Asanowicz, Timmermans, & Cleeremans, 2014; Sandberg et al., 2010; Szczepanowski, Traczyk, Wierzchoń, & Cleeremans, 2013; Zehetleitner & Rausch, 2013, for detailed comparisons between these scales).

These subjective scales have been used to investigate a variety of questions, among them, whether conscious perception is gradual or dichotomous (e.g. Overgaard, Rote, Mouridsen, & Ramsøy, 2006; Sergent, Baillet, & Dehaene, 2005; Windey, Vermeiren, Atas, & Cleeremans, 2014), how various degrees of conscious perception are related to discrimination performance (e.g. Ramsøy & Overgaard, 2004) and what factors affect the transition from unconscious to conscious perception (e.g. Anzulewicz, Asanowicz, Windey, Paulewicz, Wierzchoń, & Cleeremans, 2015; Atas, Vermeiren, & Cleeremans, 2013; Lamy, Carmel, & Peremen, 2017; Melloni, Schwiedrzik, Müller, Rodriguez, & Singer, 2011). With these scales, unconscious perception is typically defined as discrimination performance at the lowest subjective rating (e.g. Overgaard, 2012). In other words, *objective* discrimination performance is the measure by which *unconscious* processing is indexed, as illustrated in the left column (A) of Figure 5.1 (e.g. Koivisto & Grassini, 2016; Overgaard, Fehl, Mouridsen, Bergholt & Cleeremans, 2008; Ramsøy & Overgaard, 2004; Salti, Bar-Haim, & Lamy, 2012). Subjective scales are thought to be more valid the less amount of unconscious processing they indicate (i.e. the closer to chance objective performance is for the lowest rating of the subjective scale) and the more consistently subjective ratings correlate with performance accuracy (see Overgaard & Sandberg, 2012, for review). Using PAS, former iconic demonstrations of above-chance discrimination performance without subjective awareness have been called into question. For instance, Overgaard, Fehl, Mouridsen, Bergholt, & Cleeremans (2008) showed that when a blindsight patient was asked to use the PAS scale in order to evaluate her conscious perception in her blind field, her performance for the lowest rating was at chance.

To use Merikle and Reingold's (1998) terminology, in the foregoing studies, both conscious perception and unconscious processing were assessed using direct measures (a subjective measure and an objective measure of perceptual processing, respectively). However, considering that many researchers hold objective discrimination performance to index conscious processing, this measure is unlikely to be as sensitive as indirect measures of processing, such as priming, for uncovering unconscious influences on behavior. Surprisingly, however, only a relatively small number of studies have used trial-by-trial graded subjective measures of consciousness in conjunction with indirect measures of processing in order to study unconscious processing. In most of these studies, the prime stimulus parameters were set so as to ensure that participants would use the lowest rating ("no experience") on most trials. Unconscious priming was held to occur whenever significant priming was observed on those trials, and trials with higher visibility ratings were excluded from analysis (e.g. Bahrami, Vetter, Spolaore, Pagano, Butterworth, & Rees, 2010; Biderman & Mudrik, 2018; Faivre & Koch, 2014; Gelbard-Sagiv, Faivre, Mudrik, & Koch, 2016; Hesselmann & Knops, 2014; Hesselmann, Darcy, Ludwig & Sterzer, 2016). As is explained below, this approach suffers from two main problems. First, "no-experience" trials are considered in isolation, which raises serious inference problems (see Schmidt, 2015; Shanks, 2017). Second, the extent to which the process indexed by priming depends on prime visibility cannot be examined.

1.3 Objective of the present chapter

The objective of the present chapter is to argue that, while no experimental paradigm should be expected to resolve all the pitfalls associated with the study of conscious perception and unconscious processing, the liminal-prime paradigm (Peremen & Lamy, 2014a, b),[1] which has not been used until very recently (Avneon & Lamy, 2018, 2019; Kimchi, Devyatko, & Sabary, 2018; Lamy, Alon, Carmel, & Shalev, 2015; Ophir, Sherman & Lamy, 2018; Travis, Dux, & Mattingley, 2018) may be the best available method. In section 2, we describe the paradigm and discuss its advantages and drawbacks. In section 3, we illustrate how it can be employed to determine the extent to which different processes depend on conscious processing. In section 4, we show that the liminal-prime paradigm can also be used to investigate the cost of consciously perceiving an event on the processing of a trailing event (Ophir et al., 2018; Ophir, Hesselmann, & Lamy, 2019). We conclude with a set of guidelines for using the liminal-prime paradigm in future studies.

2 The liminal-prime paradigm

2.1 Description

In the liminal-prime paradigm, subjective perception of the prime is measured on every trial using the Perceptual Awareness Scale (PAS, Ramsøy & Overgaard, 2004), while the impact of this prime on responses to the target (i.e. priming) is concomitantly assessed. The prime-target sequence is similar to that used in the standard subliminal-prime paradigm (e.g. Dehaene et al., 1998) except that the method used to reduce the prime stimulus's visibility is calibrated so as to ensure that the prime is completely missed on a portion of the trials and seen with varying degrees of clarity on others. Participants are required to produce two responses: first, a speeded discrimination response to the target and then a non-speeded prime-visibility rating on a scale ranging from "0" if they had no conscious perception of the prime to "3" if they clearly perceived it.[2] Thus, with this paradigm, the impact of the prime on target discrimination performance (henceforth, the priming effect) can be assessed for each level of prime visibility. How the sequences of events differ in the subjective-objective measures, standard subliminal-prime, and liminal-prime paradigms is illustrated in Figure 5.1.

Since in the liminal-prime paradigm visibility ratings are provided by the participants and are not under the experimenter's control, their distributions can vary considerably between participants, which results in different numbers of trials for

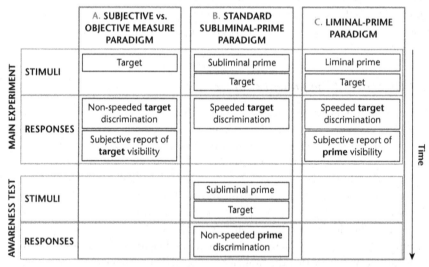

FIGURE 5.1 Sequence of events (stimuli and responses) in the main paradigms used in order to investigate unconscious processing. In the subjective vs. objective measure paradigm (column A), both a target-discrimination response and a target-visibility report (both non-speeded) are collected, typically the former before the latter (but see Wierzchoń et al., 2014, for the reverse order). In the standard subliminal-prime (column B) and liminal-prime (column C) paradigms, the prime-target sequence is similar and participants are required to provide a speeded discrimination response to the target. The main differences between the two paradigms are that (1) the prime parameters are set to make the prime subliminal vs. liminal, respectively, (2) prime visibility is assessed in a separate block after the main experiment, using a prime forced-discrimination task and with chance performance on that task attesting the subliminality of the prime in the main experiment vs. prime visibility is assessed immediately after the response to the target.

each visibility rating. Therefore, statistical models that are appropriate for handling imbalanced data structures, such as linear mixed effects models (West, Welch, & Galecki, 2014; see also Hesselmann, 2018), must be used. In addition, because some ratings do not include enough trials for meaningful analysis, they are typically grouped. While the lowest (0) rating is always considered as a separate category, either ratings 1, 2, and 3 (Lamy et al., 2015; Peremen & Lamy, 2014b) or ratings 2 and 3 (Avneon & Lamy, 2018; Kimchi et al., 2018; Ophir et al., 2018) are combined. Avneon and Lamy (2018) compared 0- and 3-visibility ratings while excluding intermediate ratings, yet such a procedure may underestimate the impact of conscious perception because of regression to the mean (Shanks, 2017) and should therefore be avoided.[3]

The liminal-prime paradigm has been used with a variety of methods for reducing prime visibility: Continuous Flash Suppression (Lamy et al., 2015; Kimchi et al., 2018; Ophir et al., 2018; Peremen & Lamy, 2014b; Travis et al., 2018), metacontrast masking (Peremen & Lamy, 2014b), sandwich masking (Avneon & Lamy, 2018a, b; Kimchi et al., 2018; Ophir et al., 2018), and degraded stimulation (Lamy et al., 2015).

Alternatives to the liminal-prime paradigm have been used, in which subjective perception of the prime was also measured with a graded scale on every trial but was combined with an objective prime-identification task (e.g. van den Bussche, Vermeiren, Desender, Gevers, Hughes, Verguts, & Reynvoet, 2013; Gelbard-Sagiv et al., 2016). However, in these studies, participants' confidence in their prime identification decision rather than the clarity of their perception was measured (see e.g. Sandberg et al., 2010, for a demonstration that visibility scales are more exhaustive and sensitive than confidence ratings). In addition, when the discriminated prime's property is the same as the discriminated target's property (e.g. van den Bussche et al., 2013), the same contamination problems arise as in variants of the standard subliminal prime paradigm in which objective prime discrimination responses are measured on a trial-by-trial basis (e.g. Koivisto & Rientamo, 2016).

2.2 Advantages of the liminal-prime paradigm

The liminal-prime paradigm does not suffer from several of the problems that burden other empirical strategies.

(a) It uses a pure measure of conscious experience that is not contaminated by unconscious processing influences and it is therefore unambiguously exclusive.
(b) It resolves the task comparability problem because the measures of conscious perception and of prime processing are collected under the same stimulus, attention, and motivational conditions.
(c) With objective measures of conscious perception, it is imperative to avoid that even just a few visible-prime trials might occur. Therefore, deeply subliminal stimuli are typically selected – at the risk of "overshooting", that is, of cutting

into unconscious processing itself. However, it is not possible to assess the magnitude of such overshooting because performance is indiscriminately at chance, irrespective of whether the critical stimulus is just under the limen of conscious perception or very far from it. As a result, null priming effects (e.g. Axelrod & Rees, 2014; Peel, Sperandio, Laycock, & Chouinard, 2018; Hesselmann, Darcy, Rothkirch, & Sterzer, 2018) are difficult to interpret. By contrast, the liminal-prime paradigm maximizes the chances of detecting unconscious processing because the prime visibility hovers around the limen.

(d) With paradigms that require subliminality of the prime, extensive participants' and trials' exclusions are not uncommon. With objective measures, participants whose performance in the awareness-test phase is above chance are typically excluded from analysis (e.g. Ansorge, Khalid, & Laback, 2016; Chiu & Aron, 2014; Hesselmann, Darcy, Sterzer, & Knops, 2015; Sklar, Levy, Goldstein, Mandel, Maril, & Hassin, 2012). Likewise, with trial-by-trial subjective measures, "no-experience" trials are considered in isolation and other trials are excluded (e.g. Bahrami et al., 2010; Biderman & Mudrik, 2018; Gelbard-Sagiv et al., 2016; Hesselmann & Knops, 2014; Hesselmann et al., 2016). These exclusion procedures make these paradigms inefficient resource-wise, but more critically, they are associated with serious inference problems (Schmidt, 2015; Shanks, 2017). By contrast, the liminal-prime paradigm does not require excluding participants on the basis of their conscious perception of the prime. Participants are excluded only if their visibility ratings are unreliable, which can be diagnosed based on their visibility ratings on catch trials, in which no prime is presented. Likewise, trials in which the prime was judged to be invisible are not treated in isolation, since the whole range of visibility judgments is considered. Imbalances in participants' ratings distributions are addressed by using appropriate statistical methods.

(e) The main advantage of the liminal-prime paradigm is that priming can be compared for various levels of subjective stimulus visibility under the same task and stimulus conditions. It is not possible to evaluate the extent to which a given process depends on conscious processing without such comparison, that is, based solely on the priming effect observed for stimuli that are not consciously perceived – especially when the magnitude of this effect is very small (e.g. Almeida, Mahon, & Caramazza, 2010; Kunde et al., 2003; Van den Bussche, Notebaert, & Reynvoet, 2009). Several authors assessed the role of conscious perception by comparing priming on weak-stimulation (subliminal-prime) trials and on strong-stimulation (supraliminal) trials (e.g. Desender, Van Lierde, & Van den Bussche, 2013; Goller, Khalid, & Ansorge, 2017; Jiang, Bailey, Xiang, Zhang, & Zhang, 2016; Kiefer & Spitzer, 2000; Lin & Murray, 2014; Tapia, Breitmeyer, & Shooner, 2010; Van Gaal, Lamme, Fahrenfort, & Ridderinkhof, 2011; Van Gaal, Naccache, Meuwese, Van Loon, Leighton, Cohen, & Dehaene, 2014). However, in this comparison, the effects of conscious perception are conflated with those of stimulation strength.

By contrast, by using constant stimulation, the liminal-prime paradigm makes it possible to categorize different cognitive processes according to their dependence

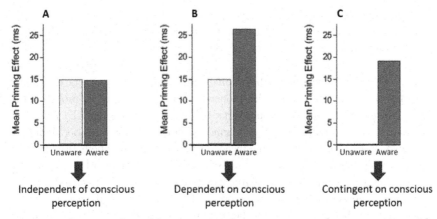

FIGURE 5.2 Interpretation of the comparison between aware- and unaware-prime trials using the liminal-prime paradigm. The process indexed by priming is (A) independent of conscious perception if priming is unaffected by prime visibility (left panel); (B) dependent on conscious perception if priming is significant on unaware-prime trials but larger on aware-prime trials (central panel); (C) contingent on conscious perception if priming is significant on aware-prime trials and null on unaware-prime trials (right panel).

on conscious processing (see Figure 5.2): if priming is stable across levels of prime visibility, then one can conclude that the process that drives the effect not only does not require conscious perception of the prime, but is in fact independent of it. Conversely, finding that priming is null on 0-visibility trials but significant when the prime is consciously perceived indicates that the process that drives the effect is contingent on conscious perception of the prime. Finally, finding that priming is significant for 0-visibility primes but becomes larger the higher the prime visibility indicates that the process does not require conscious perception of the prime but nevertheless benefits from it. Examples for each category are presented in section 3.

2.3 Potential caveats of the liminal-prime paradigm

(a) The first criticism of the liminal-prime paradigm that comes to mind is that 0-visibility ratings may not index "genuine" absence of conscious perception. Voicing this concern, Vermeiren and Cleeremans (2012) declared that the recently revived subjective approach (e.g. Ramsøy & Overgaard, 2004; Sandberg et al., 2010; Dienes, Scott, & Seth, 2010) "still faces the same issues as it did 50 years ago. Objective measures are essential when assessing awareness". These old-time problems are mainly subsumed under the criterion problem. Proponents of the PAS scale claim that using a four-step scale circumvents the criterion problem because participants are provided with clear instructions to use the lowest level only when they have absolutely no experience of the stimulus (just like on prime-absent trials), as well as with the opportunity to use intermediate ratings for stimuli of which they have even a brief glimpse. However, this argument is judged to be unsatisfactory: the claim is that subjective measures are, by necessity, less exhaustive than objective measures of conscious perception and that unless null sensitivity is demonstrated, one cannot be confident that the critical stimulus was not consciously perceived.

It is important to reevaluate this claim. With objective measures of consciousness, there is no consensus as to what property of the prime should be probed in the awareness test. Some authors stipulate that the same attribute should be judged in the priming and awareness tests (e.g. Schmidt & Vorberg, 2006, see also Merikle & Reingold, 1998). For instance, if the speeded task is to indicate whether the target is larger or smaller than 5 (and the response to the prime, also a number larger or smaller than 5, is either congruent or incongruent with the response to the target), the test of prime awareness should focus on the prime's feature that drives the priming effect: chance performance at deciding whether the prime is larger or smaller than 5 would be sufficient evidence for concluding that the prime was not perceived consciously (e.g. Ansorge et al., 2010). However, several authors (e.g. Kouider & Dupoux, 2004; Gelbard-Sagiv et al., 2016) have shown that priming driven by a high-level feature of a prime, such as the lexicality of a letter string or the identity of a face, for which participants' discrimination performance was at chance (thus presumably attesting to unconscious priming) was contingent on conscious perception of lower-level features of the prime, such as individual letters or stimulus location, respectively. Thus, which property the objective test of conscious perception relies on may critically determine whether or not priming occurs due to partial awareness of the prime.

To avoid this problem, the objective test that is most sensitive to conscious perception of the prime should be adopted, namely, a present-absent prime discrimination task. However, this test is almost never used (but see e.g. Dehaene et al., 1998; Naccache & Dehaene, 2001), probably because the stimulus parameters associated with chance performance with such a severe test of conscious perception are likely to be associated with little priming of higher-level properties, if any.

The liminal-prime paradigm does not face the problem of choosing the appropriate feature of the prime because 0-visibility ratings indicate no conscious perception of the stimulus *presence*. It is thus likely that 0-visibility trials index a lower level of visibility than does chance performance at discriminating one of the prime's features. Consistent with this conjecture, studies using four-point subjective scales and measuring both prime-discrimination performance and subjective visibility of the prime on each trial typically revealed no statistically significant above-chance performance when participants used the lowest level of the scale (e.g. Bahrami et al., 2010; Binder, Gociewicz, Windey, Koculak, Finc, Nikadon, & Cleeremans, 2017; Haase & Fisk, 2015; Lähteenmäki, Hyönä, Koivisto, & Nummenmaa, 2015; Liu, Sun, Jou, Cui, Zhao, Qiu, & Tu, 2016; Overgaard et al., 2008; Peremen & Lamy, 2014a; Ramsøy & Overgaard, 2004; Tagliabue, Mazzi, Bagattini, & Savazzi, 2016; Wyart & Tallon-Baudry, 2008). Thus, the argument that objective measures of conscious perception are necessarily more exhaustive than the PAS scale is unwarranted.

It remains nonetheless true that participants' criteria might vary when using PAS. In particular, how the "brief glimpse" rating is used seems to fluctuate considerably. Informal post-experimental reports suggest that participants may use this rating as a default when they feel they were inattentive on a particular trial or when they had a "hunch" that the prime was present but had no subjective experience of it whatsoever. Thus, brief-glimpse reports seem to be less reliable than other reports (see Ophir et al., 2018, for suggestions about how to handle these ratings).

(b) The liminal-prime paradigm can also be criticized based on the observation that it entails a dual-task situation: participants are required to respond to the target (task 1) and then rate the prime's visibility (task 2). As a consequence, responses to the target are slower in the liminal-prime than in the standard subliminal-prime paradigm, which requires performing only one task on each trial (e.g. Avneon & Lamy, 2018; Peremen & Lamy, 2014a). As a result, the liminal-prime paradigm may underestimate unconscious priming, because it has been suggested that the impact of unconscious stimuli might vanish quickly (e.g. Ansorge et al., 2010; Avneon & Lamy, 2018; Dehaene et al., 1998, fig. 2b; Greenwald, Draine, & Abrams, 1996; Kiefer & Spitzer, 2000; Kinoshita & Hunt, 2008). Accordingly, priming was shown to be smaller in dual- than in single-task conditions (e.g. Ansorge, 2004; Avneon & Lamy, 2018).

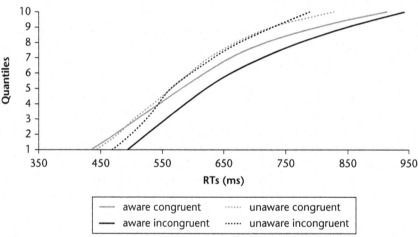

FIGURE 5.3 Illustration of the use of the vincentization procedure (Ratcliff, 1979) in the liminal-prime paradigm: quantiles of RT distributions are computed for each participant, each summarizing 10% of the cumulative RT distribution, and are then averaged to produce the group distribution (Rouder & Speckman, 2004). This nonparametric procedure is applied separately for each condition. The priming effect is the RT difference when the prime and target are associated with congruent vs. incongruent responses. In this example (Avneon & Lamy, 2019), four main findings emerge:
(a) unconscious priming is observed only for fast trials; (b) conscious priming occurs across the RT distribution; (c) conscious priming is larger than unconscious priming even for the fastest trials; (d) aware-prime trials are overall slower than unaware-prime trials (cost of awareness, see Ophir et al., 2018). Adapted from Avneon & Lamy (2019), with permission.

At least two methods can be used to address this problem. First, RT distribution analyses (such as the vincentization procedure, Ratcliff, 1979) may be used to assess unconscious priming across the RT distribution, and in particular, on fast trials, before the effect starts waning (Avneon & Lamy, 2018; see also Ansorge, Khalid, & Koenig, 2013; Kinoshita & Hunt, 2008, for the application of this procedure using the standard subliminal-prime paradigm). How this procedure can be applied using the liminal-prime paradigm is illustrated in Figure 5.3. Second, a short response deadline can be imposed in order to induce participants to provide very fast responses, thereby minimizing how much the influence of the invisible prime might decay before the target is responded to (Avneon & Lamy, 2018; see also Dehaene et al., 1998; Greenwald et al., 1996; Van Opstal et al., 2011, for the application of this procedure using variants of the subliminal-prime paradigm).

(c) A somewhat related potential problem is that in most experiments using the liminal-prime paradigm, RTs were longer for aware- than for unaware-prime trials (see section 4 for research investigating the mechanisms underlying this cost). Thus, although the liminal-prime paradigm ensures that stimulation parameters are identical in the two conditions, response latencies to the target do constitute a systematic difference between them.

Again, however, considering the whole RT distribution instead of the mean performance allows one to resolve this problem and to compare conscious and unconscious priming for the same RT bins.

(d) In the liminal-prime paradigm, visibility ratings are collected after participants make a speeded response to the target. Thus, relative to the standard liminal-prime paradigm, conscious perception of the prime is assessed with a delay. Such delay may degrade the memory of the prime and make the visibility judgments less reliable. However, in contradiction with this argument, several authors have suggested that awareness tests should be administered with a delay because conscious representations take time to develop (Vermeiren & Cleeremans, 2012; see also Reuss, Desender, Kiesel, & Kunde, 2014; Vorberg, Mattler, Heinecke, Schmidt, & Schwarzbach, 2003; Wierzchoń et al., 2014).

(e) In the priming phase of the standard subliminal-prime paradigm, participants are not required to relate to the prime and are not even informed of its presence. Thus, the prime is unattended and irrelevant to the task at the time priming is measured. By contrast, in the liminal-prime paradigm participants are required to rate the prime visibility on each trial. As suggested by Ivanoff and Klein (2003), the experimenter's attempt to measure awareness may alter the processing that the prime elicits. We measured the impact of attention and task relevance in a masked priming paradigm (Avneon & Lamy, 2018) and found them to magnify priming (see Naccache et al., 2002, for a similar role of temporal attention on unconscious priming). Thus, with the liminal-prime paradigm, the influence on performance of a stimulus that is not consciously perceived can only be assessed in the specific situation in which the prime is both attended and relevant to the task. The influence of the prime is therefore overestimated relative to the influence measured in the standard subliminal-prime paradigm, but it is noteworthy that the prime benefits from attention and task relevance on both unaware- and aware-prime trials, for which priming is compared.

3 The benefits of conscious perception

The liminal-prime paradigm was used in several experiments in order to assess the extent to which different processes depend on conscious perception. This was done by comparing the influence of a prime on behavior when this prime was consciously perceived relative to when it was not, under identical stimulus conditions. The processes underlying the priming effect ranged from relatively low-level processes, such as perceptual grouping (Kimchi et al., 2018), attentional capture (Lamy et al., 2015; Travis et al., 2018) and retrieval of stimulus-response associations (Avneon & Lamy, 2018, 2019) to high-level processes, such as semantic processing (Avneon & Lamy, 2018, 2019) and updating of object-based information in working memory (Lamy et al., 2015; Travis et al., 2018). A brief review of these findings is provided here.

3.1 Categorizing different processes according to their dependence on conscious perception

3.1.1 Attentional capture

What properties of a stimulus determine whether it will capture the observer's spatial attention against her will? A large corpus of studies show that the observer's attentional set plays an important role in attentional capture (e.g. Folk & Remington, 1998). For instance, if participants search for a red letter, an irrelevant stimulus (henceforth, cue), appearing shortly before the target, captures attention if it shares the target color (i.e. it is red) but not if it does not (e.g. if it is green). In these studies, attentional capture is measured by the spatial cueing effect: to show that the cue captures attention one has to demonstrate that responses to the target are faster when it appears at the same location as the cue than at a different location. Several authors showed that such contingent capture occurs even when the cue is not consciously perceived (Ansorge & Neumann, 2005; Hsieh, Colas, & Kanwisher, 2011; Ivanoff & Klein, 2003).

Lamy et al. (2015) extended these findings by showing that attentional capture by a color cue that matches the target color is *independent* of conscious perception of the cue. They rendered the prime liminal by using either continuous flash suppression, with the cue display presented in the suppressed eye and the target display in the unsuppressed eye (Exp. 1 and 2), or by presenting the cue for a short duration (Exp.3). They showed that the spatial cueing effect was of the same magnitude whether cue visibility was rated to be 0 or above 0 (i.e. PAS rating of 0 vs. 1, 2, and 3). This finding was replicated by Travis et al. (2018) also using CFS, as well as by Ophir et al. (2018) who used CFS (Exp.1) and sandwich masking (Exp. 2 and 3) in a very different spatial cueing task using accuracy as the dependent measure (see section 4 for details on this task).

3.1.2 Perceptual grouping

It is widely assumed that perceptual grouping of separate pieces of the visual input into coherent objects occurs early in visual processing (e.g. Rock, 1986). Accordingly, it makes intuitive sense to predict that grouping processes should occur in the absence of conscious awareness of the stimulus. However, current research on this topic draws an inconsistent picture (see Kimchi et al., 2018, for a review). Kimchi et al. (2018) suggested that this state of affairs might result from the diversity of grouping principles investigated in different studies and of methods used to render the stimulus invisible. They compared grouping by luminance similarity and grouping by connectedness using CFS and sandwich masking in a response priming task. In each experiment, the target display consisted of vertically or horizontally oriented lines and appeared shortly after a prime display consisting of dots organized either in rows or in columns. As they used the liminal-prime paradigm, Kimchi et al. (2018) could measure the extent to which grouping in the prime display depended on conscious perception. They found grouping according to both grouping principles to be fairly independent of conscious perception with sandwich masking, yet to be entirely contingent on conscious perception with CFS.

3.1.3 Retrieval of stimulus-response associations

Early demonstrations of masked response priming (e.g. Neumann & Klotz, 1994) showed that invisible masked primes can have strong and reliable effects on choice-response speed to targets. These response priming effects have been interpreted as resulting from stimulus-response connections that do not require full processing of the prime. Such stimulus-response associations have been invoked to challenge later demonstrations of unconscious semantic priming (e.g. Dehaene et al., 1998). For instance, Damian (2001) suggested that the association between a visible target and a response is learned during the experiment and unconscious low-level processing of the prime suffices to elicit the associated response. Accordingly, Damian (2001; see also Kiesel, Kunde, Pohl, & Hoffmann, 2006; Kunde et al., 2003; Reynvoet, Gevers, & Caessens, 2005; but see Naccache & Dehaene, 2001) showed that unconscious response priming occurs for prime stimuli that were encountered

The liminal-prime paradigm **131**

and responded to as targets (i.e. "used primes"), and not for prime stimuli that do not belong to the target set (i.e. "novel primes") – for which a priming effect would index purely semantic processing.

In a recent study, Avneon and Lamy (2019) applied the liminal paradigm to Dehaene et al.'s (1998) masked prime numerical-comparison task and showed that priming from used primes had the same amplitude and time course when the prime was consciously perceived and when it was entirely missed. Thus, they showed that retrieval of stimulus-response associations is strongly automatic, since it does not even benefit from conscious perception of the prime.

In a similar vein, Peremen and Lamy (2014b) compared response priming from liminal primes in an arrow-direction discrimination task (see Eimer & Schlaghecken, 1998; Vorberg et al., 2003). Primes were masked using either metacontrast masking or CFS. These authors suggested that the proportion of 0-visibility trials can be used as a proxy to assess the extent to which each method impairs prime visibility for a given set of stimulus parameters. Accordingly, they suggested that similar proportions of invisible trials indicate similar distances from the limen of subjective conscious perception. It is important to note that the notion of "distance from the limen" as defined here does not refer to how deeply or early in processing a given method impairs perceptual processing but to how effective it is at preventing conscious processing (i.e. on what proportion of the trials it does, for a given set of parameters). Peremen and Lamy (2014b) found response priming to be minimally modulated by prime visibility with metacontrast masking but to be contingent on conscious perception of the prime with CFS (but see Koivisto & Grassini, 2018, for conflicting findings), although distance from the limen was actually larger with metacontrast than with CFS.

3.1.4 Semantic processing

As explained earlier, priming from novel primes is thought to index semantic priming (e.g. Kinoshita & Hunt, 2008; Klauer, Eder, Greenwald, & Abrams, 2007; Naccache & Dehaene, 2001; Ortells, Kiefer, Castillo, Megías, & Morillas, 2016; Pohl, Kiesel, Kunde, & Hoffmann, 2010; Reynvoet, Gevers, & Caessens, 2005). Avneon and Lamy (2019) showed that, with novel primes, unconscious priming occurred only for fast responses, whereas conscious priming was stable across the RT distribution. Crucially, unconscious priming was smaller than conscious priming even for the fastest trials. These findings indicate that unlike priming from used primes, which reflect simple stimulus-response associations, semantic priming (from novel primes) is strongly dependent on conscious perception of the prime.

3.1.5 Object updating in working memory

In contingent capture studies, cues sharing the target-defining color have been consistently shown to capture attention (e.g. Folk & Remington, 1998; see Biderman,

Biderman, Zivony, & Lamy, 2017, for contingent capture in additional feature dimensions). Several studies have shown that with the same paradigm, an equally salient cue that has a color not matching that of the target produces the opposite effect: a same-location cost (e.g. Anderson & Folk, 2012; Belopolsky, Schreij, & Theeuwes, 2010; Carmel & Lamy, 2014, 2015; Eimer, Kiss, Press, & Sauter, 2009; Folk & Remington, 2008; Lamy, Leber, & Egeth, 2004; Schoeberl, Ditye, & Ansorge, 2018; Schönhammer & Kerzel, 2013; Travis et al., 2018). The mechanisms underlying this cost are currently debated. Carmel and Lamy (2014, 2015) suggested that the effect occurs at a different stage than attentional capture because the spatial cueing benefit and the same-location cost are additive. They further suggested that the same-location cost reflects the cost of updating an object's feature information in visual working memory when this feature changes across time. This conclusion was based on the findings showing that the cost emerged only when the cue and target were perceived as belonging to the same object (Carmel & Lamy, 2014). However, it is important to note that this interpretation relies on the findings of just one study and requires further empirical support.

Lamy et al. (2015) used the liminal-prime paradigm and showed that the same-location cost occurred only when the cue was consciously perceived. Consistent with this observation, Carmel and Lamy (2015) reported a same-location cost when cue exposure was long and not when it was short. Taken together, these findings suggest that the same-location cost is contingent on conscious perception of the cue, a finding that is consistent with the conjecture that the effect reflects a relatively high level of processing.

However, a recent study by Travis et al. (2018) failed to replicate Lamy et al.'s (2015) finding: they showed that the same-location cost was just as large when cue was consciously perceived as when it was not. The two studies were very similar, yet a potentially crucial difference is that Travis et al. (2018) used an analysis of variance, whereas Lamy et al. (2015) used a linear mixed-effects model analysis. Since the distribution of visibility ratings can vary considerably across participants, ANOVAs are inappropriate to analyze the data and can lead to strong distortions. This account of the discrepancy between the two studies should be examined in further analyses.

3.2 Conflicting findings with different blinding methods

The foregoing review suggests that the liminal-prime paradigm can be used to determine to what extent different processes depend on conscious perception. However, a troubling aspect of the extant findings is that the conclusions differ according to the method used to render the prime liminal. Grouping by luminance similarity and by connectivity using sandwich masking (Kimchi et al., 2018) as well S-R response priming using sandwich masking (Avneon & Lamy, 2019) and metacontrast masking (Peremen & Lamy, 2014b) were found to be largely independent of prime visibility. By contrast, with CFS, the same processes were found to be contingent on conscious perception of the prime.

In the last few years, researchers in the field have grown increasingly aware of the fact that different methods for suppressing conscious perception may interfere with processing at different stages (e.g. Almeida et al., 2010; Breitmeyer, 2015; Faivre, Berthet, & Kouider, 2012; 2014; Izatt, Dubois, Faivre, & Koch, 2014; Peremen & Lamy, 2014b). A straightforward implication of this observation for the study of unconscious processing is that methods that interfere later should be preferred over methods that interfere earlier. To illustrate this point, relying on CFS, which seems to impair processing early (see also Yuval-Greenberg, & Heeger, 2013) would lead us to conclude that both perceptual grouping and stimulus-response associations are contingent on conscious perception. Yet, this conclusion was refuted in experiments using other methods such as sandwich masking and metacontrast masking, which appear to come into play later in processing.

Breitmeyer (2015) provided a tentative hierarchy of the different methods (see also Breitmeyer and Hesselmann, Chapter 3 in this volume). However, the comparison is complicated by the fact that, within a given method, conscious perception is disrupted to different degrees depending on the specific parameters used. For instance, backward masking is more disruptive the shorter the prime-mask SOA (e.g. Enns & Di Lollo, 2000). The liminal-prime paradigm can be particularly useful for comparing the different methods because it offers a metric (i.e. the percentage of 0-visibility trials, Peremen & Lamy, 2014b), by which each method's effectiveness at preventing subjective conscious perception can be assessed and then equated by adjusting stimulation parameters.

4 The cost of conscious perception

A recurrent incidental finding that emerged in studies using the liminal-prime paradigm (Avneon & Lamy, 2018, 2019; Kimchi et al., 2018; Lamy et al., 2015; Peremen & Lamy, 2014b; Travis et al., 2018) is that responses to the target are slower when the target follows a consciously perceived prime relative to when it follows a missed prime. This cost was also often reported in studies in which subliminal primes were compared to supraliminal primes (e.g. Desender et al., 2013). These findings suggest the existence of an undocumented cost of awareness (henceforth, CoA, see Nieuwenstein, Van der Burg, Theeuwes, Wyble, & Potter, 2009, for a related finding): consciously perceiving an event (e.g. the prime) incurs a cost for processing a trailing event (e.g. the target). However, at least three alternative accounts of this effect are possible.

4.1 Alternative accounts

First, instead of considering that RTs are faster following unaware- than aware-prime trials, one may suggest that conscious perception is more likely to emerge when responses to the target are slow and the report of the prime visibility is therefore prompted after a longer delay. This conjecture is consistent with the notion that conscious representations take time to develop (e.g. Vermeiren & Cleeremans, 2012).

Second, the cost might result from response grouping (Borger, 1963). When observers are required to produce two sequential responses, they often use the strategy of withholding the first response until the second response is selected, and then group their responses, that is, produce them in close succession. This strategy results in slower response times for one task, the longer it takes to resolve the other task, and is presumably adopted because it is easier to emit two responses at approximately the same time (Miller & Ulrich, 2008). The rationale for suggesting response grouping as an alternative account of the cost of awareness relies on the premise that it may be easier (and faster) to report total invisibility of the prime than to decide on the level of its clarity when it was consciously perceived.

Lastly, attention to the prime, rather than its conscious perception, may cause the observed cost. Attention and consciousness are closely related, and attention is widely considered to be necessary for awareness (see Dehaene, Changeux, Naccache, Sackur, & Sergent, 2006; Rensink, 2002; Mack & Rock, 1998, but see Koch & Tsuchiya, 2007). Accordingly, trials in which the prime is more visible may be trials in which the prime receives more attention, and as a consequence, less attention accrues to the target. Fluctuations of attention could thus explain the CoA, that is, the higher RTs to the target when the prime is consciously perceived (because it is attended at the expense of the target) relative to when it is not.

This interpretation raises the possibility that the CoA might be a manifestation of another phenomenon, the attentional blink (henceforth, AB). The AB refers to the finding that observers' accuracy (Broadbent & Broadbent, 1987; Raymond, Shapiro, & Arnell, 1992; Weichselgartner & Sperling, 1987) and RTs (e.g. Jolicœur & Dell'Acqua 1999; Kawahara, Di Lollo, & Enns, 2001) at reporting the second of two targets are poor when these targets appear within a short temporal interval of each other, typically for intervals ranging from 150 to 600 ms (or lag 2 to 6). For targets appearing at the same location without intervening masks or distractors and at intervals below 150 ms, performance at reporting the second target often remains high – an effect known as lag 1 sparing (Chun & Potter, 1995). If one considers the liminal prime as the first target (T1) and the target that follows it as the second target (T2), then the CoA and the attentional blink could reflect the same phenomenon. Indeed, the temporal interval between the prime and target in experiments showing a CoA is typically short (<600 ms), that is, within the blink period.

4.2 A cost of awareness, attention or report?

We conducted a series of experiments to test the alternative accounts of the cost of awareness and, in particular, to determine which conditions give rise to this cost (Ophir et al., 2018, 2019). We examined whether the cost of awareness occurs for non-speeded responses with accuracy as the dependent measure. Finding this to be the case would invalidate the response-grouping and the time-to-consciousness

The liminal-prime paradigm   135

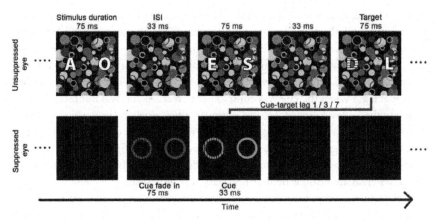

FIGURE 5.4   Illustration of the sequence of events in Ophir et al.'s (2018) study. Participants searched among heterogeneously colored letters for a red letter (indicated by horizontal lines in this figure) that could appear in one of two RSVP streams presented in the nonsuppressed eye. A non-target color cue (indicated by vertical lines) was presented in the suppressed eye (liminal cue) at lag 1, 3, or 7 prior to the target. Participants first reported the target letter and then rated the cue visibility on a PAS scale (0 to 3). Adapted from Ophir et al. (2018), with permission.

accounts of the cost: under data-limited conditions, accuracy is thought to reflect the quality of the information extracted from the display, rather than response-related processes (e.g. Santee & Egeth, 1982, Moore & Egeth, 1998). In addition, we investigated whether the cost of awareness follows the same time course as the attentional blink. Finally, we set out to disentangle the roles of attention to the first event, of its conscious perception, and of the need to report it in the cost of processing a trailing event.

In Ophir et al.'s (2018) study, we applied the liminal-prime paradigm to a task characteristic of attentional blink studies (e.g. Folk, Leber, & Egeth, 2002). The sequence of events is illustrated in Figure 5.4. On each trial, an RSVP stream of colored letters appeared on each side of fixation. Participants had to report the identity of a target defined by its color (e.g. red). A colored frame (the cue) appeared at lag 1, 3, or 7 prior to the target. The cue was rendered liminal using either CFS (as illustrated in Figure 5.4) or sandwich masking with gray frames, in different experiments. The cue appeared in either the same or the alternative stream relative to the target and was either in the target color or in a non-target color. Relying on the contingent capture account we predicted that the target-color cue would capture attention, while the non-target-color cue would not. Thus, this design allowed us to disentangle the roles of attention to and conscious perception of the cue.[4]

The results yielded four main findings. First, the cue captured attention when it was in the target color, irrespective of whether it was consciously perceived or entirely missed, in line with Lamy et al.'s (2015) finding (see also Travis et al., 2018). Second, although the target-color cue benefitted from attention in both cue awareness conditions, overall target identification accuracy was poorer when the cue was consciously perceived than when it was not, thus replicating the cost of awareness. Third, this cost shared the time course of the attentional blink: performance was poorest at lag 3 when the cue was consciously perceived and was not modulated by lag when the cue was missed. Finally, a similar, albeit smaller, lag-dependent cost of awareness was observed with non-target color cues, which did not capture attention. These findings suggest that conscious perception of a first event is a necessary condition for a lag-dependent impairment at identifying a subsequent event (i.e. the blink), whereas attention is neither necessary nor sufficient.

It is important to note that the liminal-prime paradigm requires participants to produce a report on their perception of the prime. Thus, encoding the consciously perceived prime event into working memory (WM) rather than conscious perception per se of the prime may be the crucial condition for the cost. However, the findings from many studies argue against this possibility: they showed a blink when the first event was replaced with a distractor that had to be ignored and did not require any response (e.g. Folk et al., 2002; Folk, Ester, & Troemel, 2009; Leblanc & Jolicœur, 2005; Wyble, Folk, & Potter, 2013; Zivony & Lamy, 2014, 2016). In other words, a distractor can trigger a blink when the task does not require encoding this distractor in WM. However, in these studies, the distractor matched the target-defining feature and thus most probably captured attention (see also Nieuwenstein et al., 2009). Further research is thus required to determine whether conscious perception of an event can produce a cost when this event is not attended and need not be reported.

Ophir et al. (2019) conducted a control experiment to address this question. It was similar to the dual-stream RSVP experiments reported by Ophir et al. (2018), except that participants were not required to report their subjective perception of the cue. Following the rationale used by Pitts, Martínez, & Hillyard (2012) in order to avoid inattentional blindness (Mack & Rock, 1998), we informed the participants of the presence of the cue and set the cue stimulus parameters so as to render it clearly supra-liminal. We verified that the cue had been consciously perceived on a substantial percentage of the trials during debriefing. We predicted that if conscious perception of the prime is sufficient for the cost to emerge, we should observe it here. Conversely, if encoding in WM is necessary, the blink should not occur. The results differed sharply from the results obtained when participants reported the cue visibility. We observed a lag-dependent cost of awareness only when the cue shared the target's color, whereas with non-target-color cues, performance remained high across lags, irrespective of whether or not the cue was consciously perceived.

To summarize, our findings suggest that consciously perceiving an event incurs a lag-dependent cost at processing a subsequent event only when this event is associated with a task goal: either when some information about this event must be reported (e.g. its visibility) or when it shares the target-defining feature. Although this interpretation can accommodate all the findings of our experiments, further research is required to corroborate it.

5. Conclusions and methodological guidelines

The objective of this chapter was to show that the liminal-prime paradigms has unique features that make it an especially useful tool for the study of unconscious processing and conscious perception. In particular, it retains the subjective aspect of conscious experience without sacrificing exhaustiveness relative to methods that define conscious perception using objective measures. Most crucially, it provides unique and essential insights: while subliminal-prime methods may lead only to the conclusion that unconscious attentional capture and unconscious semantic priming occur, with no possible distinction between them, the liminal-prime paradigm further reveals that attentional capture is entirely independent of conscious perception, whereas semantic priming is heavily dependent on it. In addition, this paradigm is well suited to explore the cost of conscious perception, which allowed us to shed new light on the highly investigated attentional blink phenomenon.

In order for the findings emanating from the liminal-prime paradigm to be interpretable, it is important to follow a number of guidelines. First, a sensitive four-point scale such as PAS (Ramsøy & Overgaard, 2004) should be used as the subjective measure of conscious perception rather than coarser two- or three-point scales. Second, priming should be reported for all visibility ratings rather than for a subset of these (although ratings indicating some level of conscious perception can be grouped). Third, at least 15–20 percent of catch trials (i.e. trials in which the prime is absent) should be included because these provide a measure of participants' reports reliability: participants who use high visibility ratings on catch trials are poor introspectors, or do not comply with the task (which typically happens for no more than 10 percent of the participants), and should therefore be excluded. Fourth, appropriate statistical models, such as linear mixed-effects models (LMM) for RTs and generalized linear mixed-effects model (GLMM) for accuracy, should be used to analyze the data because using more classical models, such as analysis of variance, with imbalanced data structures can lead to serious distortions. Fifth, the whole RT distribution should be considered. Relying exclusively on mean performance may mask unconscious priming because this effect occurs mainly on fast-RT trials. This is more likely to occur with the liminal-prime paradigm, because it is associated with slower RTs than paradigms in which only a speeded response to the target is collected on each trial. This problem can also be avoided by imposing a response deadline on target categorization. Sixth, in order to render the prime liminal, one should select a method known to interfere with perceptual processing as late as possible. Although a foolproof classification of existing methods is still lacking (but see Breitmeyer, 2015; Breitmeyer and Hesselmann, Chapter 3 in this volume), it seems clear that CFS should be avoided, whereas backward masking and metacontrast masking provide consistent findings. Seventh, when different "blinding" methods are compared, it is important to calibrate the stimulation parameters so as to ensure that each method is associated with a similar proportion of 0-visibility trials.

The liminal-prime paradigm is a relatively new method but it has already proved to be a very useful paradigm for the study of unconscious processing and conscious perception. However, it is likely to undergo further refinements as it gets experimented in more studies.

Author's note

Correspondence should be addressed to Dominique Lamy at domi@tauex.tau. ac.il. Support was provided by the Israel Science Foundation (ISF) grants no. 1286/16 to Dominique Lamy.

Notes

1 It is important to note that although Peremen and Lamy (2014a, b) measured priming for all four visibility ratings, the objective of their papers was to elucidate under what conditions unconscious priming is observed and not to compare conscious and unconscious priming. Such a comparison was not meaningful in their experiments because prime-mask SOAs were manipulated and each visibility rating therefore included a different mixture of SOAs (with higher average SOAs the higher the visibility rating).
2 We use a 0 to 3 scale instead of the classical 1–4 PAS scale devised by Ramsøy and Overgaard (2004) in order to better convey that the lowest level corresponds to "no experience whatsoever".
3 Note however that the priming effects observed at the intermediate levels were reported by Avneon and Lamy (2018) in supplementary materials and were in line with the conclusions of the paper.
4 Note that Nieuwenstein et al. (2009) also reported a cost of awareness. They collected dichotomous seen/unseen reports relative to a first event and found a subsequent event to suffer from an attentional blink only when the first event was seen. However, both stimuli were presented at fixation and attended. Thus, the relative roles of attention and conscious perception were not distinguished.

References

Almeida, J., Mahon, B. Z., & Caramazza, A. (2010). The role of the dorsal visual processing stream in tool identification. *Psychological Science, 21*(6), 772–8.
Almeida, J., Pajtas, P. E., Mahon, B. Z., Nakayama, K., & Caramazza, A. (2013). Affect of the unconscious: Visually suppressed angry faces modulate our decisions. *Cognitive, Affective, and Behavioral Neuroscience, 13*(1), 94–101.
Anderson, B. A., & Folk, C. L. (2012). Dissociating location-specific inhibition and attention shifts: Evidence against the disengagement account of contingent capture. *Attention, Perception, and Psychophysics,* 74, 1183–98.
Ansorge, U. (2004). Top-down contingencies of nonconscious priming revealed by dual-task interference. *Quarterly Journal of Experimental Psychology: Human Experimental Psychology,* 57A, 1123–48.
Ansorge, U., & Neumann, O. (2005). Intentions determine the effect of invisible metacontrast-masked primes: Evidence for top-down contingencies in a peripheral cuing task. *Journal of Experimental Psychology: Human Perception and Performance, 31*(4), 762–77.

Ansorge, U., Khalid, S., & Koenig, P. (2013). Space-valence priming with subliminal and supraliminal words. *Frontiers in Psychology*, *4*, 81.

Ansorge, U., Khalid, S., & Laback, B. (2016). Unconscious cross-modal priming of auditory sound localization by visual words. *Journal of Experimental Psychology: Learning, Memory, and Cognition*, *42*(6), 925–37.

Ansorge, U., Kiefer, M., Khalid, S., Grassl, S., & König, P. (2010). Testing the theory of embodied cognition with subliminal words. *Cognition*, *116*(3), 303–20.

Ansorge, U., Kiss, M., & Eimer, M. (2009). Goal-driven attentional capture by invisible colors: Evidence from event-related potentials. *Psychonomic Bulletin and Review*, *16*(4), 648–53.

Anzulewicz, A., Asanowicz, D., Windey, B., Paulewicz, B., Wierzchoń, M., & Cleeremans, A. (2015). Does level of processing affect the transition from unconscious to conscious perception? *Consciousness and Cognition*, *36*, 1–11.

Armstrong, A. M., & Dienes, Z. (2013). Subliminal understanding of negation: Unconscious control by subliminal processing of word pairs. *Consciousness and Cognition*, *22*(3), 1022–40.

Atas, A., Desender, K., Gevers, W., & Cleeremans, A. (2016). Dissociating perception from action during conscious and unconscious conflict adaptation. *Journal of Experimental Psychology: Learning, Memory, and Cognition*, *42*(6), 866–81.

Atas, A., Vermeiren, A., & Cleeremans, A. (2013). Repeating a strongly masked stimulus increases priming and awareness. *Consciousness and Cognition*, *22*(4), 1422–30.

Avneon, M., & Lamy, D. (2018). Reexamining unconscious response priming: A liminal-prime paradigm. *Consciousness and Cognition*, *59*, 87–103.

Avneon, M., & Lamy, D. (2019). Do semantic priming and retrieval of stimulus-response associations depend on conscious perception? *Consciousness and Cognition*, *69*, 36–51.

Axelrod, V., & Rees, G. (2014). Conscious awareness is required for holistic face processing. *Consciousness and Cognition*, *27*, 233–45.

Bahrami, B., Vetter, P., Spolaore, E., Pagano, S., Butterworth, B., & Rees, G. (2010). Unconscious numerical priming despite interocular suppression. *Psychological Science*, *21*(2), 224–33.

Belopolsky, A. V., Schreij, D., & Theeuwes, J. (2010). What is top-down about contingent capture? *Attention, Perception, and Psychophysics*, *72*, 326–41.

Biderman, N., & Mudrik, L. (2018). Evidence for implicit – but not unconscious – processing of object-scene relations. *Psychological science*, *29*(2), 266–77.

Biderman, D., Biderman, N., Zivony, A., Lamy, D. (2017). Contingent capture is weakened in search for multiple features from different dimensions. *Journal of Experimental Psychology: Human Perception and Performance*, *43*, 1974–92.

Binder, M., Gociewicz, K., Windey, B., Koculak, M., Finc, K., Nikadon, J., & Cleeremans, A. (2017). The levels of perceptual processing and the neural correlates of increasing subjective visibility. *Consciousness and Cognition*, *55*, 106–25.

Borger, R. (1963). The refractory period and serial choice-reactions. *Quarterly Journal of Experimental Psychology*, *15*(1), 1–12.

Breitmeyer, B. G. (2015). Psychophysical "blinding" methods reveal a functional hierarchy of unconscious visual processing. *Consciousness and Cognition*, *35*, 234–50.

Broadbent, D. E., & Broadbent, M. H. (1987). From detection to identification: Response to multiple targets in rapid serial visual presentation. *Perception and Psychophysics*, *42*(2), 105–13.

Carmel, T., & Lamy, D. (2014). The same-location cost is unrelated to attentional settings: An object-updating account. *Journal of Experimental Psychology: Human Perception and Performance*, *40*, 1465–78.

Carmel, T., & Lamy, D. (2015). Towards a resolution of the attentional-capture debate. *Journal of Experimental Psychology: Human Perception and Performance, 41*(6), 1772–82.

Cheesman, J., & Merikle, P. M. (1986). Distinguishing conscious from unconscious perceptual processes. *Canadian Journal of Psychology/Revue canadienne de psychologie, 40*(4), 343–67.

Chiu, Y. C., & Aron, A. R. (2014). Unconsciously triggered response inhibition requires an executive setting. *Journal of Experimental Psychology: General, 143*(1), 56–61.

Chun, M. M., & Potter, M. C. (1995). A two-stage model for multiple target detection in rapid serial visual presentation. *Journal of Experimental Psychology: Human Perception and Performance, 21*(1), 109–27.

Damian, M. F. (2001). Congruity effects evoked by subliminally presented primes: Automaticity rather than semantic processing. *Journal of Experimental Psychology: Human Perception and Performance, 27*(1), 154–65.

Dehaene, S., & Changeux, J. P. (2011). Experimental and theoretical approaches to conscious processing. *Neuron, 70*(2), 200–27.

Dehaene, S., Changeux, J. P., Naccache, L., Sackur, J., & Sergent, C. (2006). Conscious, preconscious, and subliminal processing: A testable taxonomy. *Trends in Cognitive Sciences, 10*(5), 204–11.

Dehaene, S., Naccache, L., Le Clec'H, G., Koechlin, E., Mueller, M., Dehaene-Lambertz, G., van de Moortele, P. F., & Le Bihan, D. (1998). Imaging unconscious semantic priming. *Nature, 395*(6702), 597–600.

Desender, K., Van Lierde, E., & Van den Bussche, E. (2013). Comparing conscious and unconscious conflict adaptation. *PLoS One, 8*(2), e55976.

Dienes, Z., Altmann, G., Kwan, L., & Goode, A. (1995). Unconscious knowledge of artificial grammars is applied strategically. *Journal of Experimental Psychology: Learning, Memory, and Cognition, 21*(5), 1322–38.

Dienes, Z., Scott, R. B., & Seth, A. K. (2010). Subjective measures of implicit knowledge that go beyond confidence: Reply to Overgaard et al. *Consciousness and Cognition, 19*(2), 685–6.

Eimer, M., & Schlaghecken, F. (1998). Effects of masked stimuli on motor activation: Behavioral and electrophysiological evidence. *Journal of Experimental Psychology: Human Perception and Performance, 24*, 1737–47.

Eimer, M., Kiss, M., Press, C., & Sauter, D. (2009). The roles of feature-specific task set and bottom-up salience in attentional capture: An ERP study. *Journal of Experimental Psychology: Human Perception and Performance, 35*, 1316–28.

Enns, J. T., & Di Lollo, V. (2000). What's new in visual masking? *Trends in Cognitive Sciences, 4*(9), 345–52.

Erdelyi, M. H. (1986). Experimental indeterminacies in the dissociation paradigm of subliminal perception. *Behavioral and Brain Sciences, 9*(1), 30–1.

Eriksen, C. W. (1960). Discrimination and learning without awareness: A methodological survey and evaluation. *Psychological review, 67*(5), 279–300.

Faivre, N., & Koch, C. (2014). Inferring the direction of implied motion depends on visual awareness. *Journal of Vision, 14*(4), 1–14.

Faivre, N., Berthet, V., & Kouider, S. (2012). Nonconscious influences from emotional faces: A comparison of visual crowding, masking, and continuous flash suppression. *Frontiers in Psychology, 3*, 129.

Faivre, N., Berthet, V., & Kouider, S. (2014a). Sustained invisibility through crowding and continuous flash suppression: A comparative review. *Frontiers in Psychology, 5*, 475.

Faivre, N., Mudrik, L., Schwartz, N., & Koch, C. (2014b). Multisensory integration in complete unawareness: Evidence from audiovisual congruency priming. *Psychological Science, 25*(11), 2006–16.

Folk, C. L., & Remington, R. (1998). Selectivity in distraction by irrelevant featural singletons: Evidence for two forms of attentional capture. *Journal of Experimental Psychology: Human Perception and Performance, 24*, 847–58.

Folk, C. L., & Remington, R. W. (2008). Bottom-up priming of topdown attentional control settings. *Visual Cognition, 16*(2–3), 215–31.

Folk, C. L., Ester, E. F., & Troemel, K. (2009). How to keep attention from straying: Get engaged! *Psychonomic Bulletin and Review, 16*(1), 127–32.

Folk, C. L., Leber, A. B., & Egeth, H. E. (2002). Made you blink! Contingent attentional capture produces a spatial blink. *Perception & psychophysics, 64*(5), 741–53.

Frings, C., & Wentura, D. (2008). Separating context and trial-by-trial effects in the negative priming paradigm. *European Journal of Cognitive Psychology, 20*(2), 195–210.

Gelbard-Sagiv, H., Faivre, N., Mudrik, L., & Koch, C. (2016). Low-level awareness accompanies "unconscious" high-level processing during continuous flash suppression. *Journal of Vision, 16*(1)3, 1–16.

Goller, F., Khalid, S., & Ansorge, U. (2017). A double dissociation between conscious and non-conscious priming of responses and affect: Evidence for a contribution of misattributions to the priming of affect. *Frontiers in Psychology, 8*, 453.

Greenwald, A. G., & De Houwer, J. (2017). Unconscious conditioning: Demonstration of existence and difference from conscious conditioning. *Journal of Experimental Psychology: General, 146*(12), 1705–21.

Greenwald, A. G., Draine, S. C., & Abrams, R. L. (1996). Three cognitive markers of unconscious semantic activation. *Science, 273*(5282), 1699–1702.

Haase, S. J., & Fisk, G. D. (2015). Awareness of "invisible" arrows in a metacontrast masking paradigm. *American Journal of Psychology, 128*(1), 15–30.

Hannula, D. E., Simons, D. J., & Cohen, N. J. (2005). Imaging implicit perception: Promise and pitfalls. *Nature Reviews Neuroscience, 6*(3), 247–55.

Heinemann, A., Kunde, W., & Kiesel, A. (2009). Context-specific prime-congruency effects: On the role of conscious stimulus representations for cognitive control. *Consciousness and Cognition, 18*(4), 966–76.

Hesselmann, G. (2018). Applying linear mixed effects models (LMMs) in within-participant designs with subjective trial-based assessments of awareness: A caveat. *Frontiers in Psychology, 9*, 788.

Hesselmann, G., & Knops, A. (2014). No conclusive evidence for numerical priming under interocular suppression. *Psychological Science, 25*(11), 2116–19.

Hesselmann, G., Darcy, N., Ludwig, K., & Sterzer, P. (2016). Priming in a shape task but not in a category task under continuous flash suppression. *Journal of Vision, 16*(3):17, 1–17.

Hesselmann, G., Darcy, N., Rothkirch, M., & Sterzer, P. (2018). Investigating masked priming along the "vision-for-perception" and "vision-for-action" dimensions of unconscious processing. *Journal of Experimental Psychology: General, 147*(11), 1641–59.

Hesselmann, G., Darcy, N., Sterzer, P., & Knops, A. (2015). Exploring the boundary conditions of unconscious numerical priming effects with continuous flash suppression. *Consciousness and Cognition, 31*, 60–72.

Holender, D. (1986). Semantic activation without conscious identification in dichotic listening, parafoveal vision, and visual masking: A survey and appraisal. *Behavioral and Brain Sciences, 9*(1), 1–23.

Hsieh, P. J., Colas, J. T., & Kanwisher, N. (2011). Pop-out without awareness: Unseen feature singletons capture attention only when top-down attention is available. *Psychological Science, 22*(9), 1220–6.

Ivanoff, J., & Klein, R. M. (2003). Orienting of attention without awareness is affected by measurement-induced attentional control settings. *Journal of Vision, 3*(1), 32–40.

Izatt, G., Dubois, J., Faivre, N., & Koch, C. (2014). A direct comparison of unconscious face processing under masking and interocular suppression. *Frontiers in Psychology*, *5*, 659.

Jiang, J., Bailey, K., Xiang, L., Zhang, L., & Zhang, Q. (2016). Comparing the neural correlates of conscious and unconscious conflict control in a masked Stroop priming task. *Frontiers in Human Neuroscience*, *10*, 297.

Jiang, Y., Costello, P., Fang, F., Huang, M., & He, S. (2006). A gender- and sexual orientation-dependent spatial attentional effect of invisible images. *Proceedings of the National Academy of Sciences*, *103*(45), 17048–52.

Jolicœur, P., & Dell'Acqua, R. (1999). Attentional and structural constraints on visual encoding. *Psychological Research*, *62*(2–3), 154–64.

Kawahara, J. I., Di Lollo, V., & Enns, J. T. (2001). Attentional requirements in visual detection and identification: Evidence from the attentional blink. *Journal of Experimental Psychology: Human Perception and Performance*, *27*(4), 969–84.

Kiefer, M. (2018). Cognitive control over unconscious cognition: Flexibility and generalizability of task set influences on subsequent masked semantic priming. *Psychological Research* (Online first), 1–15.

Kiefer, M., & Brendel, D. (2006). Attentional modulation of unconscious "automatic" processes: Evidence from event-related potentials in a masked priming paradigm. *Journal of Cognitive Neuroscience*, *18*(2), 184–98.

Kiefer, M., & Spitzer, M. (2000). Time course of conscious and unconscious semantic brain activation. *Neuroreport*, *11*(11), 2401–7.

Kiesel, A., Kunde, W., Pohl, C., & Hoffmann, J. (2006). Priming from novel masked stimuli depends on target set size. *Advances in Cognitive Psychology*, *2*(1), 37–45.

Kimchi, R., Devyatko, D., & Sabary, S. (2018). Can perceptual grouping unfold in the absence of awareness? Comparing grouping during continuous flash suppression and sandwich masking. *Consciousness and Cognition*, *60*, 37–51.

Kinoshita, S., & Hunt, L. (2008). RT distribution analysis of category congruence effects with masked primes. *Memory and Cognition*, *36*(7), 1324–34.

Klauer, K. C., Eder, A. B., Greenwald, A. G., & Abrams, R. L. (2007). Priming of semantic classifications by novel subliminal prime words. *Consciousness and Cognition*, *16*, 63–83.

Klinger, M. R., Burton, P. C., & Pitts, G. S. (2000). Mechanisms of unconscious priming: I. Response competition, not spreading activation. *Journal of Experimental Psychology: Learning, Memory, and Cognition*, *26*(2), 441–55.

Koch, C., & Tsuchiya, N. (2007). Attention and consciousness: Two distinct brain processes. *Trends in Cognitive Sciences*, *11*(1), 16–22.

Koivisto, M., & Grassini, S. (2016). Neural processing around 200 ms after stimulus-onset correlates with subjective visual awareness. *Neuropsychologia*, *84*, 235–43.

Koivisto, M., & Grassini, S. (2018). Unconscious response priming during continuous flash suppression. *PloS one*, *13*(2), e0192201.

Koivisto, M., & Rientamo, E. (2016). Unconscious vision spots the animal but not the dog: Masked priming of natural scenes. *Consciousness and Cognition*, *41*, 10–23.

Kouider, S., & Dehaene, S. (2007). Levels of processing during non-conscious perception: A critical review of visual masking. *Philosophical Transactions of the Royal Society of London B: Biological Sciences*, *362*(1481), 857–75.

Kouider, S., & Dupoux, E. (2004). Partial awareness creates the "illusion" of subliminal semantic priming. *Psychological Science*, *15*(2), 75–81.

Kouider, S., Eger, E., Dolan, R., & Henson, R. N. (2008). Activity in face-responsive brain regions is modulated by invisible, attended faces: Evidence from masked priming. *Cerebral Cortex*, *19*(1), 13–23.

The liminal-prime paradigm **143**

Kunde, W., Kiesel, A., & Hoffmann, J. (2003). Conscious control over the content of unconscious cognition. *Cognition, 88*(2), 223–42.

Lähteenmäki, M., Hyönä, J., Koivisto, M., & Nummenmaa, L. (2015). Affective processing requires awareness. *Journal of Experimental Psychology: General, 144*(2), 339–65.

Lamy, D., Alon, L., Carmel, T., & Shalev, N. (2015). The role of conscious perception in attentional capture and object-file updating. *Psychological Science, 26*(1), 48–57.

Lamy, D., Carmel, T., & Peremen, Z. (2017). Prior conscious experience enhances conscious perception but does not affect response priming. *Cognition, 160*, 62–81.

Lamy, D., Leber, A., & Egeth, H. E. (2004). Effects of task relevance and stimulus-driven salience in feature-search mode. *Journal of Experimental Psychology: Human Perception and Performance, 30*, 1019–31.

Leblanc, É., & Jolicœur, P. (2005). The time course of the contingent spatial blink. *Canadian Journal of Experimental Psychology/Revue canadienne de psychologie nexpérimentale, 59*(2), 124–31.

Lin, Z., & Murray, S. O. (2014). Priming of awareness or how not to measure visual awareness. *Journal of Vision, 14*(1), 27, 1–17.

Liu, C., Sun, Z., Jou, J., Cui, Q., Zhao, G., Qiu, J., & Tu, S. (2016). Unconscious processing of facial emotional valence relation: Behavioral evidence of integration between subliminally perceived stimuli. *PloS one, 11*(9), e0162689.

Mack, A., & Rock, I. (1998). *Inattentional Blindness* (vol. 33). Cambridge, MA: MIT Press.

Manly, T., Fish, J. E., Griffiths, S., Molenveld, M., Zhou, F. A., & Davis, G. J. (2014). Unconscious priming of task-switching generalizes to an untrained task. *PloS one, 9*(2), e88416.

Melloni, L., Schwiedrzik, C. M., Müller, N., Rodriguez, E., & Singer, W. (2011). Expectations change the signatures and timing of electrophysiological correlates of perceptual awareness. *Journal of Neuroscience, 31*(4), 1386–96.

Merikle, P. M., & Reingold, E. M. (1998). On demonstrating unconscious perception: Comment on Draine and Greenwald (1998). *Journal of Experimental Psychology: General, 127*(3), 304–10.

Merikle, P. M., Smilek, D., & Eastwood, J. D. (2001). Perception without awareness: Perspectives from cognitive psychology. *Cognition, 79*(1–2), 115–34.

Miller, J., & Ulrich, R. (2008). Bimanual response grouping in dual-task paradigms. *Quarterly Journal of Experimental Psychology, 61*(7), 999–1019.

Moore, C. M., & Egeth, H. (1998). How does feature-based attention affect visual processing? *Journal of Experimental Psychology: Human Perception and Performance, 24*(4), 1296–1310.

Naccache, L., & Dehaene, S. (2001). Unconscious semantic priming extends to novel unseen stimuli. *Cognition, 80*(3), 215–29.

Naccache, L., Blandin, E., & Dehaene, S. (2002). Unconscious masked priming depends on temporal attention. *Psychological Science, 13*(5), 416–24.

Neumann, O., & Klotz, W. (1994). Motor responses to nonreportable, masked stimuli: Where is the limit of direct parameter specification. *Attention and Performance XV: Conscious and Nonconscious Information Processing*, 123–50.

Nieuwenstein, M., Van der Burg, E., Theeuwes, J., Wyble, B., & Potter, M. (2009). Temporal constraints on conscious vision: On the ubiquitous nature of the attentional blink. *Journal of Vision, 9*(9), 18, 1–14.

Ophir, A. E., Hesselmann, G. & Lamy, D. (2019). The role of task goals in the cost of awareness. Paper presented at the annual Conference of the Israeli Society for Cognitive Psychology, February 2019, Akko.

Ophir, A. E., Sherman, E., & Lamy, D. (2018). An attentional blink in the absence of spatial attention: A cost of awareness?. *Psychological Research* (Online first), 1–17.

Ortells, J. J., Kiefer, M., Castillo, A., Megías, M., & Morillas, A. (2016). The semantic origin of unconscious priming: Behavioral and event-related potential evidence during category congruency priming from strongly and weakly related masked words. *Cognition*, 146, 143–57.

Overgaard, M. (2012). Blindsight: recent and historical controversies on the blindness of blindsight. *Wiley Interdisciplinary Reviews: Cognitive Science*, 3(6), 607–14.

Overgaard, M. (2015). The challenge of measuring consciousness. In M. Overgaard (ed.), *Behavioural Methods in Consciousness Research* (pp. 7–19). Oxford: Oxford University Press

Overgaard, M., & Sandberg, K. (2012). Kinds of access: Different methods for report reveal different kinds of metacognitive access. *Philosophical Transactions of the Royal Society of London B: Biological Sciences*, 367(1594), 1287–96.

Overgaard, M., Fehl, K., Mouridsen, K., Bergholt, B., & Cleeremans, A. (2008). Seeing without seeing? Degraded conscious vision in a blindsight patient. *PloS one*, 3(8), e3028.

Overgaard, M., Rote, J., Mouridsen, K., & Ramsøy, T. Z. (2006). Is conscious perception gradual or dichotomous? A comparison of report methodologies during a visual task. *Consciousness and Cognition*, 15(4), 700–8.

Overgaard, M., Timmermans, B., Sandberg, K., & Cleeremans, A. (2010). Optimizing subjective measures of consciousness. *Consciousness and Cognition*, 19(2), 682–4.

Peel, H. J., Sperandio, I., Laycock, R., & Chouinard, P. A. (2018). Perceptual discrimination of basic object features is not facilitated when priming stimuli are prevented from reaching awareness by means of visual masking. *Frontiers in Integrative Neuroscience, 12.*

Peremen, Z., & Lamy, D. (2014a). Comparing unconscious processing during continuous flash suppression and metacontrast masking just under the limen of consciousness. *Frontiers in Psychology*, 5, 969.

Peremen, Z., & Lamy, D. (2014b). Do conscious perception and unconscious processing rely on independent mechanisms? A metacontrast study. *Consciousness and Cognition*, 24, 22–32.

Persaud, N., McLeod, P., & Cowey, A. (2007). Post-decision wagering objectively measures awareness. *Nature Neuroscience*, 10(2), 257–61.

Persuh, M. (2018). Measuring perceptual consciousness. *Frontiers in Psychology*, 8, 2320.

Peters, M. A., Ro, T., & Lau, H. (2016). Who's afraid of response bias? *Neuroscience of Consciousness*, 2016(1), 1–6.

Pitts, M. A., Martínez, A., & Hillyard, S. A. (2012). Visual processing of contour patterns under conditions of inattentional blindness. *Journal of Cognitive Neuroscience*, 24(2), 287–303.

Pohl, C., Kiesel, A., Kunde, W., & Hoffmann, J. (2010). Early and late selection in unconscious information processing. *Journal of Experimental Psychology: Human Perception and Performance*, 36(2), 268–85.

Pratte, M. S., & Rouder, J. N. (2009). A task-difficulty artifact in subliminal priming. *Attention, Perception, and Psychophysics*, 71(6), 1276–83.

Ramsøy, T. Z., & Overgaard, M. (2004). Introspection and subliminal perception. *Phenomenology and the Cognitive Sciences*, 3(1), 1–23.

Ratcliff, R. (1979). Group reaction time distributions and an analysis of distribution statistics. *Psychological bulletin*, 86(3), 446–61.

Raymond, J. E., Shapiro, K. L., & Arnell, K. M. (1992). Temporary suppression of visual processing in an RSVP task: An attentional blink? *Journal of Experimental Psychology: Human Perception and Performance*, 18(3), 849–60.

Reingold, E. M. (2004). Unconscious perception and the classic dissociation paradigm: A new angle? *Perception and Psychophysics*, *66*(5), 882–7.

Rensink, R. A. (2002). Change detection. *Annual Review of Psychology*, *53*(1), 245–77.

Reuss, H., Desender, K., Kiesel, A., & Kunde, W. (2014). Unconscious conflicts in unconscious contexts: The role of awareness and timing in flexible conflict adaptation. *Journal of Experimental Psychology: General*, *143*(4), 1701–18.

Reynvoet, B., Gevers, W., & Caessens, B. (2005). Unconscious primes activate motor codes through semantics. *Journal of Experimental Psychology: Learning, Memory, and Cognition*, *31*(5), 991–1000.

Rock, I. (1986). The description and analysis of object and event perception. In K. R. Boff, L. Kaufman, & J. P. Thomas (eds), *Handbook of Perception and Human Performance* (pp. 1–46). New York: Wiley.

Rothkirch, M., & Hesselmann, G. (2017). What we talk about when we talk about unconscious processing: A plea for best practices. *Frontiers in Psychology*, *8*, 835.

Rouder, J. N., & Speckman, P. L. (2004). An evaluation of the Vincentizing method of forming group-level response time distributions. *Psychonomic Bulletin and Review*, *11*(3), 419–27.

Salti, M., Bar-Haim, Y., & Lamy, D. (2012). The P3 component of the ERP reflects conscious perception, not confidence. *Consciousness and Cognition*, *21*(2), 961–8.

Sand, A. (2016). Reversed priming effects may be driven by misperception rather than subliminal processing. *Frontiers in Psychology*, *7*, 198.

Sandberg, K., Timmermans, B., Overgaard, M., & Cleeremans, A. (2010). Measuring consciousness: Is one measure better than the other? *Consciousness and Cognition*, *19*, 1069–78.

Sandberg, K., Bibby, B. M., Timmermans, B., Cleeremans, A., & Overgaard, M. (2011). Measuring consciousness: Task accuracy and awareness as sigmoid functions of stimulus duration. *Consciousness and Cognition*, *20*(4), 1659–75.

Santee, J. L., & Egeth, H. E. (1982). Do reaction time and accuracy measure the same aspects of letter recognition? *Journal of Experimental Psychology: Human Perception and Performance*, *8*(4), 489–501.

Schlossmacher, I., Junghöfer, M., Straube, T., & Bruchmann, M. (2017). No differential effects to facial expressions under continuous flash suppression: An event-related potentials study. *NeuroImage*, *163*, 276–85.

Schmidt, T. (2015). Invisible stimuli, implicit thresholds: Why invisibility judgments cannot be interpreted in isolation. *Advances in Cognitive Psychology*, *11*(2), 31–41.

Schmidt, T., & Vorberg, D. (2006). Criteria for unconscious cognition: Three types of dissociation. *Perception and Psychophysics*, *68*(3), 489–504.

Schoeberl, T., Ditye, T., & Ansorge, U. (2018). Same-location costs in peripheral cueing: The role of cue awareness and feature changes. *Journal of Experimental Psychology: Human Perception and Performance*, *44*(3), 433–51.

Schönhammer, J. G., & Kerzel, D. (2013). Some effects of non-predictive cues on accuracy are mediated by feature-based attention. *Journal of Vision*, *13*(9), 76.

Sergent, C., Baillet, S., & Dehaene, S. (2005). Timing of the brain events underlying access to consciousness during the attentional blink. *Nature Neuroscience*, *8*(10), 1391–1400.

Shanks, D. R. (2017). Regressive research: The pitfalls of post hoc data selection in the study of unconscious mental processes. *Psychonomic Bulletin and Review*, *24*(3), 752–75.

Sklar, A. Y., Levy, N., Goldstein, A., Mandel, R., Maril, A., & Hassin, R. R. (2012). Reading and doing arithmetic nonconsciously. *Proceedings of the National Academy of Sciences*, *109*(48), 19614–19.

Snodgrass, M., Bernat, E., & Shevrin, H. (2004). Unconscious perception at the objective detection threshold exists. *Perception and Psychophysics, 66*(5), 888–95.

Stein, T., Utz, V., & Van Opstal, F. (2018). Unconscious semantic priming from pictures under backward masking and continuous flash suppression. *PsyAr xiv* (Sept.), 21.

Szczepanowski, R., Traczyk, J., Wierzchoń, M., & Cleeremans, A. (2013). The perception of visual emotion: Comparing different measures of awareness. *Consciousness and Cognition, 22*(1), 212–20.

Tagliabue, C. F., Mazzi, C., Bagattini, C., & Savazzi, S. (2016). Early local activity in temporal areas reflects graded content of visual perception. *Frontiers in Psychology, 7,* 572.

Tapia, E., Breitmeyer, B. G., & Shooner, C. R. (2010). Role of task-directed attention in nonconscious and conscious response priming by form and color. *Journal of Experimental Psychology: Human Perception and Performance, 36*(1), 74–87.

Timmermans, B., & Cleeremans, A. (2015). How can we measure awareness? An overview of current methods. In M. Overgaard (ed.), *Behavioural Methods in Consciousness Research* (pp. 21–46). Oxford: Oxford University Press.

Travis, S. L., Dux, P. E., & Mattingley, J. B. (2018). Neural correlates of goal-directed enhancement and suppression of visual stimuli in the absence of conscious perception. *Attention, Perception, and Psychophysics* (Online first), 1–19.

Van den Bussche, E., & Reynvoet, B. (2007). Masked priming effects in semantic categorization are independent of category size. *Experimental Psychology, 54*(3), 225–35.

Van den Bussche, E., Notebaert, K., & Reynvoet, B. (2009). Masked primes can be genuinely semantically processed: A picture prime study. *Experimental Psychology, 56*(5), 295–300.

Van den Bussche, E., Vermeiren, A., Desender, K., Gevers, W., Hughes, G., Verguts, T., & Reynvoet, B. (2013). Disentangling conscious and unconscious processing: A subjective trial-based assessment approach. *Frontiers in Human Neuroscience, 7,* 769.

Van Gaal, S., Lamme, V. A., Fahrenfort, J. J., & Ridderinkhof, K. R. (2011). Dissociable brain mechanisms underlying the conscious and unconscious control of behavior. *Journal of Cognitive Neuroscience, 23*(1), 91–105.

Van Gaal, S., Lamme, V. A., & Ridderinkhof, K. R. (2010). Unconsciously triggered conflict adaptation. *PloS One, 5*(7), e11508.

Van Gaal, S., Naccache, L., Meuwese, J. D., Van Loon, A. M., Leighton, A. H., Cohen, L., & Dehaene, S. (2014). Can the meaning of multiple words be integrated unconsciously? *Philosophical Transactions of the Royal Society B, 369*(1641), 20130212.

Van Gaal, S., Ridderinkhof, K. R., Fahrenfort, J. J., Scholte, H. S., & Lamme, V. A. (2008). Frontal cortex mediates unconsciously triggered inhibitory control. *Journal of Neuroscience, 28*(32), 8053–62.

Van Opstal, F., de Lange, F. P., & Dehaene, S. (2011). Rapid parallel semantic processing of numbers without awareness. *Cognition, 120*(1), 136–47.

Vermeiren, A., & Cleeremans, A. (2012). The validity of d' measures. *PloS one, 7*(2), e31595.

Vorberg, D., Mattler, U., Heinecke, A., Schmidt, T., & Schwarzbach, J. (2003). Different time courses for visual perception and action priming. *Proceedings of the National Academy of Sciences, 100*(10), 6275–80.

Weichselgartner, E., & Sperling, G. (1987). Dynamics of automatic and controlled visual attention. *Science, 238*(4828), 778–80.

West, B. T., Welch, K. B., & Galecki, A. T. (2014). *Linear Mixed Models: A Practical Guide Using Statistical Software* (2nd ed.). New York: CRC Press.

Wierzchoń, M., Asanowicz, D., Paulewicz, B., & Cleeremans, A. (2012). Subjective measures of consciousness in artificial grammar learning task. *Consciousness and Cognition, 21*(3), 1141–53.

Wierzchoń, M., Paulewicz, B., Asanowicz, D., Timmermans, B., & Cleeremans, A. (2014). Different subjective awareness measures demonstrate the influence of visual identification on perceptual awareness ratings. *Consciousness and Cognition, 27*, 109–20.

Windey, B., Vermeiren, A., Atas, A., & Cleeremans, A. (2014). The graded and dichotomous nature of visual awareness. *Philosophical Transactions of the Royal Society B, 369*(1641), 20130282.

Wyart, V., & Tallon-Baudry, C. (2008). Neural dissociation between visual awareness and spatial attention. *Journal of Neuroscience, 28*(10), 2667–79.

Wyble, B., Folk, C., & Potter, M. C. (2013). Contingent attentional capture by conceptually relevant images. *Journal of Experimental Psychology: Human Perception and Performance, 39*(3), 861–71.

Yang, Y. H., & Yeh, S. L. (2018). Unconscious processing of facial expression as revealed by affective priming under continuous flash suppression. *Psychonomic Bulletin and Review, 25*, 2215–23.

Yuval-Greenberg, S., & Heeger, D. J. (2013). Continuous flash suppression modulates cortical activity in early visual cortex. *Journal of Neuroscience, 33*(23), 9635–43.

Zehetleitner, M., & Rausch, M. (2013). Being confident without seeing: What subjective measures of visual consciousness are about. *Attention, Perception, and Psychophysics, 75*(7), 1406–26.

Zivony, A., & Lamy, D. (2014). Attentional engagement is not sufficient to prevent spatial capture. *Attention, Perception, and Psychophysics, 76*(1), 19–31.

Zivony, A., & Lamy, D. (2016). Attentional capture and engagement during the attentional blink: A "camera" metaphor of attention. *Journal of Experimental Psychology: Human Perception and Performance, 42*(11), 1886–1902.

6

FROM ALIENS TO INVISIBLE LIMBS

The transitions that never make it into conscious experience

Jaan Aru

UNIVERSITY OF TARTU AND HUMBOLDT UNIVERSITY BERLIN

1 Understanding consciousness: Where do we stand?

Consider a lab retreat of alien scientists. They come to earth to enjoy the winter, the fact that there is only one sun, and of course they come for the ice cream. However, as they are scientists, they also find themselves thinking about humans. Surely, humans created ice cream, but alien scientists understand that this does not explain anything about the first-person perspective of humans. They wonder what is it like to be a human with its consciousness. And, as they are scientists, to figure that out they turn to scientific papers.

If the alien scientists did their first exploration of human consciousness in this fashion then what would they think about human conscious experience? Would they know what it feels like for humans to have conscious experience? Would they actually have understood anything about what is it like to be conscious?

I do not think so. For example, from the papers about global neuronal workspace theory of consciousness, they would have read that when a single stimulus is presented at the perceptual threshold, so that it sometimes is consciously perceived and sometimes not, conscious perception co-varies with the activity of the so-called fronto-parietal network (to those alien scientists/visitors reading the current chapter I would suggest the following papers: Dehaene & Naccache, 2001; Dehaene, Changeux, Naccache, Sackur, & Sergent, 2006; Dehaene & Changeux, 2011; Dehaene, Lau, & Kouider, 2017). They would have read that when this single stimulus is consciously perceived, neural activity starts differing from the non-conscious brain activity around 270 ms (Sergent, Baillet, & Dehaene, 2005; Del Cul, Baillet, & Dehaene, 2007). Hopefully, the aliens would also read that there are scientists on planet Earth who believe and have empirical evidence for saying that local activity in sensory cortices (Fisch, Privman, Ramot, Harel, Nir, Kipervasser, Andelman, Neufeld, Kramer, Fried & Malach, 2009) and earlier negative deflections of event-related potentials are more closely tied to consciousness (for review see Koivisto & Revonsuo, 2010;

Railo, Koivisto, & Revonsuo, 2011). Are these the key facts and debates for understanding what it is like to have human consciousness? Whether the processes that correlate with consciousness appear at 200 or 270 ms and whether they appear in sensory cortex or in the frontoparietal network is not crucial to understanding what is it like to have conscious experience.

More generally, the aliens would probably be rather amused about the amount of debates scientists on Earth have about consciousness. In addition to debating whether the correlates of consciousness are to be found in the frontoparietal network or locally in sensory cortex and whether they are later or earlier in time, we debate almost everything. Are the neural correlates of consciousness in the back or front of the cortex? (Boly, Massimini, Tsuchiya, Postle, Koch, & Tononi, 2017; Odegaard, Knight, & Lau, 2017). Ee are even discussing whether the key processes constituting consciousness are in the cortex at all or is consciousness more tightly related to the activity of subcortical structures (Panksepp, 2004; Merker, 2007; Damasio, 2012). Is consciousness based on recurrent processing (Lamme, 2006), information integration (Tononi, Boly, Massimini, & Koch, 2016), neural synchrony (Melloni, Molina, Pena, Torres, Singer, & Rodriguez, 2007)? Also, we hotly debate conceptual issues. Is conscious experience rich or is it poor (Block, 2014; Lamme, 2018; Cohen, Dennet, & Kanwisher, 2016)? Is conscious perception gradual or is it all or none (Sergent & Dehaene, 2004; Overgaard, Rote, Mouridsen, & Ramsøy, 2006)? Is attention independent of consciousness or is it necessary for conscious perception (Koch & Tsuchiya, 2007; Cohen, Cavanagh, Chun, & Nakayama, 2012; Aru & Bachmann, 2013)? There are many more debates. Of course debates are a necessary part of science, but we are discussing even the most basic things. What do we agree upon? Sometimes it seems to me that the only thing the scientists on Earth have a near-consensus on is that the mechanisms of consciousness have to be in the brain.

So why do we have so many contradictory findings and theories? It has been proposed that this is due to the fact that the most widely used experimental approach – contrasting trials with and without conscious perception to unravel the neural processes that differ between the conditions – is not pure. This so-called contrastive analysis will always bring along neural processes that reflect unconscious prerequisites and consequences, in a manner and extent that is specific to the experimental paradigm used (Miller, 2007; Aru, Bachmann, Singer, & Melloni, 2012a; De Graaf, Hsieh, & Sack, 2012). This method cannot reveal the true mechanisms underlying consciousness. Hence, depending on the experimental paradigm and the exact task parameters, different confounding "correlates" of conscious processing appear in the results. What can we do about it?

I would feel a bit embarrassed in front of my alien colleagues, as despite the fact that this problem with the contrastive method has been widely known since 2012 (Aru et al., 2012a; De Graaf et al., 2012; see Miller, 2007, for an earlier treatment) and that there have been calls to arms (Aru & Bachmann, 2015; Miller, 2015), there have been really almost no radically new experimental approaches. Indeed, the aliens could point out that in top science journals papers about consciousness are still published with the same thoroughly criticized

150 Jaan Aru

method (Van Vugt, Dagnino, Vartak, Safaai, Panzeri, Dehaene, & Roelfsema, 2018). So we have endless debates and one key method that cannot resolve any of these debates. (Despite my generally pessimistic view on the progress of the science of consciousness, I would like to point out and compliment several interesting approaches to tackling the problem: Frässle, Sommer, Jansen, Naber, & Einhäuser, 2014; Pitts, Metzler, & Hillyard, 2014; Baroni, van Kempen, Kawasaki, Kovach, Oya, Howard, Adolphs, & Tsuchiya, 2017.)

2 Understanding consciousness: The alternative way

After having studied consciousness with the standard contrastive method (e.g. Aru & Bachmann, 2009a, 2009b) and with several adaptations of and improvements to it (e.g. Aru, Axmacher, Do Lam, Fell, Elger, Singer, & Melloni, 2012b; Aru, Rutiku, Wibral, Singer, & Melloni, 2016; Rutiku, Martin, Bachmann & Aru 2015; Rutiku, Aru, & Bachmann, 2016) for many years, I personally feel that I have missed the point. I think that by being focused on "when" the activity between trials with and without consciousness diverges and "where" this activity comes from, I have missed the essence of conscious experience. So far I have always put first the neural activity that can be measured and the experimental paradigm; I think that it is time to put conscious experience first – what it feels like. In some sense this is exactly what Giulio Tononi has done: starting from the key features of consciousness (consciousness is informative and integrated), he has built a theory about what consciousness is (Tononi, 2004; Tononi et al., 2016). While I am sympathetic to the approach, I do not dare leap from the features of consciousness to a full theory. Also, I think it is very hard, if not impossible to do so (see Bayne, 2018, for a thorough critique of the axiomatic approach of Tononi). However, I do think that it is an important change to focus on the characteristics of consciousness and base the research on this. The phenomenology of conscious experience has of course been well explored by philosophers and pioneers of psychology such as Wilhelm Wundt (1874) and Edward Titchener (1907), but now we might be in a position to understand how these phenomenological qualities arise from the neural machinery. (Well, maybe not, but it seems worth trying to see how far we can take this enterprise.)

I agree with Tononi's key characteristics of consciousness (consciousness is informative and integrated, it is structured and definite; Tononi & Koch, 2015). However, for me there is another feature that is quite curious – the continuity of consciousness in space and time. For me, this is an interesting and maybe a defining feature of conscious experience. If I lay in my armchair, thinking about aliens and consciousness, I have an experience of my surroundings that is stable in time, despite my eyes blinking and moving, causing constantly changing patterns on my retinae. For me it is mind boggling that our conscious experience is smooth and continuous *despite all the transitions* in the underlying neuronal activity patterns.[1]

Continuity of consciousness is curious. So why have we not studied this continuity? I see two reasons. First, historically the scientific study of consciousness got started through successes in comparing trials with and without conscious perception (Logothetis & Schall, 1989). These were exciting times, for instance there was a lot of buzz about 40 Hz oscillations (Gray, König, Engel, & Singer, 1989), first fMRI studies of conscious perception were conducted (Lumer, Friston, & Rees, 1998). With all these developments in mind Sir Francis Crick wrote about the problem of consciousness "It is not impossible that, with a little luck, we may glimpse the outline of the solution before the end of the century". He meant the end of the last century, as the quote is taken from a commentary paper in 1996 (Crick, 1996). However, all of this has turned out to be more complicated (as outlined above).

The second reason is that it is much simpler to contrast trials with and without conscious perception; it is experimentally hard to study the mechanisms of continuity (Hohwy, 2009). For example, in all the experimental paradigms, subjects are conscious of their surroundings in both cases, with and without conscious perception of the particular target. By looking at the *differences* between these two conditions we are functionally subtracting any continuity of consciousness (see Hohwy, 2009, for a longer treatment of this issue).

I think the contrastive analysis has been and will still be useful for studying consciousness. However, for me personally using advanced versions of contrastive analysis is not satisfying any more. Especially as I think that there is an interesting question to study: what grants consciousness the effortless continuity despite the restless-and-always-changing nature of the underlying neural processes? I will not pretend that one chapter can solve all the issues, but I will try to demonstrate how this shift of perspective leads to interesting questions.

3 Why don't we perceive blinking?

Let us first consider blindness to eye blinks as a clear example for continuity of consciousness over time despite the transitions in the retinal stimulation. The eyes blink once every few seconds, but one is completely oblivious to such shutters of experience – consciousness is continuous despite the fact that blinks cover the pupil for 100–50 ms (Riggs, Volkmann, & Moore, 1981). At first one could object that this is really a short time, but when darkness of such length is imposed externally, one immediately notices the dark time slice (Riggs et al., 1981; Golan, Davidesco, Meshulam, Groppe, Mégevand, Ycagle, Goldfinger, Harel, Melloni, Schroeder, & Deouell, 2016). So, here's a seemingly very simple yet profound demonstration: our conscious experience is continuous despite the eye blinks. What is happening, why are we not aware of the transitions in the neural activity created by eye blinks? Our conscious experience is maintained, but how? A key point to think about: despite the ubiquity of eye blinks, no theory of consciousness can actually explain why our experience is stable and continuous while blinking. For example, saying that consciousness is associated with the activity of the frontoparietal network does not help further: then one needs to answer why the visual cortical activity reflecting eye blinks is not chosen for ignition in the frontoparietal network. One blinks,

152 Jaan Aru

this leaves a strong trace on the early visual cortical activity (Golan et al., 2016), yet it does not reach consciousness. Why?

Both in the case of eye blinks and externally induced darkness there is a change of activity on the retina and early visual areas (Golan et al., 2016), so why is this change in one case consciously experienced and in another not? Measuring cortical responses along the visual pathway it was observed that in low visual areas blinks and saccades lead to transient responses that are quite similar to externally induced darkness and image shifts (Golan et al., 2016, 2017). In contrast, high visual areas showed a steady response without the internally generated involuntary blink- and saccade-related transients. However, the activity patterns in these areas nevertheless were affected by externally induced darkness and image shifts. In other words, the neural activity in the high visual cortex corresponded more closely to the continuity of consciousness (Golan et al., 2016, 2017). This is not to say that such activity in higher visual cortex is the key mechanism to conscious experience, but these experiments show that somewhere along the cortical hierarchy the internally generated transitions are subtracted out.

This result by itself does not explain how exactly this continuity is achieved: what mechanism holds the steady response or suppresses the transients in higher visual cortex? The obvious difference between the eye blinks and externally induced darkness is that during eye blinks the brain can predict the change in visual stimulation and hence is able to continuously fill in the experience over time. In other words, the brain has access to its own motor commands and can take these into account for creating continuous vision (Wurtz, 2008; Golan et al., 2016). During self-generated blinks and saccades the brain can predict the changes in sensory input (Golan et al., 2016, 2017). Therefore, it is possible that this prediction is used to cancel out the transients and keep consciousness continuous.

4 Potential mechanisms underlying continuity

To better understand how this might work, let us consider the potential mechanisms. With regard to the cognitive level one mechanism for subtracting the transients from entering consciousness is to withdraw attention from these transitions. Attention is a powerful mechanism for boosting signals, therefore if the transition is not attended, this transition does not disrupt the continuity of consciousness. The key idea is that the brain can take its own motor commands into account for removing attention from the self-generated transients. On the other hand, externally induced transitions cannot be predicted and they hence capture attention in bottom-up fashion. This idea makes two straightforward predictions. First, if you start paying attention to your involuntary blinks you might start seeing a short flicker of your otherwise continuous conscious experience. At least from the phenomenological standpoint this seems to be true. The second prediction is that if the brain can predict the externally imposed image shifts or the timing of external darkness, then gradually over time consciousness should stay continuous despite this externally imposed darkness. In order to better understand the suggested attentional mechanism underlying the continuity of consciousness, let us first consider further examples of transitions that never make it to our consciousness.

5 Suppressing self-generated transitions

Eye blink and saccade related activity patterns in early sensory cortices are not the only transitions that are wiped out from conscious experience. In fact, many other movements of our body affect sensory responses in a strong fashion but do not capture attention. For example, while running, one's own hands, two relatively big objects, move through the lower part of one's visual field without being experienced. Clearly, these two objects activate cells on the retina and the respective thalamic nuclei, but somewhere along the processing hierarchy these transients are suppressed. We know this, because while running or giving a talk our own moving hands do not capture our attention. Moreover, if there was an external object moving at the same position (a running dog, a moving ball) it would immediately capture one's attention. Our peripheral vision is very quick in spotting moving objects and directing our attention to them. However, our hands or legs moving does not bother us.

It seems that here too the brain actively suppresses the transients and that the mechanisms for ignoring transients might be the same as in the case of eye blinks and saccades: the brain uses predictions to withdraw attention from the transients generated by itself. How could one test this conjecture experimentally?

The basic idea to test for withdrawal of attention from the consequences of own movement is relatively simple: if attention is withdrawn from the parts of the visual field where one's own hand is currently moving then the reaction time (RT) to objects in those parts of the visual field should be longer. However, it is complicated to test this hypothesis with conventional tools of experimental psychology, as it would require that the participants see the moving objects "behind" the moving limb without seeing the moving limb itself. How to create invisible limbs? Virtual reality (VR) is the answer.

To quantify these intuitions that self-generated limb movements are associated with withdrawn attention we performed several experiments with VR (Laak, Vasser, Uibopuu, & Aru, 2017; Vasser, Vuillaume, Cleeremans & Aru, 2018; see Figure 6.1). The participants were sitting with VR goggles on. At the same time, the participants were asked to raise their hand in front of their eyes (Figure 6.1A). We captured the coordinates of hand movements precisely in time and space, but in the VR environment we only presented stimuli and we did not show the hand of the participant. Hence, we could measure any effect the movement of the hand has on the stimuli that in reality would be actually behind the hand. Now we were set to understand how the self-generated hand movement modulates perception.

In our first set of experiments (Laak et al., 2017) we presented the subjects with a visual search display (inside the VR goggles): they had to spot either a small sphere moving in the opposite direction from the rest or the sphere that changed in color (Figure 6.1B). We measured the RT of noticing the targets. The experimental

154 Jaan Aru

manipulation was that on half of the trials the stimuli appeared on the spot that would have been covered by the own hand (except that we did not show the hand). Would the fact that normally this position in space would be covered by own hand movement have any effect on the performance? Indeed, we observed that the RTs to the stimuli behind the (invisible) hand were slower than in the control conditions (Figure 6.1D). Hence, we concluded that the transients generated by own limb movement are subtracted from consciousness. Furthermore, as the study design (i.e. being a visual search task) resembled tasks used to study visual attention and the magnitude of the RT effect was similar to those from the classic visual search tasks, we concluded that the mechanism seems to be attentional.

However, in this initial work we could not demonstrate that these self-generated transitions indeed are suppressed from conscious experience. This is because RTs are a notoriously bad measure of perceptual experience. Hence, the key question remained: does this withdrawal of attention indeed also have perceptual consequences? In the follow-up study (Vasser et al., 2018) we wanted to assess whether self-generated hand movement indeed changes perception. We based our study on the experimental approach used by Carrasco and colleagues who had elegantly demonstrated that attention affects perceptual experience (Carrasco, Ling, & Read, 2004). In that paradigm, two Gabor patches with different orientations are presented, one cued and the other not, and the subjects are asked for the orientation of the Gabor with the stronger contrast (Figure 6.1C). With this experimental approach it was possible for Carrasco and colleagues to demonstrate that covert attention enhances the perceived contrast of an attended stimulus (Carrasco et al., 2004). We reasoned that if (1) attention is withdrawn from the part of the visual field where the hand is moving (Laak et al., 2017) and (2) the deployment of attention affects perceived contrast (Carrasco et al., 2004), then the subjective contrast of objects in the region of the visual field where the hand is moving ought to be reduced. Hence, we performed a study with two Gabors in our VR setting (Figure 6.1C). After initiating the hand movement, two Gabors were presented and the participants had to indicate the orientation of the Gabor patch with higher contrast. We observed that the perceived contrast of the stimulus behind the invisible hand was significantly reduced (Figure 6.1E). We replicated these results in an independent group of participants. This result again lends support for the claim that attention is withdrawn from the sensory transients generated by the brain itself. More importantly, this result shows that such self-generated transients are attenuated from experience.

To sum up: there seem to be mechanisms for actively hindering information from entering consciousness. These phenomena unravel how the brain is avoiding transitions in consciousness despite transitions in the underlying neural activity. The key mechanism for this seems to be the withdrawal of attention from these transients, where this withdrawal is enabled through the predictability of the stimulus. Can this line of reasoning bring us any closer to understanding consciousness?

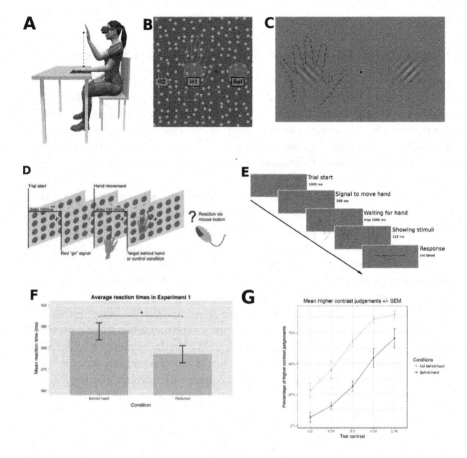

FIGURE 6.1 Self-generated movements suppress transients by withdrawing attention from them. (A) Illustration of the physical setup of the experiment: The participants were sitting behind a desk and had to make a pre-trained hand movement while the hand was kept invisible in the VR environment. The coordinates of the hand were monitored and moving targets were presented behind the (invisible) moving hand. (B) An illustrative view of the VR environment of Laak et al., 2017. In the critical condition, the targets were chosen from behind the (invisible) moving hand (position "H1" for clarity, the hand contour, the area behind the hand, and an example random target are illustrated). In control conditions, the targets were shown in the area reflected from the fixation point ("Ref"). (C) General design for a single trial in the experiments where visual sensitivity was tested (Vasser et al., 2018). Participants were instructed to perform a trained hand movement when the fixation cross changed color. This movement triggered the appearance of the two stimuli that were shown for 133 ms. The task consisted in reporting the orientation of the Gabor patch with the higher contrast. Note that participants' hand was completely invisible to them. Hand outlines and Gabor patch sizes on the figure are illustrative. (D) The mean RTs in Experiment 1 of Laak et al. (2017) for both conditions from the panel B. The participants had to react as fast as possible to moving targets either in an area currently covered by the (invisible) hand ("Behind hand", illustrated as "H1" on panel B) or a symmetric area in the other side of the visual field ("Reflected"; illustrated as "Ref" on panel B). The RTs in the experimental condition ("Behind hand") were slower than in the control condition ("Reflected"). (E) Results of Experiment 1 of Vasser et al. (2018). X axis is the value of the test contrast, Y axis denotes the percentage of trials that were reported as higher in contrast. Dark gray line shows the target stimulus appearing behind the hand and light gray line shows the target stimulus not behind the hand.

156 Jaan Aru

6 Intrinsic control of attention and theories of consciousness

Continuity of consciousness seems to be one of the key characteristics of our conscious experience. Yet, most of the theories of consciousness are only concerned with what happens to stimuli that are presented in the environment (mostly a computer screen). Or, in other words: no theory of consciousness can easily explain why and how eye blinks, saccades, or other self-generated movements are suppressed from consciousness. Continuity of consciousness is not in the focus of the theories of consciousness.

Interestingly, a particular set of computational theories that are not especially designed for explaining consciousness can readily explain the attenuation of sensory transients. In some sense this is paradoxical: why should a theory that is not meant for explaining conscious experience do a better job in explaining phenomena of conscious experience than theories of consciousness? One could also say that this is not paradoxical, but just reflects the sad state of consciousness research.

The active inference or prediction error minimization theory (Friston, 2010; Hohwy, 2013; Clark, 2015) posits that the top-down and bottom-up information flow across the hierarchical structure of the cortex implements hierarchical probabilistic inference about the causes of sensory data. Within this framework *predictions* (or beliefs) represent the hidden causes in the world that cause sensory states in the cortex. *Prediction errors* signal the discrepancy between the incoming sensory data and the predictions. Prediction errors are weighted by their *precision*. Precision determines how strongly prediction errors influence the updating of prior beliefs. According to the most widely known implementation of predictive processing, the main goal of neural computation is to minimize the (precision weighted) prediction error in the long term (Friston, 2010; Hohwy, 2013; Clark, 2015). Within this theoretical framework, performing actions is an efficient way of minimizing prediction errors by changing the sensory data to fit the predictions (Friston, 2010; Hohwy, 2013; Clark, 2015).

Crucially for the present chapter, the active inference theory suggests that movements are elicited by predicting the sensory consequences of the movement (e.g. the prediction that the hand will be moving in the visual field is the trigger for the movement). These predictions will drive the behavior so that the organism will perform movements that lead to the predicted state. However, the predicted consequences of movement are not in agreement with the current sensory data (where the hand is still in a resting position). Hence, there is a tension within the system between the prediction ("hand is moving") and sensory data ("hand is not moving"). According to the active inference theory, this tension is solved by reducing the precision of the current sensory data. This theoretical framework says that such reduction is the basis for sensory attenuation and that this reduction of the precision is necessary to allow the movement to unfold (Brown, Adams, Parees, Edwards, & Friston, 2013). Therefore, this theory explains sensory attenuation as a necessary consequence of movement: without sensory attenuation movement could not happen (Brown et al., 2013). As attention is the key mechanism for regulating the precision of the prediction errors (Feldman & Friston, 2010; Hohwy, 2013; Clark, 2015) the active inference theory proposes that the precision is reduced through the withdrawal of attention from the current sensory prediction errors. This theory might sound counterintuitive, even unnatural (for a longer treatment see Clark, 2015), but importantly for the present purposes, sensory attenuation of self-generated transients is a central part of this theoretical framework. Unlike theories of consciousness, this general computational theory can readily explain why self-generated transients are suppressed from conscious experience. In this sense, the continuity of consciousness follows naturally from this framework.

However, are we now any closer to understanding what consciousness is? There are several perspectives on how active inference could explain consciousness (Howhy, 2013; Clark, 2015; Friston, 2018). I am personally reluctant to say that active inference is the best framework for understanding consciousness, but I would conclude that active inference – although not originally a theory of consciousness – is a viable alternative to the currently prominent theories of consciousness.

Anyhow, for me the key interest has always been to understand not the computational theory behind consciousness, but the neural constituents of consciousness (Aru et al., 2012a; Miller, 2015). Does this speculation about the continuity of consciousness tell us anything meaningful about the neural processes underlying conscious experience?

7 What is the neural mechanism for cancelling out transitions?

What are the neural mechanisms for cancelling out sensory transients generated by own movement? In recent years these mechanisms have been worked out especially in mice, where technologies allow one to track and manipulate specific neural pathways. Hence, it has been established that motor cortex sends information even to primary visual (Leinweber, Ward, Sobczak, Attinger, & Keller, 2017) and auditory (Nelson, Schneider, Takatoh, Sakurai, Wang, & Mooney, 2013; Schneider, Sundararajan, & Mooney, 2018) cortex. For example, in the primary auditory cortex the axons from motor cortex have excitatory synapses but exert a primarily suppressive effect, because they also make synapses to inhibitory neurons (Nelson et al., 2013; Schneider et al., 2018). This pathway from motor cortex to sensory cortex is strong and connects to neurons in all cortical layers of the sensory cortex (Nelson et al., 2013; Leinweber et al., 2017). Hence, this projection from the motor cortex to the sensory cortex has the desired properties to reduce the effect of self-generated sensory transients: (a) information about own motor commands can be sent from motor cortex to the sensory cortex and (b) the net effect of this projection is to inhibit the incoming sensory data, making the animal less sensitive to self-generated transients.

To give one particular example, David Schneider and colleagues (Schneider et al., 2018) designed an "acoustic virtual reality system" for the mice. The idea of this setup was similar to the earlier described experiments with VR, only the association between the self-generated movement and its sensory consequences was not learned over the lifetime of the mice, but during the course of the experiment. In this setup the mice were running on a treadmill and the scientists played the mice a series of tones whose

158 Jaan Aru

rate was proportional to the running speed of mice. The advantage of doing these VR experiments in mice is that one can also monitor and manipulate the animals' neural activity, which allowed the authors to identify the neural circuit mechanisms that learn to suppress movement-related sounds. David Schneider and colleagues (Schneider et al., 2018) found that over the course of learning the connections from motor cortex to specific inhibitory neurons in the auditory cortex are strengthened so that the sounds associated to the treadmill running are selectively cancelled out. The authors proceeded to demonstrate that this learned inhibition of sensory signals leads to decreased sensitivity in a tone detection task, such that tones associated to movement are detected less well than tones not associated to movement. This finding nicely parallels the results obtained in human VR studies, where self-generated movement led to decreased sensitivity of visual information (Vasser et al., 2018). Therefore, we consider it to be plausible that this selective inhibition sent from the motor cortex to the sensory cortex is also the neural basis of the findings obtained in human VR studies.

In summary, studies with rodents have demonstrated that neural inhibition actively works in the background to keep predicted content from being processed further. To phrase it within the context of the present chapter I suggest that inhibition governs the continuity of conscious perception. In particular I propose that if the brain can predict self-generated transients (e.g. blinks, eye movements, limb movements), it will inhibit the specific sensory pathways that would process this sensory information. One could say that this is the neural mechanism of "withdrawn attention", but an alternative framing would be to say that the respective parts of the cortex are briefly disconnected from the world: inhibition cuts the specific parts of the cortex off from the input. Hence, from the perspective of the processing stages downstream from the populations receiving this inhibition it will look as if the transient never happened.

8 What is the mechanism of consciousness?

At first, it might seem that knowing the neural mechanisms of how self-generated transients are prohibited from entering consciousness will not bring us closer to understanding the neural mechanisms of consciousness. However, I personally feel that this line of thinking about consciousness does give us another angle to study the neural mechanisms of consciousness. Namely, from the current perspective we might want to understand those neural processes that co-vary with the continuity of consciousness. The main difference to the approach that is currently used is that more focus should be on trying to study those neural processes that stay the same *despite* the transitions (in cases where conscious experience stays continuous and also does not reflect these transitions). If consciousness is continuous and is not updated by a transition in the environment, the neural constituting mechanisms of consciousness should also stay oblivious or ignorant of this transition. Which neural processes are the ones that stay the same despite the transitions?

Golan and colleagues (Golan et al., 2016, 2017) had observed that in higher visual areas the self-generated transients (eye blinks and saccades) do not influence the activity. Hence, higher visual areas never witness the transients: for them this did not happen. However, this does not necessarily mean that these higher order sensory areas are the sole or the primary loci related to conscious experience. For example, the cortex is tightly connected to the higher-order nuclei of the thalamus (e.g. Halassa & Kastner, 2017). If the respective sensory cortical area is inhibited and never sends information on to these thalamic nuclei, continuity of whatever process is running there can be maintained. Hence, the present ideas are also compatible with theoretical views that put the thalamus in the center stage for consciousness (e.g. Bachmann, 1984; Ward, 2011). In any case I think we should seek for these neural mechanisms whose activity remains continuous when conscious experience is continuous despite the transitions of stimuli.

9 Going forward

Studying consciousness is hard, but sometimes I feel this "hardness" has made us – the researchers – lazy. We are still using the same experimental paradigms that were applied when the scientific study of consciousness was started (with some minor and some important modifications, of course). These experimental paradigms have fundamental problems that cannot be fixed by simply tinkering with them. I hence think that it is time to turn our attention to experimental ideas that are different. In this chapter, I favored the position that, instead of looking at the difference between trials with and without conscious perception, one could study what grants consciousness its continuity.

Acknowledgements

I would like to thank Talis Bachmann, Lucia Melloni, and Renate Rutiku for having supported me with ideas and discussions over many years. I am indebted to Madis Vasser, Laurene Vuillaume, and Kristjan-Julius Laak for conducting the virtual reality experiments.

Note

1 I thank Talis Bachmann for drawing my attention to this fact a decade ago; I thank Lucia Melloni for continuous discussion about continuity of consciousness.

References

Aru, J., & Bachmann, T. (2009a). Occipital EEG correlates of conscious awareness when subjective target shine-through and effective visual masking are compared: Bifocal early increase in gamma power and speed-up of P1. *Brain Research, 1271*, 60–73.

Aru, J., & Bachmann, T. (2009b). Boosting up gamma-band oscillations leaves target-stimulus in masking out of awareness: Explaining an apparent paradox. *Neuroscience Letters, 450*(3), 351–5.

Aru, J., & Bachmann, T. (2013). Phenomenal awareness can emerge without attention. *Frontiers in Human Neuroscience, 7*, 891.

Aru, J., & Bachmann, T. (2015). Still wanted – the mechanisms of consciousness! *Frontiers in Psychology, 6*, 5.

Aru, J., Bachmann, T., Singer, W., & Melloni, L. (2012a). Distilling the neural correlates of consciousness. *Neuroscience and Biobehavioral Reviews*, *36*(2), 737–46.

Aru, J., Axmacher, N., Do Lam, A. T., Fell, J., Elger, C. E., Singer, W., & Melloni, L. (2012b). Local category-specific gamma band responses in the visual cortex do not reflect conscious perception. *Journal of Neuroscience*, *32*(43), 14909–14.

Aru, J., Rutiku, R., Wibral, M., Singer, W., & Melloni, L. (2016). Early effects of previous experience on conscious perception. *Neuroscience of Consciousness*, *2016*(1).

Bachmann, T. (1984). The process of perceptual retouch: Nonspecific afferent activation dynamics in explaining visual masking. *Perception and Psychophysics*, *35*(1), 69–84.

Baroni, F., van Kempen, J., Kawasaki, H., Kovach, C. K., Oya, H., Howard, M. A., Adolphs, R., & Tsuchiya, N. (2017). Intracranial markers of conscious face perception in humans. *NeuroImage*, *162*, 322–43.

Bayne, T. (2018). On the axiomatic foundations of the integrated information theory of consciousness. *Neuroscience of Consciousness*, *2018*(1), niy007.

Blakemore, S. J., Wolpert, D. M., & Frith, C. D. (1998). Central cancellation of self-produced tickle sensation. *Nature Neuroscience*, *1*(7), 635.

Boly, M., Massimini, M., Tsuchiya, N., Postle, B. R., Koch, C., & Tononi, G. (2017). Are the neural correlates of consciousness in the front or in the back of the cerebral cortex? Clinical and neuroimaging evidence. *Journal of Neuroscience*, *37*(40), 9603–13.

Block, N. (2014). Rich conscious perception outside focal attention. *Trends in Cognitive Sciences*, *18*(9), 445–7.

Brown, H., Adams, R. A., Parees, I., Edwards, M., & Friston, K. (2013). Active inference, sensory attenuation and illusions. *Cognitive Processing*, *14*(4), 411–27.

Carrasco, M., Ling, S., & Read, S. (2004). Attention alters appearance. *Nature Neuroscience*, *7*(3), 308.

Clark, A. (2015). *Surfing Uncertainty: Prediction, Action, and the Embodied Mind.* Oxford: Oxford University Press.

Cohen, M. A., Cavanagh, P., Chun, M. M., & Nakayama, K. (2012). The attentional requirements of consciousness. *Trends in Cognitive Sciences*, *16*(8), 411–17.

Cohen, M. A., Dennett, D. C., & Kanwisher, N. (2016). What is the bandwidth of perceptual experience? *Trends in Cognitive Sciences*, *20*(5), 324–35.

Crick, F. (1996). Visual perception: rivalry and consciousness. *Nature*, *379*, 485–48.

Damasio, A. (2012). *Self Comes to Mind: Constructing the Conscious Brain.* New York: Vintage.

De Graaf, T. A., Hsieh, P. J., & Sack, A. T. (2012). The "correlates" in neural correlates of consciousness. *Neuroscience and Biobehavioral Reviews*, *36*(1), 191–7.

Dehaene, S., & Changeux, J. P. (2011). Experimental and theoretical approaches to conscious processing. *Neuron*, *70*(2), 200–27.

Dehaene, S., & Naccache, L. (2001). Towards a cognitive neuroscience of consciousness: Basic evidence and a workspace framework. *Cognition*, *79*(1–2), 1–37.

Dehaene, S., Changeux, J. P., Naccache, L., Sackur, J., & Sergent, C. (2006). Conscious, preconscious, and subliminal processing: a testable taxonomy. *Trends in Cognitive Sciences*, *10*(5), 204–11.

Dehaene, S., Lau, H., & Kouider, S. (2017). What is consciousness, and could machines have it? *Science*, *358*(6362), 486–92

Del Cul, A., Baillet, S., & Dehaene, S. (2007). Brain dynamics underlying the nonlinear threshold for access to consciousness. *PLoS Biology*, *5*(10), e260.

Feldman, H., & Friston, K. (2010). Attention, uncertainty, and free-energy. *Frontiers in Human Neuroscience*, *4*, 215.

Fisch, L., Privman, E., Ramot, M., Harel, M., Nir, Y., Kipervasser, S., Andelman, F., Neufeld, M.Y., Kramer, U., Fried, I., & Malach, R. (2009). Neural "ignition": Enhanced activation linked to perceptual awareness in human ventral stream visual cortex. *Neuron*, *64*(4), 562–74.

Friston, K. (2010). The free-energy principle: A unified brain theory? *Nature Reviews Neuroscience*, *11*(2), 127.

Friston, K. (2018). Am I self-conscious? (Or does self-organization entail self-consciousness?). *Frontiers in Psychology, 9.*

Frässle, S., Sommer, J., Jansen, A., Naber, M., & Einhäuser, W. (2014). Binocular rivalry: Frontal activity relates to introspection and action but not to perception. *Journal of Neuroscience*, *34*(5), 1738–47.

Golan, T., Davidesco, I., Meshulam, M., Groppe, D. M., Mégevand, P., Yeagle, E. M., Goldfinger, M. S., Harel, M., Melloni, L., Schroeder, C. E, & Deouell, L. Y., Mehta, A.D., Malach, R. (2016). Human intracranial recordings link suppressed transients rather than "filling-in" to perceptual continuity across blinks. *eLife*, *5*, e17243.

Golan, T., Davidesco, I., Meshulam, M., Groppe, D. M., Mégevand, P., Yeagle, E. M., Goldfinger, M.S., Harel, M., Melloni, L., Schroeder, C.E., & Deouell, L. Y. (2017). Increasing suppression of saccade-related transients along the human visual hierarchy. *eLife*, *6*, e27819.

Gray, C. M., König, P., Engel, A. K., & Singer, W. (1989). Oscillatory responses in cat visual cortex exhibit inter-columnar synchronization which reflects global stimulus properties. *Nature*, *338*(6213), 334.

Halassa, M. M., & Kastner, S. (2017). Thalamic functions in distributed cognitive control. *Nature Neuroscience*, *20*(12), 1669–79.

Hohwy, J. (2009). The neural correlates of consciousness: New experimental approaches needed? *Consciousness and cognition*, *18*(2), 428–38.

Hohwy, J. (2013). *The Predictive Mind*. Oxford: Oxford University Press.

Koch, C., & Tsuchiya, N. (2007). Attention and consciousness: Two distinct brain processes. *Trends in Cognitive Sciences*, *11*(1), 16–22.

Koivisto, M., & Revonsuo, A. (2010). Event-related brain potential correlates of visual awareness. *Neuroscience and Biobehavioral Reviews*, *34*(6), 922–34.

Laak, K. J., Vasser, M., Uibopuu, O. J., & Aru, J. (2017). Attention is withdrawn from the area of the visual field where the own hand is currently moving. *Neuroscience of Consciousness*, *3*(1).

Lamme, V. A. (2006). Towards a true neural stance on consciousness. *Trends in Cognitive Sciences*, *10*(11), 494–501.

Lamme, V. A. (2018). Challenges for theories of consciousness: Seeing or knowing, the missing ingredient and how to deal with panpsychism. *Philosophical Transactions of the Royal Society B*, *373*(1755), 20170344.

Leinweber, M., Ward, D. R., Sobczak, J. M., Attinger, A., & Keller, G. B. (2017). A sensorimotor circuit in mouse cortex for visual flow predictions. *Neuron*, *95*(6), 1420–32.

Logothetis, N. K., & Schall, J. D. (1989). Neuronal correlates of subjective visual perception. *Science*, *245*(4919), 761–3.

Lumer, E. D., Friston, K. J., & Rees, G. (1998). Neural correlates of perceptual rivalry in the human brain. *Science*, *280*(5371), 1930–4.

Melloni, L., Molina, C., Pena, M., Torres, D., Singer, W., & Rodriguez, E. (2007). Synchronization of neural activity across cortical areas correlates with conscious perception. *Journal of Neuroscience*, *27*(11), 2858–65.

Merker, B. (2007). Consciousness without a cerebral cortex: A challenge for neuroscience and medicine. *Behavioral and Brain Sciences*, *30*(1), 63–81.

Miller, S. M. (2007). On the correlation/constitution distinction problem (and other hard problems) in the scientific study of consciousness. *Acta Neuropsychiatrica*, *19*(3), 159–76.

Miller, S. M. (ed.) (2015). *The Constitution of Phenomenal Consciousness: Toward a Science and Theory* (vol. 92). Amsterdam: John Benjamins Publishing Co.

Nelson, A., Schneider, D. M., Takatoh, J., Sakurai, K., Wang, F., & Mooney, R. (2013). A circuit for motor cortical modulation of auditory cortical activity. *Journal of Neuroscience, 33*(36), 14342–53.

Odegaard, B., Knight, R. T., & Lau, H. (2017). Should a few null findings falsify prefrontal theories of conscious perception? *Journal of Neuroscience, 37*(40), 9593–9602.

Overgaard, M., Rote, J., Mouridsen, K., & Ramsøy, T. Z. (2006). Is conscious perception gradual or dichotomous? A comparison of report methodologies during a visual task. *Consciousness and Cognition, 15*(4), 700–8.

Panksepp, J. (2004). *Affective Neuroscience: The Foundations of Human and Animal Emotions.* Oxford: Oxford University Press.

Pitts, M. A., Metzler, S., & Hillyard, S. A. (2014). Isolating neural correlates of conscious perception from neural correlates of reporting one's perception. *Frontiers in Psychology, 5*, 1078.

Railo, H., Koivisto, M., & Revonsuo, A. (2011). Tracking the processes behind conscious perception: A review of event-related potential correlates of visual consciousness. *Consciousness and Cognition, 20*(3), 972–83.

Riggs, L. A., Volkmann, F. C., & Moore, R. K. (1981). Suppression of the blackout due to blinks. *Vision Research, 21*(7), 1075–9.

Rutiku, R., Aru, J., & Bachmann, T. (2016). General markers of conscious visual perception and their timing. *Frontiers in Human Neuroscience, 10*, 23.

Rutiku, R., Martin, M., Bachmann, T., & Aru, J. (2015). Does the P300 reflect conscious perception or its consequences? *Neuroscience, 298*, 180–9.

Schneider, D. M., Sundararajan, J., & Mooney, R. (2018). A cortical filter that learns to suppress the acoustic consequences of movement. *Nature, 561*(7723), 391.

Sergent, C., & Dehaene, S. (2004). Is consciousness a gradual phenomenon? Evidence for an all-or-none bifurcation during the attentional blink. *Psychological Science, 15*(11), 720–8.

Sergent, C., Baillet, S., & Dehaene, S. (2005). Timing of the brain events underlying access to consciousness during the attentional blink. *Nature Neuroscience, 8*(10), 1391.

Titchener, E. B. (1907). *An Outline of Psychology.* New York: Macmillan.

Tononi, G. (2004). An information integration theory of consciousness. *BMC Neuroscience, 5*(1), 42.

Tononi, G., & Koch, C. (2015). Consciousness: Here, there and everywhere? *Philosophical Transactions of the Royal Society B, 370*(1668), 20140167.

Tononi, G., Boly, M., Massimini, M., & Koch, C. (2016). Integrated information theory: From consciousness to its physical substrate. *Nature Reviews Neuroscience, 17*(7), 450.

Tsuchiya, N., Wilke, M., Frässle, S., & Lamme, V. A. (2015). No-report paradigms: Extracting the true neural correlates of consciousness. *Trends in Cognitive Sciences, 19*(12), 757–70.

Van Vugt, B., Dagnino, B., Vartak, D., Safaai, H., Panzeri, S., Dehaene, S., & Roelfsema, P. R. (2018). The threshold for conscious report: Signal loss and response bias in visual and frontal cortex. *Science, 360*(6388), 537–42.

Vasser, M., Vuillaume, L., Cleeremans, A., & Aru, J. (2018). Waving goodbye to contrast: Self-generated hand movements attenuate visual sensitivity. *bioR xiv*, 474783.

Ward, L. M. (2011). The thalamic dynamic core theory of conscious experience. *Consciousness and Cognition, 20*(2), 464–86.

Wundt, W. M. (1874). *Grundzüge de physiologischen Psychologie* (vol. 1). Leipzig: W. Engelman.

Wurtz, R. H. (2008). Neuronal mechanisms of visual stability. *Vision Research, 48*(20), 2070–89.

INDEX

0-visibility trials, liminal-prime paradigm 125–9, 131–2, 133, 138
40 Hz oscillations 151

absolutely-clear-image trials, Perceptual Awareness Scale (PAS) 120
accuracy-based measures, breaking CFS (b-CFS) 20–2, 26, 28–9
acoustic virtual reality systems, mice 157–8
active inference theory, intrinsic control of attention and theories of consciousness x, 156–9; *see also* prediction error minimization theory
adaptation aftereffects 4, 5–6, 81–2, 96
affective blindsight 96
affective learning, breaking CFS (b-CFS) 14–15
affective priming 96
afterimages, contrast response functions (CRFs) 81–5
alien scientist research explanation scenario, consciousness research ix–x, 148–59
almost-clear-image trials, Perceptual Awareness Scale (PAS) 120
alternative viewpoints on understanding consciousness ix–x, 39–59, 150–9
amygdala 12–13, 92, 94, 96–109; damage effects 108; roles 107–9; social information and the unconscious 12–13, 92, 94, 96–109; tagged visual input 108; *see also* emotional expressions; eye gaze; neuroscience
analysis of variance (ANOVA) 52, 132, 137

angry faces, social information and the unconscious 95, 98–9
antisocial personality disorder, social information and the unconscious 103–6
anxiety, social information and the unconscious 103–6, 109
arrow-direction discrimination task, liminal-prime paradigm 131
Aru, Jaan ix–x, 148–62
attention x, 15–16, 25–6, 40–59, 100–2, 128–30, 131–2, 134–8, 152–9; breaking CFS (b-CFS) 15–16; continuity of consciousness studies 152–9; eye gaze 100–2; intrinsic control of attention and theories of consciousness x, 156–9; liminal-prime paradigm 128–30, 131–2, 134–8; withdrawal studies x, 152–9
attentional blink 72, 77, 79, 134–8; liminal-prime paradigm 134–8
attentional capture processes 15–16, 25–6, 41–4, 129–30, 131 2, 134–8; liminal-prime paradigm 129–30, 131–2, 134–8
attentional cueing 4, 15–16, 129–30, 131–2, 135–6
attractiveness, facial characteristics 12–13, 45, 93
auditory cortex 55–6, 157–9
auditory modality 16–17, 55–6, 157–9
autism spectrum disorder (ASD) ix, 17, 57–8, 103–6; social information and the unconscious ix, 17, 57–8, 103–6; *see also* psychiatric disorders

164 Index

averted eye gaze, autism spectrum disorder (ASD) ix, 57–8, 104–6; social information and the unconscious ix, 12–13, 57–8, 100–2, 104–6, 107–9

Avneon, Maayan ix, 118–47

aware-unaware prime trial comparisons, liminal-prime paradigm 124–6, 127–9

baby faces 12–13

backward masking suppression viii, 5–6, 8, 25–6, 27–9, 40–1, 72, 75, 77, 83, 108–9; critique viii; definition viii, 5, 8, 29; *see also* suppression methods

Baroni et al (2017) 150

basketball 46–7

Bayesian methods 49, 53

bias 17, 54, 58, 76–7, 93, 98, 100, 102–3, 108–9

binocular rivalry suppression viii, 9, 22–3, 25–6, 41–2, 43–4, 47, 48–9, 71–3, 76–7, 81–3; critique viii, 41–2, 71–3, 76–7, 81–3; definition viii, 41, 71–2; *see also* suppression methods

blinding techniques vii–viii, 3–10, 40–1, 59, 71–85, 106, 132–3; critique 71–85; definition vii, 40–1, 59, 71–5, 79; inattentional blinding methods 79; *see also* masking

blindsight-like studies 3, 4–10, 20–2

blink periods, liminal-prime paradigm 134–8

boosted stimuli ideas, breaking CFS (b-CFS) 26–7

bottom-up information flows, active inference theory x, 156–9

breaking CFS (b-CFS) vii–viii, 2–29, 43–58; assumptions 2–29; attention 15–16; background vii–viii, 2–29, 43–58; boosted stimuli ideas 26–7; clinical studies 17; comparisons with other psychophysical techniques vii, viii, 5–6, 25–9; comparisons to classic dissociation paradigms 3, 4–10, 11–12, 24–9; conclusions 29, 48–59; confounds vii, 11, 13–14, 20–1, 26–9, 41, 44, 50–2, 57; control conditions 10, 22–6, 29, 43–6, 50, 57–9; control for post-perceptual factors vii, 18–20, 23–6, 29; critique vii, 7, 10, 25–9, 44, 48–58; definition vii–viii, 2–3, 6–7, 25–6, 43–4; detection responses 6, 7–8, 14–15, 19–29, 55–9; detection-discrimination dissociation proposal 27–9; differential unconscious processing 6–10, 58–9;

experimental manipulations 10–22, 28–9, 58–9; faces 5–6, 7, 11–17, 19–22, 24–9, 45, 48–58; false positives 18; future research 3, 21–2, 25–9; high-level processing 10–11, 13–14, 39–59; implementation factors 9–29; isolation of CFS-specific processing 24–5; localization 6–8, 15, 18–29, 74–83; low-road of visual processing 10–13, 14–15, 54–9; multimodal integration 16–17, 55–6; non-orthogonal discrimination RT tasks 19–22; non-speed accuracy-based measures 20–2, 26, 28–9; objects 11–13, 15–16, 18, 28–9, 46–7, 52–8; orthogonal discrimination RT tasks 19–22; overview of common tasks/measures 3; parsimonious summaries of the field 53–9; pendulum-swinging studies 50–3; perceptual and affective learning 14–15; priming studies 15–16; proposals 26–9; publications 2–3, 5, 7–8, 9–25, 43–58; rationale 3–8, 9–25; recommendations 3, 25–9; review of b-CFS studies 9–25, 43–58; speeded RT-based measures 18–22; suppression speeds 10–13, 18–22; tasks and measures 18–22; threshold-detection proposal 26–7, 29; transition times 8, 15, 18–19, 43–4; uses vii, 2–29, 43–58; visual integration and replication issues 17–18, 48–58; words and phrases 13–14, 15–16, 18, 45–6, 48–9, 51–8; working memory 15–16; *see also* continuous flash suppression

Breitmeyer, Bruno G. viii, 5, 40, 48, 71–91, 108, 124, 133, 137

brief-glimpse trials, Perceptual Awareness Scale (PAS) 120, 126–7

Brown et al (2013) 156

callous–unemotional trait 106

cancelling-out neural mechanisms, transitions 157–9

Carrasco et al (2004) 154

change blindness 79

Chinese ideographs 45, 104

Clark, A. 156–7

clinical studies, breaking CFS (b-CFS) 17

cognitive functions vi, vii–x, 1–29, 40–59, 93–4, 103–6; overview of the book vi, vii–x

cognitive neuroscience *see* neuroscience

cognitive psychology 1–29

color cues, attentional capture processes 10, 15–16, 129–30, 131–2, 135–6

Index **165**

complete facial features, social information and the unconscious viii–ix, 92–109

conditioning context, social information and the unconscious 56–7, 97–100, 107–9

conference shortfalls 49

confidence ratings (CRs) 120–38

confounds, breaking CFS (b-CFS) vii, 11, 13–14, 20–1, 26–9, 41, 44, 50–2, 57

conscious perception trials, liminal-prime paradigm 129–38

consciousness, active inference theory x, 156–9; alien scientist research explanation scenario ix–x, 148–59; alternative viewpoints on understanding consciousness ix–x, 39–59, 150–9; controversies ix, 1–2, 39–40, 118, 148–59; current understandings ix–x, 148–51; definitions 39–40, 78–9, 148–59; dissociation paradigms 2, 3–10, 11–12, 24–9, 43; intrinsic control of attention and theories of consciousness x, 156–9; mechanism of consciousness questions 158–9; neural mechanisms for cancelling-out transitions 157–9; objective/subjective measures of awareness 43–4, 118–38; overview of the book i, vi–x; perceiving-blinking questions 151–2; perspectives on theoretical and methodological questions i, vi–x, 1–2, 3, 9–29, 41–59, 72–85, 92, 107, 108–9, 137–8, 148–59; phenomenological approaches 78–9, 150–1, 152–3; vegetative states 39–40; *see also* continuity of consciousness studies; transitions

contamination problems 29, 123

continuity of consciousness studies x, 150–9; active inference theory x, 156–9; attention 152–9; eye blinks 151–9; future research 159; hand movements 153–4, 156–9; intrinsic control of attention and theories of consciousness x, 156–9; perceiving-blinking questions 151–2; potential mechanisms 152–3; saccade related activities 152–4, 156, 158–9; suppressing self-generated transitions x, 152, 153–9; *see also* consciousness

continuous flash suppression (CFS) vii–viii, 2–29, 39–59, 72–83, 108–9, 123, 129–30, 132–3, 135–6; assumptions 2–29; background vii–viii, 2–29, 39–59, 72–83, 132–3; comparisons with other psychophysical

techniques vii, viii, 5–6, 25–9, 41–3, 72–83; conclusions 29, 48–59, 83–5; confounds vii, 11, 13–14, 20–1, 26–9, 41, 44, 50–2, 57; control conditions 10, 22–6, 29, 43–6, 50, 57–9; critique vii, 7, 10, 25–9, 43–4, 45–59, 72–83, 132–3; definition vii–viii, 2–3, 6–7, 41–2; direct/indirect measures of unconscious processing overview 42–4; dissociation paradigms 3, 4–10, 11–12, 24–9; examples 42; faces 5–6, 7, 11–17, 19–22, 24–9, 45, 48–59; file-drawer problems 49–50; future research 3, 21–2, 25–9, 83–5; high-level processing vii, 10–11, 13–14, 40–59; invisible stimuli vii, 3–4, 6–9, 40–59; localization 6–8, 15, 18–29, 74–83; natural scenes 46–7, 52–9; numerical processing 47, 48–51, 53–9; objects 11–13, 15–16, 18, 28–9, 46–7, 52–8; parsimonious summaries of the field 53–9; pendulum-swinging studies 50–3; publications 2–3, 5, 7–8, 9–25, 43–59, 72–83; recommendations 3, 25–9, 83–5; review of studies vii, 9–25, 41–59, 72–83; Type 1 errors 49–50, 52; uses vii–viii, 3–29, 41–59, 129–30, 132–3, 135–6; visual integration and replication issues 17–18, 48–59; words and phrases 13–14, 15–16, 18, 45–6, 48–9, 51–9; *see also* breaking CFS; masking; suppression methods; visual processing

contrast response functions (CRFs) 80–5

contrastive analysis critique ix–x, 6–7, 40–1, 71–2, 75, 77, 80–5, 123, 131, 132–3, 148, 149–59

controls, breaking CFS (b-CFS) conditions 10, 22–6, 29, 43–4; intrinsic control of attention and theories of consciousness x, 156–9

controversies ix, 1–2, 39–40, 118, 148–59

cooperative research practices vii

cortex viii, 48–59, 71–85, 96, 101–2, 148–59; *see also* neurofunctional hierarchical scheme

cortical anatomy, neurofunctional hierarchical scheme 73–4, 80–5

cost of awareness (CoA), liminal-prime paradigm 133–8

costs of conscious perception, liminal-prime paradigm 121, 133–8

costs/benefits of awareness, liminal-prime paradigm ix, 118, 121–38

Craik-O'Brien-Cornsweet illusion 55

Crick, Francis 151

166 Index

crowding suppression 8, 25–6, 72–5, 77–85, 108–9; *see also* suppression methods
current consciousness understandings ix–x, 148–51

danger, visual processing 93–6, 98–100, 104–6
darkness contrasts, eye blinks 151–3
decision-making high-level cognitive operations 94, 96, 129–30
Decoded Neurofeedback 92
degraded stimulation methods 123
Dehaene et al (2006) 148
Dehaene et al (2017) 148
detection-discrimination dissociation proposal, breaking CFS (b-CFS) 27–9
dichoptic stimulus presentation paradigm 41–59; definition 41; *see also* continuous flash suppression
differential unconscious processing, breaking CFS (b-CFS) 6–10, 58–9
direct eye gaze, autism spectrum disorder (ASD) ix, 57–8, 104–6; social information and the unconscious ix, 12–13, 45, 57–8, 100–2, 104–6, 107–9
direct-direct dissociation paradigm 3, 4–10, 28–9, 43; definition 3, 4–5, 6, 28; *see also* dissociation paradigms
direct-indirect dissociation paradigm 3–10, 43; definition 3–4, 6, *see also* dissociation paradigms
discrete transition point debates 8–9, 20–6; *see also* transitions
discrimination performance at chance level ix, 26, 118–38
dissociation paradigms 2, 3–10, 11–12, 24–9, 43; breaking CFS comparisons 3, 4–10, 24–9; continuous flash suppression (CFS) 5–10, 11–12; definition 3–5, 6, 7; direct-direct dissociation paradigm 3, 4–10; direct-indirect dissociation paradigm 3–10, 43; uses 3–6, 7
distance-dependent priming 52–4
Donne, John 92
dorsal stream processing 47–8, 55–6, 76–7, 84–5
double-blind placebo-controlled studies 106
drift-diffusion model 58
dropouts, double-blind placebo-controlled studies 106
dual-task situation critique 43–4, 127–8

Ebbinghaus illusion 54–5
EEG studies 52

electrical shocks 14–15, 56–7, 97–8
emotional expressions, eye gaze viii–ix, 45, 48–59, 92, 100–2, 104–9; facial characteristics viii, 11–16, 17, 45, 48–59, 93–109; photographs 94–5
empirical studies, continuity of consciousness studies x, 150–9; contrastive analysis critique ix–x, 6–7, 148, 149–59; current consciousness understandings ix–x, 148–51; future research 3, 8, 21–2, 25–9, 83–5, 159; lazy researchers 159; meta-analysis challenges 84–5; overview of the book i, vi–x; pessimistic viewpoints ix–x, 92, 109, 121, 125–6, 148–59; sample sizes 109; *see also individual topics*; liminal-prime paradigm; research trends; subliminal-prime paradigm
evolution, emotional expressions 95
exclusions, liminal-prime paradigm 124; subjective measures of awareness 124–5
experimental manipulations, breaking CFS (b-CFS) 10–22, 28–9, 58–9
extrafoveal target letters 78
extrastriate cortex 80–3
eye blinks x, 134–8, 150–9; continuity of consciousness studies 151–9; darkness contrasts 151–3; higher visual cortex 151–2; perceiving-blinking questions 151–3
eye dominance 10–11
eye gaze, attention 100–2; emotional expressions viii–ix, 45, 50–1, 57–9, 92, 100–2, 104–9; psychiatric disorders 57–8, 104–6; social information and the unconscious viii–ix, 12–13, 17, 45, 50–1, 57–9, 92, 100–2, 104–6, 107–9; *see also* visual processing
eye whites 102

face processing viii–ix, 5–6, 7, 11–17, 19–22, 24–5, 26–9, 45, 48–59, 92–109, 126–7; breaking CFS (b-CFS) 5–6, 7, 11–17, 19–22, 24–5, 26–9, 45; conditioning context 56–7, 97–100, 107–9; many roads of face processing 93–7; race/age groups 12
face shapes 50–1
facial characteristics viii–ix, 5–6, 7, 11–17, 19–22, 24–5, 45, 48–59, 92–109, 126–7; attractiveness 12–13, 45, 93; emotional expressions viii, 11–16, 17, 45, 48–59, 93–109; social information and the unconscious viii–ix, 5–6, 12–16, 45, 48–59, 92–109, 126–7; trustworthiness 12–13, 45, 50–1, 93–4, 95–6

facial dominance, social information and the unconscious 12–13, 45, 50–1, 95–6
facial mimicry 96
facial muscle contractions 98
false positives, breaking CFS (b-CFS) 18
familiar faces 1, 13, 50–1
familiar words 14, 46
famous faces 12–13, 55–6
fear-conditioned orientations 14–15, 27–9
fearful faces, social information and the unconscious 12–13, 15, 17, 45, 50–1, 93–5, 96–7, 98–102, 104–6
feature integration, visual cognition hierarchy viii, 14–15, 71, 78
Feynman, Richard 59
file-drawer problems, continuous flash suppression (CFS) 49–50
flanker interference 56–7, 78–9
fMRI studies 78, 84, 151
food consumption, cognitive functions 93–4
fools 59
forced-choice detection, objective measures of awareness ix, 20–1, 120–38
forward masking suppression 40–1, 75–6
fractionation 44–59, 77–85
framing differences in suppression times 56–7
Frässle et al (2014) 150
Friston, K. 156–7
frontoparietal network 148–59
fusiform face area (FFA) 101–2, 108
future research 3, 8, 21–2, 25–9, 83–5, 159; see also perspectives on theoretical and methodological questions

Gabor patches 42, 82–3, 85, 154–5; see also contrastive analysis critique
generalized linear mixed effects models (GLMMs), liminal-prime paradigm 137–8
global space work model 73–4
Golan et al (2016, 2017) 151, 152, 158–9
gorillas, invisible gorilla video 79
gratings 16–17, 19–20, 57

hand movements 17, 153–4, 156–9; continuity of consciousness studies 153–4, 156–9; running 153–4, 156–9
happy eyes 102
happy faces 12–13, 45, 102, 103–4
haptic gratings 16–17, 19–20
heartbeats 17
Hesselmann, Guido i, vi–x, 1, 4, 5, 13, 17–18, 27, 40, 44, 48, 51–6, 59, 71–91, 108, 138

high-level processing vii, 1–29, 40–59, 71–85, 93–4, 96–7, 129–38, 152; continuous flash suppression (CFS) vii, 10–11, 13–14, 40–59; Type 1 errors 49–50, 52; see also cognitive functions
high-level stimulus property vii, 1–29, 40–59, 96–7, 129–38, 152; see also sensory stimuli
higher visual cortex 151–3, 157–9; eye blinks 151–3
Hohwy, J. 156–7
holistic (identity) face processing, social information and the unconscious viii, 45, 54–9, 107–9, 126
houses 20–1, 28–9

illusions 11, 54–6, 81–2
imbalanced data structures, liminal-prime paradigm 123–38
impoverished intensity stimuli 40
inattentional blinding methods 79
intraparietal sulcus (IPS) 101–2
intrinsic control of attention and theories of consciousness x, 156–9
inverted faces 7, 11–13, 17, 19–22, 24–9, 45, 50–1, 57–9
inverted words 13–14, 45–6, 51–2
invisible gorilla video 79
invisible stimuli vii, 3–4, 6–9, 40–59, 71–85, 121–38, 148–59; rendering processes 40–1, 71–2
iris of the eye 102
isolation of CFS-specific processing, breaking CFS (b-CFS) 24–5

Jiang et al (2007) 2–3, 7, 18, 45–6

Kanizsa targets 11–12, 54–5
Koch, C. 2–3, 41, 74

Laak et al (2017) 153–5
lag 1 sparing effects 134–5
Lamy, Dominique ix, 118–47
lateral geniculate nucleus (LGN) 73
lateral occipital cortex (LOC) 78
lazy researchers 159
learning, breaking CFS (b-CFS) 14–15; cognitive functions 14–15, 93; perceptual and affective learning 14–15
lexicality of letter strings 13–14, 45–6, 48–9, 51–9, 71–2, 78–9, 126–7, 129–30, 135
liminal-prime paradigm ix, 118, 121–38; 0-visibility trials 125–9, 131–2, 133, 138; advantages/drawbacks 121–32,

137–8; alternatives 123–4, 133–4; arrow-direction discrimination task 131; attentional capture processes 129–30, 131–2, 134–8; aware-unaware prime trial comparisons 124–6, 127–9; background ix, 118, 121–38; blinding methods' conflicting findings 132–3; caveats 125–9; conclusions 137–8; conscious perception trials 129–38; cost of awareness (CoA) 133–8; costs of conscious perception 121, 133–8; definition ix, 121–5, 137; dual-task situation critique 127–8; exclusions 124; generalized linear mixed effects models (GLMMs) 137–8; linear mixed effects models (LMMs) 123, 132, 137–8; masked prime numerical comparison task 131; perceptual grouping processes 129, 130–1, 133, 134–5; perspectives on theoretical and methodological questions 137–8; retrieval of stimulus-response association processes 129, 130–1, 133; same-location costs 129, 132–4; semantic high-level cognitive operations 129–30, 131–2, 137; trailing events 121, 133–8; uses ix, 121–38; vincentization procedure uses 127–8; working memory object updates 129–30, 131–2, 136–8; *see also* Perceptual Awareness Scale; subjective measures of awareness
linear mixed effects models (LMMs), liminal-prime paradigm 123, 132, 137–8
lip movements, social information and the unconscious 103
low-road of visual processing viii–ix, 10–13, 14–15, 54–9, 71–85, 92–101, 105–6; breaking CFS (b-CFS) 10–13, 14–15, 54–9; definition 93–4; social information and the unconscious viii–ix, 54–9, 92–101, 105–6; *see also* subcortical visual processing

Madipakkam, Apoorva Rajiv viii, 12, 17, 57–8, 92–117
magnocellular channels 105–6
major depressive disorder (MDD), social information and the unconscious 17, 103–6
many roads of face processing, social information and the unconscious 93–7
masked prime numerical comparison task 47, 48–51, 53–9, 131
masking vii, viii, 5–10, 40–59, 71–85, 102, 106, 108–9, 123–4, 129–32; critique 40–1, 132–3; types vii, viii, 5–6, 8, 25–6, 27, 40–2, 71–4, 123, 129–32; *see also* backward masking suppression; continuous flash suppression; metacontrast masking suppression; sandwich masking suppression; suppression methods
measures of awareness ix, 4–29, 43–59, 118–38; *see also* objective measures of awareness; subjective measures of awareness
mechanism of consciousness questions 158–9
meta-analysis challenges 84–5; *see also* empirical studies
metacontrast masking suppression 40–1, 71–2, 75, 77, 123, 131, 132–3; critique 71–2, 75, 77, 132–3; definition 71–2; *see also* suppression methods
mice, acoustic virtual reality systems 157–8
Michelson contrasts 80
middle temporal and inferior frontal gyri 101
Mondrian mask 42, 74–5
Moors, Pieter vii, 2, 39–70
motor cortex 157–8
mouth region, social information and the unconscious 50–1, 103
moving speeds 10–13
MRI studies 78, 84, 151
multimodal integration, breaking CFS (b-CFS) 16–17, 55–6

Naka-Rushton equations 80, 82, 85
natural scenes, object-scene congruency 46–7, 52–9
neural circuits, social information and the unconscious vi, ix–x, 12–13, 40–59, 92–109
neural correlates vi, ix–x, 40–59, 71–85, 148–59
neural reinforcement 92; *see also* Decoded Neurofeedback
neurodevelopmental disorders, social information and the unconscious 104–6
neurofunctional hierarchical scheme viii, 59, 71–85, 108, 133, 137; background viii, 71–85; conclusions 84–5; cortical anatomy 73–4, 80–5; definition viii, 72–4, 84–5; future research 83–5; recommendations 83–5; tentative hierarchy schematic 72–3, 76, 84
neuroimaging studies viii, 48–9, 78, 84–5

Index

neuroscience vi, vii, viii, ix–x, 1–29, 40–59, 71–85, 92–109, 133, 137, 148–59; mechanisms for cancelling-out transitions 157–9; *see also* neurofunctional hierarchical scheme

no-experience trials, Perceptual Awareness Scale (PAS) 120–1, 124–5, 138

non-orthogonal discrimination RT tasks, breaking CFS (b-CFS) 19–22

non-speed accuracy-based measures, breaking CFS (b-CFS) 20–2, 26, 28–9

not-seen judgments 4, 43, 108

novel primes, retrieval of stimulus-response association processes 131

null sensitivity, definition 3–6; problems 43–4, 49–50, 58–9, 119, 124–5; publication considerations 58–9

numerical processing, masked prime numerical comparison task 47, 48–51, 53–9, 131

object recognition, visual cognition hierarchy viii, 71

object-scene congruency, natural scenes 46–7, 52–9

object-substitution masking (OSM) 72, 73, 74–5, 77–8, 83–4

objective measures of awareness 4–6, 20, 43–4, 118–38; background 4, 6, 43–4, 118–38; controversies 43–4, 118–20, 125–6; critique 4, 43–4, 123–6, 137; definitions 4, 6, 118–19, 122–3, 126; exclusions 124–5; problems 4, 43–4, 123–6, 137; *see also* present-absent prime discrimination task; subliminal-prime paradigm

objects, breaking CFS (b-CFS) 11–13, 15–16, 18, 28–9, 46–7, 52–8

observers, sensory stimuli vi–vii

occipital cortex 96, 101–2

occipitotemporal lobe regions 101–2

open research practices vii

Open Science Framework 59

Ophir, Eyal ix, 118 47

opinions, overview of the book i, vi–x

orthogonal discrimination RT tasks, breaking CFS (b-CFS) 19–22

overestimated unconscious processes, social information and the unconscious 99–100

Overgaard, Morten ii, 118–26, 137–8

overshooting risks, subliminal-prime paradigm 123–4

overview of the book i, vi–x

pacmen stimuli 11

pedestal masking 81, 84

pendulum-swinging studies, continuous flash suppression (CFS) 50–3

perceiving-blinking questions, eye blinks 151–3

perception vii, 1–29, 121, 129–38, 149–59

Perceptual Awareness Scale (PAS) 43–4, 120–1, 125–38; absolutely-clear-image trials 120; almost-clear-image trials 120; background 43–4, 120–1, 125–38; brief-glimpse trials 120, 126–7; definition 43, 120, 125, 137; no-experience trials 120–1, 124–5, 138; *see also* liminal-prime paradigm; subjective measures of awareness

perceptual defenses 14

perceptual grouping processes 11–13, 129, 130–1, 133, 134–5; liminal-prime paradigm 129, 130–1, 133, 134–5

perceptual learning, breaking CFS (b-CFS) 14–15

peripheral vision 153–4

perspectives on theoretical and methodological questions i, vi–x, 1–2, 3, 9–29, 41–59, 72–85, 92, 107, 108–9, 137–8, 148–59; alien scientist research explanation scenario ix–x, 148–59; continuity of consciousness studies x, 150–9; contrastive analysis critique ix–x, 6–7, 148, 149–59; current understandings ix–x, 148–51; future research 3, 8, 21–2, 25–9, 83–5, 159; lazy researchers 159; liminal-prime paradigm 137–8; overview of the book i, vi–x; social information and the unconscious 107, 108–9; *see also individual topics*

pessimistic viewpoints, research trends ix–x, 92, 109, 121, 125–6, 148–59

phenomenological approaches, consciousness 78–9, 150–1, 152–3

photographs, emotional expressions 94–5

Pitts et al (2014) 150

Poggendorff illusion 81

Ponzo illusion 54–5

post-decision wagering (PDW) 120–38

post-perceptual factor controls, breaking CFS (b-CFS) vii, 18–20, 23–6, 29

prediction error minimization theory, intrinsic control of attention and theories of consciousness 156–9; *see also* active inference theory

170 Index

present-absent prime discrimination task, definition 126; rare uses 126; *see also* objective measures of awareness

prime-awareness test phase, subliminal-prime paradigm 118, 121–38

priming ix, 3–10, 15–16, 42–3, 118–38

priming effect ix, 42–3, 118, 121–38; definition 121–3, 124; liminal-prime paradigm ix, 118, 121–38; *see also* subliminal-prime paradigm

priming phase, subliminal-prime paradigm 118–38

priming-like studies, direct-indirect dissociation paradigm 3–10, 43

psychiatric disorders ix, 13, 17, 57–8, 92, 103–6, 109; eye gaze 57–8, 104–6; psychotropic medication 109; social information and the unconscious ix, 13, 17, 57–8, 92, 103–6, 109; treatments 103–6, 109; types 17, 57–8, 103–4, 106, 109; *see also* autism spectrum disorder

psychopathy, social information and the unconscious 17, 106; *see also* callous–unemotional trait

psychophysical experiments, overview of the book vi–x

psychotropic medication 74, 109

pulvinar 94

questionnaire-based personality traits 13

race/age groups, face processing 12

random walks 27

rapid serial visual representation technique 8, 25–6

regression to the mean 123

relative functional levels of unconscious processing 84

research trends i, vi–x, 1–2, 3, 8, 21–2, 25–9, 83–5, 92, 109, 121, 125–6, 148–59; alien scientist research explanation scenario ix–x, 148–59; continuity of consciousness studies x, 150–9; contrastive analysis critique ix–x, 6–7, 148, 149–59; future research 3, 8, 21–2, 25–9, 83–5, 159; lazy researchers 159; overview of the book i, vi–x; pessimistic viewpoints ix–x, 92, 109, 121, 125–6, 148–59; *see also* empirical studies

retina 10–13, 39, 41, 79, 81–2, 152–3

retrieval of stimulus-response association processes, liminal-prime paradigm 129, 130–1, 133

roses, smells 16

Rothkirch, Marcus viii, 12, 17, 18, 56–8, 59, 75, 92–117, 118, 124

RSVP streams of colored letters 135–6

running, hand movements 153–4, 156–9

saccade related activities, continuity of consciousness studies 152–4, 156, 158–9

sad faces 12–13, 17, 103–4

same-location costs, liminal-prime paradigm 129, 132–4; working memory object updates 132

sample sizes 109

sandwich masking suppression 25–6, 40–1, 123, 130, 132–3, 135–6; critique 132–3; *see also* suppression methods

schizophrenia, social information and the unconscious 17, 103–6

Schneider et al (2018) 157–8

selective attention, visual cognition hierarchy viii, 71

self-generated transitions, continuity of consciousness studies x, 152, 153–9

semantic high-level processing vii, viii, 1–2, 5–6, 10–11, 13–14, 15–16, 40–59, 71–85, 129–30, 131–2, 137; continuous flash suppression (CFS) vii, 10–11, 13–14, 40–59, 74–83; liminal-prime paradigm 129–30, 131–2, 137

sensory attenuation movement, active inference theory 156–9

sensory cortex viii, 96, 101–2, 148–59

sensory stimuli vii, 1–2, 3–29, 40–59, 94–109, 120–38; overview of the book i, vi–x; *see also* high-level stimulus property; *individual topics*; suppression methods; visual processing

Simon, Daniel 79

simulation studies 52, 74–85

simultaneous brightness illusion 81

simultaneous noise masking 8

skin conductance responses (SCRs) 57, 97–100

smells, roses 16

SOAs 43, 133, 138

social information and the unconscious viii–ix, 12–13, 45–59, 92–109, 126–7; amygdala 12–13, 92, 94, 96–109; antisocial personality disorder 103–6; anxiety 103–6, 109; autism spectrum disorder (ASD) ix, 17, 57–8, 103–6; background 12–13, 45, 92–109; conclusions 106–9; conditioning context 56–7, 97–100, 107–9; danger 93–6, 98–100, 104–6; eye gaze viii–ix, 12–13, 17, 45, 50–1, 57–9, 92, 100–2,

104–6, 107–9; facial characteristics viii–ix, 5–6, 12–16, 45, 48–59, 92–109, 126–7; facial dominance 12–13, 45, 50–1, 95–6; fearful faces 12–13, 15, 17, 45, 50–1, 93–5, 96–7, 98–102, 104–6; holistic (identity) face processing viii, 45, 54–9, 107–9, 126; low-road of visual processing viii–ix, 54–9, 92–101, 105–6; major depressive disorder (MDD) 17, 103–6; many roads of face processing 93–7; overestimated unconscious processes 99–100; perspectives on theoretical and methodological questions 107, 108–9; psychiatric disorders ix, 13, 17, 57–8, 92, 103–6, 109; psychopathy 17, 106; schizophrenia 17, 103–6; trustworthiness 12–13, 45, 50–1, 93–4, 95–6; unconsciousness viii–ix, 12–13, 92–109

spatial cueing benefits, working memory object updates 132

speeded RT-based measures, breaking CFS (b-CFS) 18–22

spiders 13

staircase procedures 20–1

stare-in-the-crowd effect 100

startle reflex 98

Stein, Timo vii, 1–38, 40–5, 48, 50–1, 55, 57, 59, 95–6, 99–108, 119, 124

stimulus fractionation 44–59; definition 44

striate cortex viii, 71–3, 75–6, 80–2

subcortical processing 12–13, 72–85, 93–101, 105–6, 149

subcortical visual processing 12–13, 72–85, 93–101, 105–6, 149; definition 93–4; social information and the unconscious 12–13, 93–101, 105–6; see also low-road of visual processing; visual processing

subjective measures of awareness ix, 4, 6, 43–4, 118–38; background ix, 4, 6, 43–4, 118–38; conclusions 137–8; controversies 43–4, 118–20; critique 4, 43–4, 118–20; definitions ix, 4, 6, 121–5, 137; exclusions 124–5; see also liminal-prime paradigm; Perceptual Awareness Scale; trial-by-trial graded subjective measures

subliminal faces, social information and the unconscious 56–7, 93–4, 97–100, 101–2, 107–9, 126–7

subliminal-prime paradigm 44–5, 118–38; contamination problems 123; definition 118–19, 122–3; exclusions 124–5; overshooting risks 123–4; problems

123–6, 137–8; see also objective measures of awareness

superior colliculus 94, 101

superior temporal sulcus (STS) 101–2

suppressing self-generated transitions, continuity of consciousness studies x, 152, 153–9

suppression methods vii–viii, x, 5–29, 40–59, 92–5, 100–4, 106, 108–9, 123–38, 152, 153–9; critique 40–1, 132–3; neurofunctional hierarchical scheme viii, 59, 71–85, 108, 133, 137; overview of the book vii–viii; types vii, viii, 5–10, 25–6, 27, 40–2, 71–85, 108–9, 123, 129–33; see also backward masking suppression; binocular rivalry suppression; continuous flash suppression; crowding suppression; masking; metacontrast masking suppression; sandwich masking suppression

suppression speeds, breaking CFS (b-CFS) 10–13, 18–22

supraliminal faces, social information and the unconscious 93–4, 97–100, 107–9

supraliminal-prime strong-stimulation paradigm 124, 136

suprise-induced blindness 79

tagged visual input, amygdala 108

task comparability problems, subliminal-prime paradigm 119–20, 123–4

tasks and measures, breaking CFS (b-CFS) 18–22

thalamic nuclei 153, 159

threshold-detection proposal, breaking CFS (b-CFS) 26–7, 29

Titchener, Edward 100, 150

Tononi et al (2016) 150–1

Tononi, Giulio 150–1

top-down information flows x, 55, 156–9

trailing events, liminal-prime paradigm 121, 133–8

transition times, breaking CFS (b-CFS) 8, 15, 18–19, 43–4

transitions, alien scientist research explanation scenario ix–x, 148–59; continuity of consciousness studies x, 150–9; discrete transition point debates 8–9, 20–6; neural mechanisms for cancelling-out transitions 157–9; overview of the book i, vi–x; perspectives on theoretical and methodological questions i, vi–x, 1–2, 3, 9–29, 41–59, 72–85, 92, 107, 108–9, 137–8, 148–59; suppressing

172 Index

self-generated transitions x, 152, 153–9; *see also* consciousness; continuous flash suppression; unconsciousness
transparent research practices vii
trial-by-trial graded subjective measures 43–4, 121, 123–4; *see also* subjective measures of awareness
trustworthiness, facial characteristics 12–13, 45, 50–1, 93–4, 95–6; social information and the unconscious 12–13, 45, 50–1, 93–4, 95–6
Tsuchiya, N. 2–3, 41, 74
Type 1 errors, continuous flash suppression (CFS) 49–50, 52

unconsciousness i, vi–x, 1–29, 39–59, 71–85, 92–109, 131, 133, 137; contrast response functions (CRFs) 80–5; controversies ix, 1–2, 39–40, 118; definitions 1–2; dissociation paradigms 2, 3–10, 11–12, 24–9, 43; eye gaze viii–ix, 45, 50–1, 57–9, 92, 100–2, 104–6; facial characteristics viii–ix, 12–13, 45, 48–59, 92–109; high-level stimulus property vii, 1–29; liminal-prime paradigm ix, 118–38; neurofunctional hierarchical scheme viii, 59, 71–85, 108, 133, 137; numerical processing 47, 48–51, 53–9, 131; objective/subjective measures of awareness 43–4, 118–38; overestimated unconscious processes 99–100; overview of the book i, vi–x; perspectives on theoretical and methodological questions i, vi–x, 1–2, 3, 9–29, 41–59, 72–85, 92, 107, 108–9, 137–8, 148–59; *see also* continuous flash suppression; social information and the unconscious; suppression methods; transitions
understandings, current consciousness understandings ix–x, 148–51
upright faces 7, 11–13, 19–22, 24–9, 45, 50–1
used primes, retrieval of stimulus-response association processes 131

V2–V4 areas 78
Van Boxtel, J. J. A. 82–5
Vasser et al (2018) 153–5
vegetative states 39–40
ventral stream processing 48, 76–7, 84–5

verbal communications, social information and the unconscious 103
vincentization procedure uses, liminal-prime paradigm 127–8
virtual reality environments (VR) x, 153–9
visibility trials 4–5, 125–38; liminal-prime paradigm 125–38
vision-for-action pathway 76–7
vision-for-perception pathway 76–7
visual cognition hierarchy viii, 14–15, 71
visual cortex 48–59, 71–85, 151–3, 157–9
visual illusions 11, 54–6, 81–2
visual integration and replication issues, breaking CFS (b-CFS) 17–18, 48–59
visual processing vii–x, 1–29, 39–59, 71–85, 92, 93–101, 105–6, 108, 122–38, 151–2; conditioning context 56–7, 97–100, 107–9; contrast response functions (CRFs) 80–5; cortical anatomy 73–4, 80–5; danger 93–6, 98–100, 104–6; neurofunctional hierarchical scheme viii, 59, 71–85, 108, 133, 137; overview of the book vii–x; reflections on studies 58–9; social information and the unconscious vii–x, 45–59, 92, 93–101, 105–6; trustworthiness 12–13, 45, 50–1, 93–4, 95–6; *see also* continuous flash suppression; eye; low-road of visual processing
visual search technique 8, 25–6
The Visual (Un)conscious and its (Dis)contents (Breitmeyer) 73

white noise burst 97–8
withdrawal studies, attention x, 152–9
WM *see* working memory
word frequencies 51–2
words and phrases, breaking CFS (b-CFS) 13–14, 15–16, 18, 45–6, 48–9, 51–9
working memory 15–16, 129–30, 131–2, 136–8; breaking CFS (b-CFS) 15–16; liminal-prime paradigm object updates 129–30, 131–2, 136–8; object updates 15–16, 129–30, 131–2, 136–8
workshop shortfalls 49
writing systems vii, 13–14
Wundt, Wilhelm 150

Yang et al (2014) 74–5